Curlew: Home

Curlew: Home

Essays & a Journey Back

Tom Montag

tom montag

Midday Moon Books
Waite Park, Minnesota

CREDITS:

The material in "A Short, Irregular History of Curlew, Iowa"
is drawn (some of it, word-for-word) from "Our Centennial:
Memories of Yesteryear, Hopes for Tomorrow, Curlew, Iowa,
1884-1984." We must all be grateful to the committee
that compiled Curlew's history.

"Her Most Perfect Day Ever" first appeared in
The Journal of Unconventional History.

"Soda," "Welcome Jones," "Iced Tea at the Neighbors,"
"Killing Rats," "Killing Pigeons," and "Riding the Horses" were
previously featured in *Midday Moon.*

"Shelling Corn" was first published by *Flyway.*

"Moving the Elevator" appeared in *Cream City Review.*

"Allergy" was published in *Bellowing Ark*

"Why I Don't Hunt" appeared in *Chiron Review*

Black and white cover photo is of the author, his mother,
a brother and two sisters. See reference to photo on p. 33.

Midday Moon Books
P.O. Box 368, Waite Park, Minnesota 56387
ISBN: 0-9711874-0-1

Generation after Generation

for my parents, Bill & Oma Montag,
my wife, Mary
and daughters, Jenifer and Jessica

The seasons turn,
And we turn with them

Contents

Part One

Part Two

Part Three

Part One

The Journey:

Fairwater, Wisconsin,
Monday, October 23, 2000, Morning

One starts such a journey with some apprehension. I have risen at 4:00 a.m. as I usually do, yet I won't be spending time at my desk today before heading to my day job; instead I shall be driving to Iowa to poke around for a week in the place I grew up, a very specific locale: Curlew, Mallard, West Bend, and Emmetsburg, Iowa. To Palo Alto County, where I spent my first fourteen years. This is where "home" was. A farm one mile south and a quarter mile west of Curlew. Grade school and church at St. Mary's in Mallard. Sunday dinners at Gramma Allen's in West Bend. Grocery shopping with my parents once a week at Ted's Super Valu in Emmetsburg.

For several months I have been recording what I remember of my early years spent on that Iowa farm, engaging that home through the lens of memory, putting myself at the edge of that place in another, earlier time. Of course the world glows with the shimmer memory gives it. Memory is not enough. I must see the place itself.

There are no accidents. I think it was no accident that I came across a quote from Franz Kafka last night–to the effect that if you remain quite still and solitary, "the world will freely offer itself to you to be unmasked, it has no choice, it will roll in ecstasy at your feet." Will it? I am an empty cup. What will show itself?

My parents had moved from Curlew by the time I was a senior at Trinity Prep in Sioux City, Iowa; they'd bought a farm at Dows, Iowa, in Wright County. Dows was never home for me. Having gone off from Curlew to board at high school in Sioux City, and from there to further training and college, I had stayed at Dows only for short visits. One does not set roots during temporary layovers. One sends down roots in the early, formative years, I think, the first fourteen. We find the world as it is and accept it early on and give ourselves to a certain roll of landscape ever after, to a certain lay of light. That is always home. Mine was my Curlew home.

Everyday the sun rises, the sun sets. The seasons turn. The years run away. Why would a fellow want to go back to where he grew up? Now I have established a home here in Fairwater, I have roots here, I belong. What do I expect to find at Curlew?

I think who I am was shaped early on by the swell of the land, the cycle of seasons, the scrape of voices I was familiar with at Curlew. The land and the people, farm and school and church, small town, wind, flash of sunset– these were all peculiar and special to a certain time and place in my youth. I go back not to recapture them–because I know the world changes; not to evaluate them–because I don't know enough to judge; not to dismiss them–because I cannot, the images, the memories have claws. Rather I go back to see what moves me–I had belonged, I left, I no longer belong. What will the land say to me, what will the old buildings say? Will the neighbors know me?

One goes back partly to see what is left, perhaps. And to see what he may have left there. Anything? A fellow wonders.

Any answer seems like just so much smoke.

Any answer except the going. The only truth will be leaving Fairwater, leaving what I am and what I know, and heading back to a place that exists only in its present circumstance yet reverberates for me in the power of memory. I want to immerse myself in that other place, to see if I can understand why and how I am who I am, where I am.

My Curlew home will not be changed by my going back so much as I will be changed. Why do certain images hold me, I want to know, why do certain words catch in my throat? I think I am going away so I can come back wiser. A wise man knows himself. I'd like a clearer understanding, some brighter wisdom. The more I understand my Curlew home, the more I will understand the world, perhaps.

I want to go back to Curlew as something of an outsider, with some distance from my own heart. I want to walk unrecognized on Curlew's streets, on the roads leading into and out of town. Shall I be moved by what I see? Shall I be disappointed? I don't know, one can't. I am excited at the prospect of returning to Curlew, yet I am a little apprehensive. Still I cannot turn away from this adventure.

I make the journey, or the journey makes me. How could it be otherwise?

Dodgeville, Wisconsin,
Monday, October 23, 2000, Morning

8:00 a.m. Dodgeville, Wisconsin. I've been on the road for a couple of hours and now I have stopped for breakfast at the Courthouse Inn Restaurant on Iowa Street. My usual restaurant breakfast consists of two pancakes, two eggs, two sausage patties; here that's called "the Clerk's Breakfast." Isn't the clerk the fellow who writes everything down? Sometimes I feel as if my task is recording the world's business. It is not an obligation I reject. I order my usual breakfast.

Near my booth there's a table with six old fellows and one woman seated at it. These folks are talking when I come into the restaurant, and they will still be at it when I leave.

I go back to Curlew believing truth and beauty can be found in common places. The human condition can be seen in an artist's suffering, sure, but it may also be found in conversation around an ordinary breakfast table in a small town restaurant. In the talk of folks like those gathered here.

"She's president of the organization," I overhear one fellow say, "she's full of good ideas, but all she does is sit on her fat butt. You can bet when it's time to do the work, you won't find her."

"I hear corn is running a hundred fifty bushels to the acre out in South Dakota," another fellow says.

"They didn't need a new house," a third one offers, "but they bought one. I suppose you make that much money you got to spend it."

"He did say it won't be long and they'll have to be fixed," a fellow explains, "but he didn't actually say they were in bad shape."

"If there are seven of you, and he's Grumpy," says the waitress, "who are the rest of you?"

"Are you calling me Grumpy?" the first fellow wants to know.

"You called me a smart-ass," the waitress responds, "what am I supposed to think?"

＝＝

The lilt of the talk in the restaurant, the clink of silverware on the table, the thunk of thick plates set down heavy. As I'm heading back to Curlew, this restaurant in

Dodgeville is not my destination yet it is like my destination. Ordinary folks at an ordinary breakfast in an ordinary place. There are commonplaces that are holy; they reveal themselves in flashes. Dodgeville is not unlike Curlew. The sacred moments wink at me. I make note of them, it is my duty. It is a serious obsession, my desire to speak for so many who may not speak for themselves and who may get lost in the fog of time. My obsessions do not make me special: the small gift I have been given is also a burden. You eat your breakfast, you tip the waitress well, you go on doing what you have to do. Middle western duty.

Postville, Iowa, Monday,
October 23, 2000, Morning

As I crossed the Mississippi at Prairie du Chien, I couldn't see the river from the bridge. A heavy mist and the rain. Even down at the level of the river itself in Marquette, Iowa, visibility was less than an eighth of a mile. The "Mighty Mississippi," sure. Yet it was not so fierce today, when a little gloom and doom could hide it.

To my mind, crossing the Mississippi has always been more significant than crossing the Missouri. As a youngster, when I crossed the Missouri into Nebraska, I saw mostly corn–corn and more corn. Crossing the Mississippi into Wisconsin–well, that was Wisconsin, land of small dairy farms with tidy barns, snow on wooded knolls, roads that curve, trees and lakes and rivers. Back then, Wisconsin seemed nothing like Iowa at all.

The grey wetness this morning is thick, like gauze on a wound. The sky drips. It would be a good day to roll over and go back to sleep, yet I won't let the day's grimness make me gloomy. I pause briefly at the gas station here, drinking coffee and making notes; soon I am moving west again, towards Curlew and Mallard, West Bend and

Emmetsburg, towards my Curlew home.

It is still morning. I am still heading west. I hear myself say, "It can't be an ice cream parlor when all you've got is a recipe for ice cream." No one is listening. Art is a lonely drive, and you spend a lot of time talking to yourself.

Waverly, Iowa,
Monday, October 23, 2000, Early Afternoon

Now I have stopped for some lunch at the Coffee Depot in Waverly, Iowa. I order a cup of the "Depot Blend" (and I mean LARGE cup, with a saucer nearly the size of a dinner plate) and a chicken salad sandwich with a serving of fresh fruit on the side.

"Fruited or unfruited?" the girl asks.

"Pardon me?" I say. I thought I'd ordered the fruit.

"Do you want the chicken salad with fruit in it, or plain? The fruited has pineapple and orange."

"Oh," I say, "I'll have the fruited."

I find a table. Behind me as I eat there is a posting that invites area writers to join a local group to "write your memoirs of your life for your family." Such a sign, here, as I'm driving back to Curlew to work at a memoir of my own? If a fellow put that bit of foreshadowing into fiction, it wouldn't be believable. Yet here it is, real as daylight.

I know I am writing my story for those close to me. I will also offer it as a gift for those unable to write their own similar stories. I do not expect there will be many interested in our small lives out here in the middle of the middle, yet I will hold tight to my local notions, to my belief that beauty and truth can reside in common places, in the world of my childhood, even in the "fruited chicken salad" at the Coffee Depot in Waverly, Iowa. I want to write of the small beauties, the small truths, the common place I grew up.

⌒ The Journey ⌒

Highway 3 in Iowa, Heading West,
Monday, October 23, 2000, Afternoon

Only a few fields of corn and soy beans still stand in Iowa between here and the Mississippi behind me; around Fairwater there are many fields remaining to be harvested. Part of the reason for the difference is the dryness of the season here; Iowa farmers have been able to put corn in the bin without too much need to take the moisture out of it. I have heard of thousand-acre fires in cornfields this season in Iowa and southern Minnesota. It has been that dry.

It is not dry now; the sky still spits occasional mist and rain. At times the sun wants to break through the overcast.

I am heading west on Highway 3, and suddenly I realize this is not the landscape of my childhood. Many of the trees here are not much older than I am.

Hampton, Iowa,
Monday, October 23, 2000, Afternoon

I reach my parents' house in Hampton much earlier than I'm expected. The smell of supper cooking fills the kitchen. I will have supper here tonight; I will visit during the evening with my parents and will sleep here before continuing west.

"Hello," I yell into the house.

"Hello, hello, come in," my parents yell back from the TV room.

"What are you doing here so early?" my mother asks. She is settled back in her chair with a blanket across her lap and legs. I motion that she doesn't have to get up. My dad is tipped back in his chair, too.

"I thought I'd do to you what you do to us when you come visit–you always show up way earlier than planned."

Asking one's parents "Why am I a poet?" is a little like asking God "Is any of this supposed to make sense?" You don't expect to get the real answer but you are interested in what might be said.

I remember, one winter, my class had been reading Longfellow's *Snowbound*; it might have been when I was in fifth grade, or sixth. Then a great blizzard hit us. School was canceled. I had never seen so much snow, such winds.

My father spent most of that day on the tractor with the front end loader, pushing snow, opening a path to the barn, clearing the yard and the driveway. He would come into the house every hour or so and call out "Coffee, woman" –his affectionate signal he was ready for some coffee, hot and black. Then he'd go back out at it, fighting the storm, knowing he couldn't win, knowing tomorrow would look like today.

I spent most of my day upstairs in the bedroom I shared with my brother Flip. This was about the only private place a fellow could find in a house filled with brothers and sisters. I had been given a leather-bound notebook for Christmas. I started writing in it, a long poem about the blizzard, twenty pages of snow and blow. Was this my *Snowbound*? It was the first hint that *writing* was a choice an Iowa farm boy could make. I don't know where the impulse came from; I wrote and wrote, filling one page and another and another. Was the poem any good? No, of course not. If anything was good, it was the storm. The storm snarled and raged.

I was sixteen, I think, when I saw in my mind a lonely shore, a sand beach, a cliff behind it, waves lapping the edge of the sand. I saw a sunset, the last bird, the end of the world. I felt an immense loneliness. I was filled with emptiness.

⌒ *The Journey* ⌒

It was summer vacation, I was home from high school in Sioux City, it was evening, and I was writing the poem. I could not imagine where the poem was coming from, yet I kept writing. My aloneness ached. I scrawled at the image; it was hung with all the meaning I could give it. I knew no poets, I had no model, I wasn't sure what I was doing. I pushed forward, alone, and I kept pushing.

The following Christmas break I made a bus ride home from Sioux City. I had a notebook with me. I was writing in it. The steam of breath, the smell of those who must travel by bus. I was feeling like a writer, like I would be the fellow with the Great American Novel in the bib pocket of my overalls, I was in my Thomas Wolfe phase, I guess. I remember not caring if people thought I was a hick. You ache, you don't know what the ache means, you poke long enough, something bleeds out. Poem? Essay?

So here I am, thirty-six years later, asking my parents "Why am I a poet?"

"You loved books," my mother says. "You used to rhyme words when you were little."

Fair enough, I think. Then she goes too far: "You're a sensitive person and you love people." I love the idea of people, maybe; real people, I wouldn't go that far.

"You could correct my English when you were in third grade," she says. Later she will add "Oh, I hated it when you did that. Maybe I don't speak correct English, but I didn't need you telling me."

"I think being a poet was partly a way for you to get away from the farm," she says.

My father answers the question with a story. "A farmer a few miles west of here had a beautiful farm, good cows, and three sons. All three of those sons left home. None of them wanted to farm. The farmer had to sell his cows and sell the farm."

That's all he says about me and poetry.

"I had nine kids," my mother says. "Everyone of them is completely different. Don't ask me how they got that way."

Asking a farmer and the farmer's wife "Why am I a poet?" cannot possibly elicit a full answer, because of course they don't know why. They cannot know. The poet himself doesn't know. Yet the poet wants to return to that elemental place, the farm at Curlew, and re-examine the essential images out of his childhood. How does the farm boy come to cadenced speech? What forces his utterance? What moves me to speak for the people I remember back then, and for others like them? For my parents, our neighbors, the folks in town, for people who often enough do not choose to speak for themselves?

Looking back at my life I can see a mosaic has been dropped and the pieces are scattered; I need to pick them up, re-work them, try to see what they mean. I know going back to Curlew that the best I can hope for is only a hint. Only a hint at the source of my need to explore the swirl of images I've lived with all these years. These images continue to shape me.

Of course the impulse to poetry cannot be understood by family and neighbors; you don't understand it yourself. For me there has been a fierceness, an urgency. My world was changed by my drive towards poetry. Why expect his parents or siblings to understand the fire that burns in a poet's belly? All artists are aliens to some extent, more so in small town Iowa in the middle of the twentieth century. What experience does family have of the poet's fire?

Sometimes the artist wants to be alienated and fosters alienation. He measures how he is different instead of what he has in common with family and neighbors and companions. Sometimes we choose the pain of exclusion, taking pride in it. Yet we haven't always sought to be excluded, I know that too, and we aren't always excluded on purpose; life is sometimes strangely bent.

For myself, I've now come to the point in my life where I want to find what I might have in common with my fellows. The difference that makes me a poet is only a small difference. The elemental experiences that have their claws in me and won't let go, the memories that rise up insistent—these I share with family and Curlew neighbors, don't I?

That family loves us doesn't mean they understand us. Sometimes we think the failure to understand is the sin; it's not. The sin is the failure to love.

It occurs to me, too, that sometimes artists are not loved because they are not loveable. That would be a story different from this one, I hope.

Sometimes you might wish the family would stand back out of the way; yet it is seldom in the nature of family to stay out of the way. So a poet makes do. He counts his blessings and thanks his lucky stars and starts to set down one word, then another, and he is surprised to hear them sing.

Why am I a poet? Sometimes the answer to the question is simply having asked it, nothing more.

Hampton,
Tuesday, October 24, 2000, Morning

It is 5:00 a.m. My parent's house is quiet. Last night I saw my brother Flip here, and his wife Vickie, and their son Little Phil. Little Phil is Little Phil as Little John was little. We had supper together, conversation.

The world is never as we wish it to be: we are all afraid George W. will be elected. We all think everything the fellow says is code for "Give more money to the rich people."

"It scares me a lot to think Bush will be president," my father said. Reagan had been my dad's earlier nightmare, Reagan, the man presiding over a previous looting of America.

The house is quiet at this hour except for the insistent buzz of the refrigerator and the tock tick tock of a grandfather clock.

Once again my mother has taken charge of things. You raise nine kids, I suppose it's hard to give up giving orders, hard to stay out of the poet's way. Remember: "When I say Thomas, come here, you come here." She wants me to go to breakfast at my sister Marilyn's this morning. She and Dad will come too. I had to call Marilyn yesterday afternoon to tell her to expect us; Marilyn will make biscuits and gravy.

"I didn't come out here to visit family," I'd told my mother, who gazed at me blankly as if she hadn't heard me. Perhaps she had not, she is going a little deaf now. Or perhaps she intended to will the world to be the way she wanted it.

So I go with the flow. The trip back to Curlew is partly about the world offering itself. I give up resistance and look forward to seeing Bill and Marilyn's new place, a house in the country, some few acres, a new dog, their thousand cats.

I take down a collage of photographs from the bedroom where I've slept, to examine the pictures more closely. I know this collection had been put together for the celebration of my folks' fiftieth wedding anniversary a few years ago, all these old photos on a piece of corkboard.

My parents' wedding picture is in the center. Below that, a photo of my mother in 6th grade. I'd once thought she looked like she was in high school when the photo was taken, but later she corrected that notion. Above the wedding picture, a photo of my mother with brown hair, four babies, a little girl I don't recognize, and a woman who looks like an Indian. Or she could be a dark-skinned immigrant. It is my Aunt Minerva, Grandpa Allen's sister.

There are other wedding photos. Photos of my father in uniform, a soldier boy gone off to fight Hitler. Photos of my Gramma Allen appearing more suave than I ever remember her. Here, Grandpa and Gramma Allen leaning up against a black hump of automobile, an old woman with them, a young boy. The woman is Grandpa's mother, the boy is my Uncle Larry. There, a photo of my mother with my dad's sister, the one we call Sis; they are standing in front of my grandfather's truck while Grandpa looks out the open window of the cab. Sis lived with Grandpa and Gramma Allen while her husband, my Uncle Phil, Mom's brother, served in the Navy during World War II. Another photo, grey and faded, of a couple men standing belly to belly in bib overalls, Grandpa Allen and a cousin of his from Oklahoma. They are laughing. You can tell it is a contest to see who has the greatest belly. Grandpa wins. Gramma stands out in the hog pen in another photo; there are five or six large, dark sows in front of her. She wears a pork pie hat. Shadow is on her face, hiding her smile at the joke–pork pie hat in the hog pen.

A photo of my mother, "the year I lost so much weight." She is sitting on a chair in the yard just north of the farm house at Curlew. She has a pan of apples on her lap and a paring knife in her hand. There is a chair in front of her with a pan of peeled apples on it. The scene is backlit softly with heat and a little breeze.

In the upper left corner of the collection of photos there is one of my mother with me and Kack and Nancy, Flip, Marilyn. I am six years old perhaps. We are standing in front of the farm house at Curlew. There is snow on the ground. We have our winter coats on, I have a cap with big wool ear flaps. My mother bends over us bare-armed in a short-sleeve blouse. Kack looks away. Flip smiles.

Nancy squints and with her high cheek bones she looks like an Indian. This was so long ago.

What the Distance Knows

A man reaches the age where his astonishment trumps his certainty. Old men spend a lot of time sitting on benches and thinking. I was more than fifty years old before I started to understand why. There's a lot for old men to think about. The more you think about it, the more astonished you become: how does a fellow get to where a fellow is?

The middle west was the bottom of an ocean, wasn't it? It is a great, flat accumulation. It is home for me, because I need trees and a great humming greenness, I need the turn of seasons, I need the ice. I was born here in the middle of it, in Iowa, in our only truly middle western state.

Ohio is too much Pennsylvania and West Virginia to be middle western. Indiana is too southern. Michigan has too much water. Wisconsin and Minnesota have too many lakes, too much forest, and these states might be partly Canadian, ey? Kansas and Nebraska, South Dakota and North–half of each of these is western. Missouri is too much like Arkansas.

That leaves Illinois and Iowa, doesn't it; yet Illinois has Chicago at one end and Cairo at the other, so what remains as the only true middle western state is Iowa. Of course it has taken more than fifty years for me to appreciate this. All our lives we want to run from that which we should be embracing.

Home is where you start from.

Perhaps home is not something you inhabit so much as something that would inhabit you.

Home is a seed planted in a little clay pot you can carry with you the rest of your life.

Home is where you hurt the most when you get hurt, where you shout with exuberance when you realize you are loved by good family.

Home is the hope that life means something; it is a wasp's nest crawling with questions, the place the sun stands still at noon, rain during a dry spell.

You cannot go home again, Thomas Wolfe whispers from behind my left shoulder. Looking for home is quintessentially middle western, I respond. A fellow has got to turn over rocks, looking. He has got to go back, to see what remains of his memories, to see what it was that shaped him, and whether those ghosts still walk. Who am I, who were those people, what place was that? How did I get where I am?

Life is a series of train wrecks. Some of them are happy accidents, and some of them are disasters. Although you can see only in the rearview mirror, you cannot go back to live there, you move instead into the unmarked future. I do not mean to suggest we are not responsible for our fate, each of us. We are. Yet I also believe we are shaped and molded by unseen forces—the land around us, the people on the land, what those people believe, how they behave, what came before.

What I know of flatness, I learned in Iowa, not North Dakota. I should be different had I grown to manhood in North Dakota. Not better, not worse—different. North Dakota's great enormous reach of empty sky would have humbled me, surely. The great stretch of endless miles between nowhere and nowhere else would have worn me out. Riding AmTrak's Empire Builder home from a visit to Montana a few years ago, I remember waking at night in my cramped sleeping berth. "Where am I?" I asked myself in the darkness. "Oh, yeah," I said with my Iowa smugness, "I'm sleeping my way across North Dakota at 79 m.p.h.–the only way to cross it." It's not that Iowa is any more interesting, there's just not so much of it.

I remember wind in South Dakota, it was not a hugging wind. My parents had *finally* taken us on vacation. They were cooped up in the station wagon with the nine of us kids, heading west to the Black Hills, to see Mount Rushmore. We stopped for a picnic lunch along the way, brought out our sandwiches and something to drink. We were hungry kids, yet before we ever got a bite of that Wonderbread and baloney, the wind had turned the white slices hard as shingles. Tank tank tank, you could pound your sandwich on the picnic table. "Mom, look at this!" Tank tank tank.

A few years ago, my wife and I pulled off a country road in the Sand Hills of Nebraska, onto a two-rut ranch track. The end of this particular wagon path promised us a look at Old Jules' farmstead and orchard, promised us the opportunity to pay our respects at the grave of Mari Sandoz. Driving onto private land, the Iowa farm boy in me felt as if he were trespassing. Deeper in we went. "Close the gate behind you," a sign directed where we had to stop and let ourselves through a fence line. "Watch for calves on the road," it warned. When we met a car coming out as we were halfway in, we stopped to talk. "Is it worthwhile getting this far off the road?" I asked. The two woman in the other car, a mother and her grown daughter who was driving, looked at each other then back at us and they laughed. "If you love Mari Sandoz, it is," the daughter said, "and we love Mari." They were from Lincoln, Nebraska, and had made a special trip. My wife and I went on. We arrived at Mari Sandoz's grave site, within view of the Old Jules farmstead. So many trees had been bull-dozed out of the orchard, heaped up. Mari's grave was surrounded by a fence to keep cattle from tramping it. We had a view across the brown valley with only the greenness of some few trees. That South Dakota wind was blowing in the Sand Hills of Nebraska, too. "This is Desolation Hill," I thought. It wasn't, of course. Yet I'd never felt a place so remote, so absolutely removed from the world, and I consoled myself that Mari Sandoz was buried in ground she loved, however lonesome it seemed to me.

We were tromping around Chase County, Kansas, my wife and I, following in the footsteps of William Least Heat-Moon. I had read *Prairy Erth*. I had wondered how a fellow could write more than six hundred pages about a piece of ground with some two thousand inhabitants and not much of anything on it. "Deep history" is what it's called. I call it local curiosity. We wandered from town to village to ghost town. The history was deep because it surely is not on the surface. We stopped at the museum in Cottonwood Falls and got one ear full about William Least Heat-Moon from the curator who followed us room to room, talking; we got the other ear full about Chase County and its history and its inhabitants and about others who had stopped at the museum because they'd read *Prairy Erth*. Yet later when we found ourselves pulled off along the side of a raw road somewhere amongst the ranches between Homestead, Kansas, and Wonsevu, I recognized desolation with a capital D for its very deep and local history.

How do we end up where we are? "Everybody's gotta be some place," says the fellow hiding in the bedroom closet. Yeah, I know, but how do we get there?

The first reason is we're born there. For some, home is

where you are born and raised and if there is no compelling reason to leave that is where you live and die. Family ties are the argument for staying. You hear people say they don't want to move too far from family.

My native place was Curlew; the farm was a fine piece of black dirt. I am the eldest son of Bill and Oma Montag. Curlew was, in those years, a grey village of about one hundred people laid alongside the train tracks, not far from Mallard and Plover, not far from nowhere. When I started high school, I left the farm and my family and went off to high school in Sioux City because I'd thought God had called me to be a priest. Turns out God was just muttering to himself and wasn't talking to me at all; yet I'd left home and couldn't seem to find my way back, at least I couldn't go back to stay.

A second reason we might live where we do: we're trapped there and can't manage to go anywhere else. How often do we hear–in literature or in life–"If I could, I'd get out of this one horse, two-bit town. I'd blow this pop stand." Can't a fellow get up the money for bus fare? Can't a woman put together a grub stake that would let her start fresh some place else? Sometimes we simply don't have the will we need to change our circumstances. Sometimes we come to depend on the pain we suffer. Sometimes what little we have is enough for us.

My Grandma Allen belonged. She never felt a need to leave, not even when her husband died and left her widowed. She would never have thought she was trapped even though she was sixty years old before she ever got much more than twenty miles from home.

The world has changed. This day is gone: a little girl takes lunch as her father drives a team and wagon. She bites into a banana, spits it out. She thinks the skin is too tough to chew, she didn't know to peel it. The man in charge of the horses was my Grandpa Allen; I never knew him, he died before I was born. The little girl with a mouthful of banana skin is, of course, my mother. She did not know much about bananas. Nor did she feel any need, early on, to go very far from family. Curlew is about twenty miles from West Bend; on a clear day, you could see the West Bend elevator gleaming to the east, its late afternoon shadow laid across Grandma Allen's yard.

Some of us live where we do for mercenary reasons—for our job, for the sake of advancement, for the opportunity to make it big, strike it rich, whatever. Think of the Forty-Niners heading to the goldfields of California. The source of that impulse: great opportunity. Remember when there were great jobs in Chicago or Detroit, and the migration to those cities? Or is Dallas where the money is? Writers go to New York because that is where writers make it. The wannabe starlets head to Hollywood, even if they have to wait tables or make dirty movies, some of them, to pay their rent.

My parents moved to Dows to own a farm. None of my siblings ever stayed close to Curlew, yet none of them ever went marching off in pursuit of shimmering gold, either. I thought God had called me to be a priest; my sister Kack thought she was supposed to be a nun. I'm married to a nurse I met in Milwaukee, Wisconsin; Kack is married to a Minnesota plumber. Nancy married another Minnesota boy, a Coca Cola route salesman. My brother Flip married a girl he met after the folks had moved to the farm at Dows, when he thought *he* might be the farmer in the family, though it never was so easy he could be. None of my siblings ever strayed so far from home as I did; I am the black sheep, though none of them settled close to Curlew, either. My youngest brother, Randy, died driving truck when he was not yet twenty-one and is buried a few miles east of our old farmstead at Curlew, in the cemetery for St. Mary's Church. That's about as far from home as you can go and still lie down within shouting distance.

A fourth reason we might live where we live is aesthetic. The beauty of a region may call to us. I've heard some people say they moved to Colorado simply because they wanted to be near the mountains; they managed to find jobs and make livings, yet that's not why they're there.

There are more subtle manifestations of this, too: my wife and I could not settle in Wyoming nor parts of South Dakota because we'd be too far from trees. Even Iowa sometimes feels a little naked to me, now, after my years in Wisconsin. There are trees in Iowa, don't get me wrong, yet mostly the view is unobstructed. In a grey, drab spring you look out across the rolling, bare ground and watch the grey grass in the ditches and farm yards start to green up tenderly. You would say to yourself "this is home, this is home, this is home," as if saying it could keep the world from changing. You are bent by the Iowa wind just as the Iowa trees are.

We might live where we do for reasons of climate. Now when you get damned tired of Wisconsin's harsh winters, you may choose something warmer, Florida or Arizona or southern California. The Sunbelt is peopled with retired Iowa farmers in long pants and John Deere caps.

Yet I don't know if it would ever have occurred to the Iowa neighbors I grew up amongst in the 1950s that they could leave. Giving up was not an option they would consider. They intended to grow where they'd been planted. They put bales of straw around the house to keep the wind from coming in where the frame met the foundation. In the great blizzards, when the snow was piled up all the way to the second story windows, they pushed their way outside to milk the cow, feed the chickens, break open the ice in the water tank so the cattle could drink. I don't remember that anyone ever thought he was trying to prove something; we were simply doing what we had to.

Sometimes we live here in order not to live there. For someone who doesn't want to live in the mountains, or in California, or on the Great Plains, then Wisconsin is a pretty good choice. What you don't want defines what you do want.

I find myself drawn to a very old photograph of my mother's family. The photo is cracked and torn and marked with water spots. Grandma Allen is holding a baby, that must be my Uncle Larry, or else it's my oldest cousin. Grandma's hair is brown, not white; I don't ever remember her hair being brown. Only nine or ten of Grandma's thirteen children are in the picture. The girls are Opal, Sunny, and Oma–Opal has a string of pearls around her neck, a dress with matching hat; Sunny and my mother are in white dresses, both of them are smiling. My mother is five years old. I am trying to see into her eyes, I am trying to see *me* in my mother's eyes, but she is squinting in the bright sunlight in front of the house, in front of the vines growing on the lattice in front of the porch. I cannot see the future in my mother's eyes. I cannot begin to tell which of the boys are which of my uncles. All of them, from tallest to smallest, wear bib overalls. The three eldest sons have denim caps. One of the boys has his head cocked to the side and his face bent to a smirk; he could pass for my brother Flip. My mother has hold of her brother's hand, reassuring him. Could this be Larry? Who of these is still alive? My mother, Sunny, Steve, Larry? Grandma Allen stares straight ahead, her chin set firmly. She thinks she has everything she wants. There is nowhere else.

We might choose the place we live for philosophic or political reasons. Think of the Mormans in Salt Lake City. Think of the Phalanx at Ceresco near Ripon in the 1840s. If you want to hang out with guys who jump out of airplanes, my friend says, you have got to jump out of airplanes. Fifty years ago, it was family gathered around me, Iowa farmers.

Now I am holding another photograph. I see my mother crouched on one knee, my brother Flip on her lap. Flip is in diapers, he looks blankly to the side like some hungry pioneer child in some desolate past. My sister Kack is hooked in my mother's left arm, she has her hand to her mouth, her mouth is open as if she would speak, her eyes raise questions I cannot answer. My sister Nancy pushes up to my mother's lap from the right side, already her face is browed with worry. My mother is not looking into the camera, nor is Kack, Nancy, and Flip. My mother wears a long polka dot dress, white anklets, white shoes. Her hair is up in a braid around her head like a halo. Flip and my sisters have white socks and white shoes. My mother looks upward expectantly, as if something great is about to happen and she knows it.

I am in the photograph, too, dressed in bib overalls cut off at the knees, my hair already falling down over my forehead. My feet are in dark shoes, and the shoes look as if they have already taken root right where I stand. I am the only one in the photo who looks into the eye of the camera. I am looking into the heart of the camera. My eyes in the photo seem to me dark and bold and eternal. I have my hands in my pockets and a broken smile on my face. I *look* like a poet, I look like a poet should look at four years of age. As I stare at the boy in the photograph, the boy I was is staring back at me. None of it confuses him yet. If that boy has doubts, he doesn't let them show.

I do not know where the photograph was taken. There is an old car in the gravel driveway behind us. There seems to be a slash of sidewalk just in front of us. Over my mother's left shoulder, the fabric of some bush. Beyond the driveway, some buildings whose shape and meaning I can't quite make out. Let me guess where it was taken. We were at my grandmother's house in West Bend: the indistinct buildings in back, the bush. It is late spring: the grass is four or five inches long, Flip would have been born the preceding August. The year is 1951: I am four years old in the photograph, looking out at myself who will be looking back half a century later.

The final reason we might live where we do is some combination of the choices we've made. We make choices all the time and they pile up on one another, the weight of them heavy on us.

The choices I'm aware of that led me to Fairwater, Wisconsin, stretch all the way back to seventh grade, St. Mary's School, Mallard, Iowa. What I thought I was going to do with my life determined where I went to school. I thought God had touched me. Where I went to school opened other possibilities that wouldn't have been available to me had I stayed on the farm. One thing leads to another. The next thing you know, I was going to school in Wisconsin; I met a good woman there and married her. We started a family in Milwaukee. But I was never entirely comfortable in the city and wanted to get back to something more rural. We headed northwest out of Milwaukee, towards Marquette County where Mary's parents had a summer place, 120 acres of sand and trees. "You call this 'The Farm?'" I said. I laughed. I was from Iowa: "The Farm" looked like a big sandbox to me.

We knew it would be difficult to make a living on the Marquette County sands—ask anyone who lives there—so we looked for something nearby. Mary found a job as a nurse at the hospital in Ripon. I thought I could write anywhere. We had a place to settle.

We knew what we wanted in a house—it had to be out in the country, on two acres, with a fireplace and a big porch wrapped around the side. Ha! Not in our poor church mouse price range. I was a poet, after all, and we were as patched as a poet's family is supposed to be. Finally, we toured the Hankerson house in Fairwater. It had been the Laper house before that. Seventy-five years old, it had been owned only by those two families. We walked in the front door to the shine of wood floors, oak woodwork, a built-in hutch that took our breath away. The price was right and we compromised to get it—no fireplace, no porch, no two acres.

Eventually I had to give up the notion that I could make a living as a writer. I had to take a "real" job. At some point when you don't want to start over somewhere else, you recognize you are trapped by the choices you've made.

Yet chance struck circumstance long before I was ever in seventh grade, long before we moved to Fairwater. Back in 1900, what if the railroad had not put a line through Sac City, Iowa, heading west towards Sioux City? What if the tracks had not cut my greatgrandfather's farm in half. What if he hadn't sold the property, disgusted that it had been ruined by the train tracks running through? What if my greatgrandfather had chosen to re-settle his family somewhere other than West Bend? What if his son, Henry, hadn't lived just down the road from that fetching girl, Luna, who would become my grandmother? What if Grandpa and Grandma Montag had been just too tired the night my father was conceived?

Maybe life is like a game of pinball, ka-ching, ka-ching, ka-ching.

Perhaps none of this is random, perhaps it only looks like chaos.

You have *got* to wonder how you got here. How can you not try to explain it to yourself. I am a poet grown off that farm near Curlew. I have to wonder: how did it happen that *I* am a poet? Sometimes I am so much like my father it scares me. The older I get, the more I sound like him, think like him, act like him. Just when you think you are your own person, you see how much you're not. Now my father would never say he is a poet, would he? Yet how close his terse and well-chewed farm talk comes to poetry. He had no self-consciousness about what he would say, that's part of it: his talk was work, not art. Working a farm one is so given to the task at hand it's a wonder any farm boy can come to poetry at all. And if he does–if the farm boy tries to write–there'll be dirt left with the words, weeds, the smell of hog manure not far off.

Well east of Fairwater, set in the Kettle Moraine area, there's a heap of earth called Ashford Hill. It's a stony mound of dirt where a glacier dumped what it had left when all was said and done. It's a hill, you'd say, part of which is fenced to pasture a farmer's cows. Holsteins click their hooves against stones there as they graze.

Yet you stand back and squint and look carefully, you wonder why the stones are set in lines perpendicular to the crest of the hill, as regular as rib bones. Walking the hill, you wonder at the great heap of stone here and here, another cairn there, another over there, like horns and eyes and snout. A hundred years ago, you'd have seen lines of ribs running down the other side of the hill.

You can't see it standing close up. You need some distance. Ashford Hill appears to be a buffalo effigy spread across many acres, using the shape of the hill to suggest a buffalo at rest. One Cheyenne fellow came all the way from the Black Hills of South Dakota and pinned the site: it's sacred, he says, it is the center of the Cheyenne universe. The farmer who pastures his cows on the hill let some elders construct a sweat lodge at the edge of the site. The elders prayed and sweated and, one supposes, had visions.

The center of the Cheyenne universe? You don't say. In Wisconsin?

Be the Cheyenne fellow. Stand atop Ashford Hill. Get out your medicine bag. Lay out the Cheyenne map of the sky. Look closely, then look at the landscape that surrounds you. Why are there hills in this direction, and that, and that, that correspond to markers on the map. And when you put down your marker for "the direction the thunder rolls in from," why do you set it intuitively on the very spot that would correspond to "Lightning Strike Hill" if you could lay the map across the landscape?

Why is Ashford Hill one of five sacred sites forming a straight line more than twenty miles long pointed directly at the summer solstice sunset? One of the other sites is a vision quest pit dug out of the Niagara Escarpment near Oakfield, Wisconsin. There is a figure pecked into the stone there that resembles some of those found at the Jeffers Petroglyph site in southwestern Minnesota, halfway to the Black Hills.

Why is there a forty-foot tall petroform–locally called "Star Man"–laid out on the ground not much more than fifteen miles north of Ashford Hill, and why does it mirror the constellations as you'd have seen overhead if you'd been standing there fifteen hundred or two thousand years ago?

Did the Iowa farm boy become a writer so he could leave poems and essays about the land as emblems set like cairns, like the buffalo effigy that is Ashford Hill, to mark his sacred sites? Is the physical place a way into the spiritual world for me?

There are unseen forces at work in the world, and some of them rise right out of the landscape that surrounds us. The landscape of home is perhaps a metaphor for hope and family and what we choose to believe when the hard choices come. Man is an animal who builds things, and he also builds notions about how things are. We look for pattern and meaning and message. We are tugged this way and that. We try to impose order on the world around us, and the world imposes its order on us.

Here in the middle west, section lines and grid lines

have been laid incessantly upon the land. We have fenced so much in, we have fenced so much out. We have cut down trees here and have planted them there. Our plows opened the skin of earth and exposed the soil to wind and water erosion. We have dammed the rivers and drained the lakes. We have tried to farm our marshes. We put houses here, houses there. Our roads cut through hill, fill the dale. Power lines and telephone poles compose the view for us. Our feet tramp paths hard as concrete. We have changed the weather with our black fields retaining the heat of a weak spring sun. We have polluted the water. Wild game has become scarce. We planted exotics, and they drive out our native species.

Because we are the animal with tools—some of them very big tools—we are able to shape the world, to mine its resources, to build cities, to lay out roads and lines of communication. We are able to farm bigger and bigger swatches of it, with water pulled from deeper and deeper within the earth. At the same time, the world pushes back: the length of the days, the turn of the seasons, the advance and retreat of glaciers, these create rhythms. The fertility of the land determines how close our neighbors can be.

On the treeless plains, our greatgrandmothers burned buffalo chips for cooking fire and for heat. We have seen photographs of the pioneer women in their long dresses and their wheelbarrows; the women are out picking up the buffalo chips and perhaps they're asking themselves how *ever* has it come to this? The emigrant women who went west—how did the land change them? The full answer to such a question is more than I can imagine.

Settlers moved west. Train tracks crossed the rolling land and villages sprang up alongside at regular intervals. Look to the Hi-Line of Montana for proof, follow the railroad across northern North Dakota or southern Kansas. Town could never be much farther off than a farmer could drive his team and wagon in a day. Steam locomotives required water at regular intervals, required someone to keep the tracks in good repair.

Why is the western personality flintier than the middle western? Here in the middle west when we plant our seeds in spring we are confident we'll have a crop to harvest in due course. Settlers in Montana might have held that notion a season or two, in their mistaken belief that rain follows the plow. Soon enough, though, the western sky revealed its truth: the West is arid. Those who stayed had to adapt. The dry plains make a dry man.

To the far north, the Inuit eat whale fat and like it. No, they don't just like it, their bodies crave it: survival in those harsh conditions requires it. Need is one side of the coin of opportunity: now *that's* a middle western notion.

Go back far enough and ask: Wasn't it a kind of prairie that encouraged our ancestors to stand up on two feet, to learn to walk upright? However much we change the world, the world changes us too, deep in our core; it determines how we walk, what we can see, what we can think, what we will be affected by.

What makes a place what the place is?

Bedrock geology, of course. Topography. Was the place an inland sea once, under water, with coral reefs rising here and there, with sediment being laid down? Did a glacier sculpt the earth here, did wind and rain change its face the way a pretty girl changes with the beauty of her aging?

Latitude and longitude affect the place. The angle of the sun, the distance from the Arctic Circle. The distance from the mountains, from the sea.

What of clime and climate. Certainly latitude and longitude condition the weather, as–again–do sea and mountain. A thunderstorm rolls across the Nebraska plains in a way not possible perhaps in Maine, not possible even in Wisconsin maybe. Does the weather bring moisture enough to support a thickness of trees, or only enough for rough desert grasses? What of the animals of a place, do they thrive in the lowlands or the highlands, in wet or dry? What of the flowers and shrubs? The conditions of the place make their presence possible; their presence changes the nature of the place, no? Can farmers farm here? The difference between farm and ranch is measured in inches–inches of rain. (I admit the difference may also be a matter of the heart.)

What of altitude? Altitude is related to climate, which alters the possibility of animal and plant, the possibility of man. Compare my lung capacity to that of an Indian in the Peruvian Andes, for instance. How greatly would the nature of a piece of prairie close to sea level be changed should it be uplifted twelve thousand feet? What is the difference between Nebraska and the Tibetan plateau?

What of the "scale" of things? Certainly the American west would be far different for us were it only three hundred miles from Des Moines, Iowa, to San Francisco, California, instead of eighteen hundred some. Part of what makes Big Sky Country is the sheer scale of it; you could not coop up that landscape and get the same breathless effect. I think perhaps it is because of its scale that Wallace Stegner suggests the west is more about motion than about place. Rootlessness requires an elsewhere.

We middle westerners, we chose to settle here. We are settled along the path to the west, it is not the west. Those who stopped here and stayed did so by choice, not because they'd butted up against mountains, or an ocean. Yes, at some point Green Bay, Wisconsin, was the western edge of settlement, the eastern edge of wilderness. Still, the path went west, to Portage, to Prairie du Chien, across the Mississippi into Iowa. The great land rolled onward, all the way to the edge of the continent.

By living along the path, instead of at the edge, we are different and the difference may help define the "middle" part of the middle west. Perhaps, here, we recognize more clearly that we have made the conscious choice to stay; as we watch the sun setting in the west, the possibility of moving onward is lit for us. We have not drifted to the point we can drift no more. We have not yet exhausted our possibilities. This place, this life, what we have chosen –for us, it is not the end of the road.

A contrary argument might be made in some of our towns and villages where live, perhaps, those who have no gumption, those who would be king of junkyard and mobile home, who would have washing machine and sofa sit out on the open porch through the winter, who take no pride in who they are or what they have or how they do. We have such folks. One wonders whether they have examined life's possibilities and chosen freely; or have they simply taken their cards, cursed their gods, and continued to do what their daddies did?

We who live along the path, along the way, we render service to passersby–we are innkeepers and merchants and middlemen. We feed the world. The quintessential middle westerner is a small town butcher, up to his elbows in the blood stuff of life; he accepts his predicament, yet he is hopeful that his sons and daughters become something more than he is. Living along the path, we welcome the weary traveler; we are glad to see his money; and, soon enough, we are happy to send him on his way. Perhaps we don't trust those coming through; there is some unease, some discomfort, and we exercise caution, carefully watching the strangers among us. For fifteen years after we bought our house in Fairwater, it remained "the Hankerson house." In the eyes of our careful neighbors, it was half a generation before the house we owned truly belonged to us.

Sometimes, living here in the middle of things, along the path instead of run up against the mountains or at the western edge of the continent, we make a vice of our virtue. Our righteousness becomes sinful. We are much too smug hunkered down in our good homes here, watching the doings of the outlaws and the mountain men farther west. We have the solid earth beneath us, and we know it: the certainty of the earth makes us conservative, rather than daring; smug, rather than humble. We have so much with which to gamble we are afraid to gamble any. We may take too much comfort in the fact that we have set up shop along the way between.

Here in the middle west we are a community of "citizens," I think, rather than a gang of "outlaws," in Tobias Wolff's distinction. We are generally sober and settled and stern, not drunk and noisesome and dangerous, and not, perhaps, fun. Eventually the strictures of our seriousness force the outlaw out. We expect those who stay to have a job, to contribute, to become pillars. Sure, we have had our fur traders, we have had our lumberjacks, but they are gone now. We are a community of innkeepers with shotgun kept behind the counter where it's handy when needed. And we will use it. The dogs of chaos must be kept away.

The land I grew up on had its certain character. The people I grew up among had theirs. I came away a poet, and I'm not yet sure why, though I'm going to keep asking. The times were different; the times were no different. There are no sure answers, only hints at the shape of an answer.

We like to think we've had some say in the choices we've made. We like to believe the course of our lives has not been predetermined. We hope there is no unseen hand pulling our strings. Yet in the quiet of an evening, as a fellow sips his beer and thinks about life, he might begin to see just how much chance has played in everything.

How did I get where I am? It's hard to say. Why am I

asking? Well, that's the Iowa farm boy's need to know.

Memory is a poor filter and words a poor substitute for the experience itself. I was raised on an Iowa farm in those grey Republican 1950s–that experience shaped me irredeemably. Yet I shaped my life to some degree as well. Part of life is what we imagine it to be; part of it is what we insist upon; part of it is what lands on us. Does the wind bend the reed or does the reed's resilience alter the course of the wind? Do we define home, or does home define us?

What do we inherit? The sum of the influences that have acted on us plus the sum of the choices we have made. We may come away with a template for the ideal landscape, the perfect home, the good family. We may come away shaped by the temperament of the people we grew up with. At the same time, some of us have managed to re-fashion those inheritances, or have attempted to reject them. How did I come to choosing poetry when none of those around me did? Something pushed me. Few others choose to write of that land, my Iowa farm home, the people I grew up among. Something tugs at me. Something in my own "deep history" insists that I write of my middle western farm home.

I think again about the Ashford Hill, a marker on the landscape ultimately not unlike the marks I want to leave as I write. What the distance knows is that you must step back if you want to see it, whatever it is; the farther back you step, the more you can see. What the distance also knows is that you must examine it closely, very minutely, if you are to understand it. Understanding where he's come from and what he's come to, what he's part of and what that means, that might be a man's life work. That might be a task I choose to accept.

Over my left shoulder Thomas Wolfe whispers once more: "You can't go home again." Is this what he means: home has changed you and, having changed you, home changes? The land. The people. The ghosts. The memories. What I have seen, is it like the infinite regression of an image in mirrors, or like a knot we might untangle if we can find the end of the string? Where is the end of the string? Shall I ever find my way back?

The Journey:

Whittemore, Iowa,
Tuesday, October 24, 2000, Late Morning

To get to Marilyn's for breakfast by 9:00 a.m., we left my parents' house at 7:50 a.m. Visibility in the fog was only an eighth of a mile at first, then a quarter of a mile, then more. There was a mile's visibility by the time we got to Marilyn's house in the country northwest of Belmond, Iowa, and there was the promise of sun burning through and blue sky. The promise that the world would open itself.

Marilyn had sausage gravy and biscuits and my folks brought cinnamon rolls. We had coffee and breakfast and talk after a quick tour of the house. Marilyn's husband Bill was at work. I petted the dogs and scritched the kitties afterwards, after we ate, after my parents left. Mom got herself in a hurry to go home, she always does. She has always been better with the going than the getting there. It's like she was homesick for the chickens again, though she no longer has chickens. Some things don't change.

On the drive from Hampton to Marilyn's house, when I told her I was planning to visit the cemetery where my brother Randy is buried, Mom had said: "I always get so excited when we're going there, going to see Randy. And when I get there, I'm always disappointed. There's nothing there."

Whittemore,
Tuesday, October 24, 2000, Late Morning

I left Marilyn's and right away a fellow in a pick-up who was stopped at a gravel crossroad had to wave a big Iowa welcome at me, not just a quick wink of finger but the whole hand, wide.

At the cemetery just east of Corwith, Iowa, I saw that all the stones face east, perpendicular to the road. I'm a little obsessive about graveyards so which way the stones face is something to notice.

As I came into Corwith, a woman in a van was pausing at the stop sign as required by law. She waved broadly at me. The sun was bright, burning at the haze. The metaphor seemed to hold–the world reveals itself. On Main Street in Corwith, a kid driving towards me waved; a girl at a stop sign at the other edge of town waved too; so did a kid driving into town behind her. I'd say it's probably not neighborly to go through Corwith without waving at everyone you meet.

Whittemore,
Tuesday, October 24, 2000, Late Morning

I remember last night Flip told a story about a neighbor of his at Dows. The fellow had gotten some weed killer splashed on him; this happens, he didn't think anything about it. The poison got into his system "and made him crazy for a couple days."

"Did he get back to normal?" Mom wondered.

Flip: "Well, he always was a little screwy, so it's hard to tell."

Whittemore,
Tuesday, October 24, 2000, Late Morning

I have been traveling Iowa's gravel roads this morning. We don't have as many gravel roads in Wisconsin. It is good to hear again the shaky lullaby a car sings on gravel. I turned west where a sign said "No Snow Removal." A red-tail hawk led my way, the poet's good omen.

I was noticing what's left of many farmsteads out in this part of Iowa: only ghostly groves, trees like mist, the house and outbuildings gone.

I made another turn, to another gravel road, another red-tail hawk. Off to my left, thirty-five buffalo collected in the corner of a pasture. The land swelled like a hump of buffalo shoulder.

Half a mile farther, another red-tail. What was different than my memory of Iowa? There are so few fences now.

Another mile, another red-tail hawk.

Then all of a sudden, fog closed down the view like a curtain dropped at the end of a show. The world can play hide and seek any time it wants. Suddenly it was foggy enough that my feet felt damp, as if I'd been standing in water.

As I came into Algona from the east, then again left Algona heading west, all the crows were clumped in threesomes.

Rodman, Iowa,
Tuesday, October 24, 2000, Noon

The sign says: "Welcome to Rodman, The Small Town with the Big Heart." There is no business district, there are no businesses remaining. Even the grain elevator has been shut down. The Rodman Consolidated School, a nice dark brick structure, has been boarded up for a very long time. Looking about, I feel some dull, vague ache of sadness, like a wave washing over me.

Rodman is where the story began. My folks lived a mile south of here and half a mile east when I was born.

South of Rodman,
Tuesday, October 24, 2000, Afternoon

The land is all that one color of brown. Or is it grey? Is it a tawny tan? The sky is grey. The wind is an invisible whistler. Only the Riverside Cemetery south of Rodman has green grass and birdsong. I look at gravestones.

The marker for the fellow born the earliest belongs to James W. Pearson–1843-1927. What a stretch of life: at one end, a Gold Rush, the Panic of 1857, the Civil War; at the other end, World War I and the Roaring Twenties, almost the Depression.

There are a lot of markers here for folks born in the 1870s. And this sadness: a tiny concrete marker for "Lula Hildebrand and Infant Son Eugene, 1934." A marker for Anna M. and David Sloan, "Co K 1 Wis H.A."–am I related to these Sloans?

I leave the cemetery and in less than half a mile I pass by the farmstead where my folks had lived when I was born. A red-tail hawk settles onto a power pole there, as if to confirm my notion. The hawk is the color of drabness, like a field emptied of soy beans. The farmstead draws no attention to itself; I'll return to it for my own reasons.

Her Most Perfect Day Ever

Her most perfect day ever had started as just another day in March, 1947. They were farming eighty acres and living in a drafty house near Rodman and had another two hundred acres over closer to West Bend. It was their first year of marriage, their first year farming. The young farm wife was making pancakes for breakfast that morning, as she had done often. They ate, then, did the farmer and his wife; he was a veteran of the recent war, a farm boy gone off to soldiering, and now he was home and he was going to farm. They put butter and syrup on those pancakes that morning–butter the color of the sun melting into the morning's sweetness.

If she wanted cold water, she had to pump it at the sink in a grey corner of the kitchen, had to work the long handle of the noisy pump by hand until water splashed into the pan in the sink, or into a pitcher; hot water she took from a big pot kept on the wood-burning cook stove. She prepared a pan of warm water for dishes, a little soap in it. Then she washed the breakfast dishes, as she had done often.

She was just finishing up dishes when the farmer came back into the house from chores. Ma, he said to her, you want to go with me to look at that oat seeder? They had seen a seeder advertised in the Farm Bureau's paper, a used oat seeder for sale over west of Emmetsburg. This was their first season at seeding and planting and when the soil warmed enough they would need an oat seeder.

Old Tom Maury's farm was five miles west of Emmetsburg. Emmetsburg was fifteen miles west of Rodman. The young farmer and his wife climbed into their 1940 Ford sedan. In those days you could buy an auto painted just about any color you wanted–that was the joke–as long as it was black. It was a black 1940 Ford. They were going to Tom Maury's over west of Emmetsburg and they were going to buy an oat seeder.

Old Tom Maury had farmed all his life. He lived in a big white house set square to the road. He was big and jovial and his eyes tended to well up when he laughed. He was near retirement age now and maybe that was why he'd put his oat seeder up for sale. The black Ford pulled into the farm yard and Tom Maury came out to greet the young couple who got out of the car.

The young farmer asked the old farmer if he was the fellow with the oat seeder for sale.

Yes.

Can we see it? the young farmer asked.

Yes.

And together the three of them, the old farmer, the young one, and the young wife, angled over to the machine shed where the seeder was kept. It was old. It had been well-used. Yet there still was a little paint left on it.

An oat seeder of this kind is set into the tailgate section of a farm wagon. A chain from the wheel of the wagon runs up to a sprocket on the seeder and spins a pair of trays to spray seed out in an arc of about twelve feet. Someone drives tractor and pulls the wagon across a worked field. Someone else stays in the wagon, shoveling seed into the hopper. You go up the field and back. Repeat the process until the whole field is seeded. Up and back.

Now the young farmer stood at the edge of the light

in the machine shed, not far from the seeder; he stood a little sideways to the older man; he looked down at his shoes, then up into the face of Tom Maury.

How much would you be wanting for the seeder? the young man asked.

Old Tom said he'd probably have to have forty dollars.

The young farmer said he could probably give thirty-five.

The old farmer looked down at his own shoes. He paused. There was a bird in the machine shed, making noise. Old Tom looked up into the face of the young farmer. Then he looked over at the softened roundness of the wife not yet four months pregnant.

On such a fine day as this, the old farmer said, for such a fine young couple, I suppose I could let it go for thirty-five.

Together the old farmer and the young one set the oat seeder into the trunk of the Ford and tied it into place for the drive back to Rodman. The young wife had been studying Tom Maury's house and buildings and fields from her vantage point in the doorway of the machine shed and now she offered how it was a beautiful place he had. She might have been a little green with envy, and wistful; she might have thought Tom Maury had everything. And Tom— he was proud of his spread, sure. He beamed a little bit at the compliment. But maybe Tom envied their youth, their whole lives stretched out before them. That kind of envy was not something he could put in words.

There you go, then, he said instead, pulling tight the last knot in the rope holding the seeder in place.

They left Tom Maury's late in the morning, the young couple did, to drive home. They were headed back to their little rented farm. To a house without running water. With an outhouse for plumbing. With an icebox, not a refrigerator. In the trunk behind them, the oat seeder rattled and creaked. They would use it later that spring, putting in oats and flax. They'd continue using it as long as they raised oats, all their lives, as long as they farmed, but they didn't know that yet. Still, driving home, the young couple talked of the future. They didn't stop for lunch in Emmetsburg, they went home to bean soup. The sun shone bright all across the Iowa farmland. In the ditches along the roadside there was a faint dreaming hint of green. The young farmer had been to war and did not talk much ever; he was a man of very few words; but even he talked of his plans, his hopes, his dreams. The young wife, she talked too. They talked about everything, the whole life they'd share.

They might have talked about the children they would have. The woman would have told her farmer-husband that if he didn't want a dozen kids, he shouldn't have married her. They might have talked about finding a better farm to rent next year, better than what they were farming now, better soil, better buildings, more acreage; about a big, old empty house that would stand on the place, and how they'd proceed to fill it with children. They might have talked about buying a farm at some future time, once they'd gotten their feet under them good, once they had some experience behind them and some credit built up, once they had sons and daughters to help with the work.

They might have talked about old Tom Maury and how maybe they'd name their first-born after the old farmer.

They might have talked about the first refrigerator they would ever buy; how they'd get it at Wilson Hardware in West Bend, a new Kelvinator model called the Shelvador, how they'd pay for it with some of the one hundred dollars a month the young farmer had earned as a soldier fighting the Nazis.

They might have talked about earning a reputation for paying their bills. That would get them good credit.

Why, in the year or so that the rural electric cooperative made such information public, three times it announced this young farm couple had been the very first to pay their electric bill this month, and this month, and this. Do you get that bill and always run right out to pay it? a jealous sister would ask the young farmer when she saw his name in the paper time and again.

They might have talked about grandchildren and great-grandchildren, about fifty-some years of married life, a life busting full of happiness, a life with its sadnesses as well.

Maybe they didn't talk about the lonesomeness in those early years. About the day the young farmer would be planting corn in the near field. His wife would be so lonesome for him, she would want an excuse to go out and visit with him. They would have had bean soup for lunch. She'd think: I'll take him a bean sandwich and talk with him while he eats it. Bean sandwich! the farmer would exclaim. Whoever heard of a bean sandwich! Well, the wife would say, in my family we have bean sandwiches all the time. We have bean soup for dinner and then a bean sandwich for supper. The young farmer would go ahead and eat his and the couple could talk.

Driving home from Tom Maury's farm, the oat seeder rattling in the trunk, maybe they didn't talk about the morning the young farmer and the hired hand headed off to work the other two hundred acres over near West Bend. The young wife still had chicken chores to do, but they didn't have to be done right away so she went back to bed. Along comes a knocking at the door and there's a young fellow who says he's selling magazines to work his way through college. I don't have any money for magazines, the wife would tell him, but I sure get bored out here. Tell you what, she says, you help me to do the chicken chores, and I'll play cards with you. So that's what she did. The young wife and that magazine salesman did up the chicken chores, then they went to playing cards all morning. Along about half past eleven, the wife told that young salesman that her husband and the hired man would be coming home for dinner at noon and he'd have to get moving along. It wasn't until years later she wondered what nosy neighbors might have thought about her entertaining a young fellow all morning while her husband was away. She was still that innocent.

Maybe they didn't talk about the coming August. The young farmer would be working with the threshing crew to get the flax in. His wife would see in the paper there was a 320 acre farm at Curlew for rent, from an important man in Graettinger. The young wife would have the nerve to call that important man and say to him: would you mind not renting that farm until my husband can come see you about it? And the important man would say: let me see if I have this right—you want me to hold off renting my farm until your husband has time to come see me? Yes, that's right, the young wife would say, we want to rent it.

The very first day they could, the young couple went to see the important man with the farm for rent. They sat with their straight backs in their straight chairs in front of the important man's wide desk. He told them what was obvious—they didn't have money enough to farm his land, they didn't have equipment enough, they didn't have sons to help with the work. It all sounded hopeless.

The young wife spoke up. She said: if we had enough money and equipment and sons, we could afford to buy a place of our own, we wouldn't have to rent yours.

Let me call my brother, Charles, at the bank in Emmetsburg, the important man said. Charles said the young farmer had had an account at his bank for years and if he could get his father to co-sign the lease, the young couple could rent the farm.

Then two weeks later the couple would have a son and they would call him Tom and would send a birth announcement to the important man.

They started to fill up that big old farmhouse with children and every winter one more baby had to endure its draftiness–wind came in around the windows in the bedrooms, in all the rooms.

It would be another autumn, another winter approaching. The farmer would be out harvesting corn. His wife would be hauling the corn up to the crib, unloading it, taking the wagon back to the field for another load. As she waited at the end of the field for the corn picker to come around with a full load, she'd bend to pick up the corn that had dropped onto the headland. The cornpicker loses some ears when it is turned around.

One of those chilly autumn days, it would be a Saturday afternoon, the farmer's wife was out there again at the end of the field, waiting for another load of corn, bending to pick up ears that had dropped. Into the field would drive the landlord–the important man with his important Cadillac. The young wife would think this is as good a time as any to ask the very important man for storm windows for the second floor of the farmhouse. In winter, frost came into the corner of the ceiling of the stairwell and piled up two or three inches thick in there; something had to be done about it.

So she would ask for storm windows, the young wife would.

The important man would say: no, we can't buy you storm windows. We have forty-some rental houses and we couldn't possibly afford storm windows.

So the farm wife would bend and pick up an ear of corn. You can see her, it's almost like slow motion. She throws the ear into her empty wagon, just as she had been doing all day, just as she had done often, but she throws it hard. When the ear of corn hits the far side of wagon, nearly all the kernels explode off of it—she threw that hard and the corn was that dry. If you can't get us storm windows, the farm wife says to the important man, you can bet that's the last damn ear of corn I'm picking up for you.

The young farmer, when he heard about this exchange, would be furious. He would say: Mother, it's just things like this that's going to cause us to have to move.

That would be a Saturday afternoon. On Monday morning, even before the sun was up, 5:30 a.m., the phone rings in the drafty old farmhouse. The young wife answers. Ah, says the important man on the other end, I got the boss. I wanted to talk to you. Charles and I were visiting yesterday and we thought it would be a good idea if you had the fellow at the lumberyard in Curlew come out and measure the house for storm windows. You want to have him put storm windows on the first floor, too.

The couple farmed that land near Curlew for more than fifteen years. Every year they worried this would be the year they'd have to move. They didn't know that the important man would tell them, once they'd made a down payment on a farm of their own, that he would never, not ever, have made them move. But buy a farm they would, that couple, no longer as young as they once were.

They'd go to the bank in Emmetsburg to tell the very important man's brother, Charles, that they'd bought a farm. The hell you did, Charles would say. Your account is overdrawn.

Well, that's what we need to see you about, the farmer would say. We wrote another check yesterday, for a $5000 down payment, and we need you to cover it.

All this lay before the young couple, lay off in the future. As they drove home that morning in March, maybe they talked about how 1947 would not be a good year for farming, or maybe they did not talk of it. A storm on May 28 would put four inches of snow on their fields. The corn that had been cultivated already was killed. The corn that had not been cultivated, that corn survived. Did they talk about the hail storm that would come on the sixth of June, followed by another one two weeks later, chopping at the crops; then the heavy, wet weather until the Fourth of July? About the rest of the summer without a drop of rain? About the beans that had been replanted because of the hail and that wouldn't sprout until the end of September?

Maybe they didn't talk about this: after their first year farming, they had less money than they had started with. On their tax return for the year, they would include this note to the IRS: "As near as we can tell, you owe us money."

Never would they remember exactly what all they talked of that day, driving back to Rodman from Tom Maury's farm with the oat seeder clattering in the trunk of the old black Ford. They never talked to old Tom Maury again, though they drove past his farm a hundred times over the years. Every time they did, the farm wife would relive her most perfect day. That morning of making plans for the rest of their lives, that day in spring, long ago now, in March, 1947. The snow of winter was gone then–none was left in the ditches, none along the fence rows. As the young couple drove back towards their first home, they could smell the freshness of the new earth. They could feel the weight of the sun against their skin, the wind at the hairs of their forearms. The whole world was throbbing around them, through them, in them. Their whole life together was rolling out before them. Electric. As alive as anything can be.

The Journey:

West Bend, Iowa,
Tuesday, October 24, 2000, Afternoon

As I drive into West Bend, I'm looking for the grain elevator that in my memory *is* West Bend. It remains hidden in the haze. I am a block and a half from it before the elevator finally shows itself. West Bend.

Where my Gramma Allen's house once stood, now there is J.B. Mertz's farm implement dealership, an AMPRIDE gas station, a worked field. There is no sign anywhere this piece of ground has stories. By neglect or intent we erase ourselves from the land. There is a big old tree in front of Mertz's shop; it has been trimmed back severely yet I think I recognize it as an old friend. I think I have played in its shade.

Downtown West Bend has a sad look, as if so much has been lost; yet enough business remains that in my rearview mirror I see a fellow run across Main Street in white shirt and tie.

I drive past St. Peter and Paul's Church and the Grotto of the Redemption but I don't stop. The Grotto Restaurant looks closed. The surface of the pond just north of the Grotto, and the land along the edge of it, these are covered with Canadian geese. The geese call thickly: wronk, wuck, wuck. An old fence surrounds the pond, it may be the very fence Father Dobberstein had to put up when the pond was dug out. Wuck, wuck say the geese. There is a pair of swans out on the water, with more elegance in a single toenail than the whole flock of geese can muster.

On the Porch???

I don't have the least electric tendril of a memory: what I know of the story is what my mother told me as she teased me about it.

We had been to one of those Sunday dinners at Gramma's house in West Bend, I suppose. We had eaten fried chicken, mashed potatoes and gravy, cherry pie. And I suppose we were outside sitting with a cool breeze in the shade of the big old cottonwood at the corner of the yard, along the drive from the south. Someone would have been telling about a friend or neighbor or acquaintance who kept a sow on the porch of his house, where it had farrowed. A litter of pigs born right on the porch, can you imagine that?

Some years later I was also appalled to learn that our hired girl's family kept a few chickens penned into the corner of their dining room. That family ate dandelion gravy, too. Whoever heard of such things?

So it was Sunday after dinner at Gramma's. We were in the shade of the cottonwood. People were talking the way people talk after dinner on Sunday, nowhere to go 'til chore time. Someone spoke of that sow farrowing on the porch.

Supposedly I exclaimed "On the porch???"–my nose turned up in astonishment, my voice full of great surprise. "On the porch???"

❧ On the Porch??? ❧

No family is large enough that you ever live anything down. Not something like this—"On the porch???" I'd just be congratulating myself that I hadn't heard the story for quite some time, then my mother or grandmother would haul it out to remind a whole great gathering of relatives. "Oh, Tom was so surprised to hear about that sow on some farmer's porch," my mother might say. "He said 'On the porch???'" Her voice was round and turned upward. Astonishment, you console yourself, is one of the first qualities of poetry.

The Journey:

West Bend and Mallard, Iowa,
Tuesday, October 24, 2000, Afternoon

I used to think the land here was flat. I had not yet been to Kansas.

The land rises and falls with swells like a moderate ocean. There have been more fields of soy beans than corn here this past season. The road between West Bend and Mallard is paved all the way now. Much of it used to be gravel.

All of a sudden I'm upon the curve I slid my car through ass-end first back when I was seventeen-years-old and still believed I'd live forever. My heart skips a beat, reminding me of my good fortune. A quarter-mile farther on another red-tail hawk rises on the wind.

Distant farmsteads shine through the haze. I think of last October, southern Alberta. My wife and I had been driving the prairies looking for Writing-on-Stone Provincial Park east of Milk River. In the distance, across the border into Montana, the Sweetgrass Hills. That's what I'm seeing here, farmsteads in the afternoon haze shining like sweetgrass hills.

Registering for First Grade at St. Mary's School in Mallard

It is a clear and powerful image, the memory of registering for first grade at St. Mary's Catholic School in Mallard. Mallard was a few miles south and east of our farm. We went to Mass faithfully in Mallard, at the Catholic Church there adjacent to the school.

There was a long, wide sidewalk leading up the incline to the brick school house and its double-door entrance on the east side. I was bare-foot and in bib overalls. My mother was talking with the nun, getting me set to start first grade the coming September. The room was filled with fuzzy light, dirty pools of it. A smell lingered in the hallway, of unwashed farm children. The nun was a study in quiet severity, black and white. My bib overalls. My bare feet.

I stretched out a leg to touch my toe to the wrought iron framework of one of the school desks. My big toe caressed the ironwork.

Was there some question whether I was ready for first grade? I'd had only the six weeks of kindergarten offered by the public school in Curlew, I was a farm kid who seldom got off the farm, and there I stood all tow-headed and barefoot. Perhaps this was not what the good nun expected when she'd said her vows and made her promises to God. Maybe she hadn't considered that she'd have to spend her life ministering to such young heathens as I was. Of course every dollar of tuition was one dollar less the parish had to set aside to support the school, and I represented a few dollars of tuition. I was the oldest of several farm kids who might follow me through the grades. So my mom and the nun got it all untangled and I was registered for school.

To our right as my mother and I walked back down the broad sidewalk from the school to our car, across the fence to the south, a farm field was being worked. A farm field off to our right hand, the church off to our left, and now I was signed up for the best adventure a farm kid could want—a little schooling, some book learning, a way through and beyond the fences that marked the edges of the world.

The Journey:

Mallard,
Tuesday, October 24, 2000, Afternoon

Mallard seems about as prosperous as it ever did, although the buildings on Main Street are obviously fifty years older than they used to be. I don't look so good myself.

The front steps and main doors of St. Mary's Church are only half as wide as I remember them. The grade school I attended—St. Mary's—is gone. An empty light fills the space the school had occupied. There is a parking lot there now. "You don't know what you've got 'til it's gone." The field south of where the school stood is only grey stubble, the soy beans have been taken. There is a smatter of wet leaves in the street.

All of a sudden the air is charged with brightness. I look again at the empty space where the school had been. I am immensely sad. I recognize that part of me has been lost. "Oh, don't it always seem to go...." A ragged American flag flaps in the breeze at the church entrance.

I make three passes through downtown Mallard, just to be sure it's really there. It is not a mirage. It is more than memory. Along Main Street a "Commercial Enforcement Vehicle" has a truck pulled over. My dad used to call these fellows "Weigh-boys." I'm not sure anything on the back of the flat-bed this Weigh-boy stopped has been strapped down securely; apparently the officer isn't convinced either. A handful of fellows stand around close, surveying the situation, appearing ready to help, smiling because it's not their problem.

Between Mallard and Curlew, Iowa,
Tuesday, October 24, 2000, Afternoon

Halfway between Mallard and Curlew, I stop at the Rush Lake Cemetery. I don't remember ever stopping here when I lived at Curlew, it's not the Catholic cemetery. Yet here I am: somebody has got to walk the cemeteries and I guess I got the job.

Stone: "John Dilocker, born in Wislemberg, Germany, March 13, 1812, died at Curlew, Ia., July 7, 1897."

Stone: "Harriet Talbert, wife of Jas. McCreary, August 11, 1834-Dec. 3, 1910. James McCreary, July 11, 1830." No date of death is given for McCreary. I wonder where he is buried.

Stone: "Dean Backstrom, 1927-1987, parents of Dennis, Debra, and Dale." Why does that name sound familiar?

Stone: "Edwin N. Anderson, 1923-1990. Neoma M., 1922-1993. Parents of Betty, Shirley, Richard, and Alan." These were the Andersons, near neighbors.

The sky is full of the sound of what I believe are A-10 Warthog war planes playing tag overhead. There are fields on three sides of the cemetery and across the road, the stubble of corn, soy beans. The stone markers want to speak: "God damn," they want to say, "year after year, up and down the tractors go, back and forth. They give us no peace and now the sky is filled with more unhappiness."

Stone: "Elmer Lowman, 1912-1975." This is another name I half recognize, or should. Or this one: "Homer Lowman, 1897-1970." One of these fellows was our gas man.

I look to the east. More than an eighth of a mile off in that direction, a red-tail hawk sits on a fence post, watching.

Stone: "Eddie Seagren, 1912-1978." This is a brother of Squeek, who ran the grocery store in Curlew; I think Eddie ran the garage.

Stone: "Oral M. Headrick, 1912-1992. Bertha A., 1917-1987. Gerald R., 1942-." Relatives of mine. A shudder of chill recognition, that we are ashes.

Stone: "Leslein, Leonard E., 1920-. Mary E., 1921-. Parents of Marilyn, Connie, and Joy." The Lesleins have not died yet but they appear prepared for that eventuality, their stone in the Leslein family plot.

Stone: "Ruth Wermersen, 1929-1994. Robert, 1925." Ruth helped my mother with laundry and cleaning sometimes, and she baby-sat us at times. Was it Robert who ran the hog-buying station in Curlew?

Overhead the A-10s make another rumbling pass. The sound of the wind in the pine trees is lost in the roar. The ground almost trembles.

The Eclipse

The eclipse is only an image now, memory's photograph. I could not have been more than five years old. I was standing in the farm yard, midway between the northeast corner of the farmhouse and the southwest corner of the barn. My mother was off somewhere to my left or behind me. Perhaps she was putting wash on the clothesline. The sky was growing dark, the air was fuzzy with darkness, the darkness was like dust blotting out the world. My father drove a team of horses into the yard; the horses were pulling a wagon. I remember the play of light and darkness in the wheels of the wagon. I remember how the horses seemed to have blankets hanging off them. Blankets of darkness.

"Don't look at the sun," my mother said. The sun was dark now and I was staring up at it, a little scared. The sun was at the 11:15 a.m. position in the Iowa sky and it was not shining any more. The air was heavy with shadow, as if some great storm was coming strong. As if the world was holding its breath. As if I had plenty of reason to be scared.

I remember the play of light and darkness in the spokes of the wagon wheels as my father brought the team into the yard. The wheels were turning as if in slow motion. Everything was moving as if in slow motion, until the instant everything stood still.

☞ *The Eclipse* ☜

Memory's photograph: the dark sun; the air diffused with darkness; the boy in the farm yard, scared; the team of horses coming on. That instant.

Farming With Horses

We still used horses on the farm when I was young. I remember having to water the pair of them at the big, round water tank to the east side of the barn. I'd stand at the tank, a line for each horse in hand, thinking about the old saying "You can lead a horse to water but you can't make him drink." Ours drank just fine, and they were somewhat noisy about it.

They weren't big horses. They weren't a lovely matched set. And we didn't use them for any of the heavy work. They'd pull wagons full of corn; they'd haul manure out to the field. Maybe they pulled the buck rake we had, raking hay, though I don't remember it. We had a horse-drawn mower, too, though again I don't remember seeing the horses hitched to that.

I do remember the day we got rid of the horses. Oral Headrick, relation of my mother who lived in Curlew, hauled livestock for a living; my dad hired him to take the horses off to wherever it is old horses go—the glue factory, I guess. My brother Flip was four or five years old at the time; and he was not very happy to see the horses loaded onto the truck, not happy to see the truck roll off down the road. It was seven or eight years later, a long time since we'd seen Oral Headrick, when Flip and the truck driver met at a family reunion.

"Do you remember who I am?" Headrick asked Flip.

"Yeah," Flip said. "You're the son of a bitch who hauled away our horses."

Learning To Drive

When I tell people I drove tractor before I started school, they say yeah sure and shake their heads, thinking that I'm making it up. One of my earliest memories is hauling a load of corn to the neighbor's place a quarter mile east of us and three quarters of a mile north, just at the edge of Curlew, the place my Uncle Larry would later farm. I was driving our Ford tractor, following along behind my father who was pulling our feed mill with the Farmall "M." We were going to the neighbor's to grind some feed. As I remember, steering wasn't difficult–the Ford was always an easy tractor to handle. The tricky part for a five-year-old was getting stopped at the stop sign a quarter mile east of our driveway, then stopping again in the neighbor's yard. Success! When you are the eldest son in a farm family, you do what you've got to. It had been grey and ragged that spring day, but all of a sudden–accomplishment!–the world was bright.

I wasn't much older when I drove my uncle's car a quarter mile along our gravel road and into the farm yard. My uncle worked as our hired man then. We'd gone west out of the driveway to herd some cows to the barn. My uncle thought that once he got them going, they'd move along to the barn, but they didn't, they needed someone to push them, and that would be my uncle. He pointed the car towards home for me, I held onto the steering wheel and swung my foot down to engage the clutch. My uncle reached in through the window and put the car in low gear. I couldn't put my foot on the gas and see out the windshield at the same time, so the car rolled home at an idle, a slow crunch of gravel beneath the tires. My uncle pushed the cows along the lane off to my left, yee-hah, and he kept an eye on the kid in his Kaiser.

A distinct memory: hauling in oats from the field in the full heat of summer. I was in second or third grade perhaps. My father was in the field with the combine, filling wagons with rich yellow oats, a good harvest. My mother was at the farmhouse, and every time I rolled in with another wagon-load of oats, she'd help me unload it. We had to use the wagon hoist to lift the front end of the wagon high enough that all the oats slid to the tailgate of the wagon, into the elevator, up into the bin in the crib. I'd put the wagon in its proper place and unhook it from the Ford tractor. My mother was on the Farmall "H" and started the elevator. I'd pop open the tailgate of the wagon to get the oats running out and my mom used the "H" to raise the front end of the wagon high off the ground. I remember how even the most well-greased elevator creaked and screeched. The dangerous part of it was having the front end of the wagon some six feet in the air. The dust of the oat field was in my nose, was caught in the hairs of my arms like sunlight. I felt like I was contributing. Creak screech went the elevator, and then the wagon was empty. We'd lower the hoist, I'd hook the Ford back up to the wagon and head to the field to bring in another load.

I was in fourth grade perhaps when my father said Yes you can take the pickup out to the hayfield and teach yourself to drive it. It was an early 1950s Ford pickup with three on the floor. We'd just baled hay, the field was short stubble. I had forty acres to turn 'round in. It was late afternoon, chores were done, light lay like a fine dust on everything. There was a badger hole out in the middle of the field, black dirt kicked up at the entrance to it. I stopped the pickup briefly in the long light to watch the badger grumbling about the area. I maintained my distance because the fellow was broadly-built and looked fierce. I'd never seen a badger before and took its appearance while I was learning to drive the pickup as a good omen. Those were the days when I was young and the world was still tender; I could take most anything as a good sign of something.

The Grove

The grove of trees around the old farmstead sheltered the house from that Iowa wind. This wasn't South Dakota, so the wind didn't run us to death; it just left us tired. There were no great trees in the grove itself, none stand in the memory as giants.

There were mulberry trees, two or three of them, heavy with berries in summer, berries the size of nipples. Sometimes we'd climb into those mulberry trees and pick the berries by hand; sometimes we'd lay sheets on the ground around the trees—it looked as if a girl may have dropped her slip to the floor—and then we'd shake the trees and shake them. Berries pelted the sheets and stained them.

Was there a honeysuckle hedge somewhere along the edge of the grove? I think so.

Did the grove keep light coming through even as it deflected the wind? The way light wanted to worm its way among the trees was the most astonishing thing. Speckled, splotched, freckled, the ground danced with diffused brightness and shadow—at dawn, at high noon, near sunset. The light among the trees was never sharp and dangerous, more like a moist kiss, your lover's warm breath soft about your neck. The light had a clinging quality and it tugged at you; enough of it made you lonely.

Sometimes we'd put up a big old canvas tent within

the shelter of the trees. Sometimes we'd leave the tent up all summer, rain or shine. When you stepped into the tent, you'd notice the musty smell, you could almost feel the moisture in the thick grey fabric. After a run of hot summer days, the air in the tent would choke you. On an evening, my brothers and I might sleep out in the tent, listening to strange sounds in the night, a blanket beneath us, another blanket to cover our fear, our noses close to the musk of earth. Another night, my sisters might sleep out there and I don't know what frightened them.

Sometimes my dad would burn scraps of lumber and branches and other useless pieces in one of the more open places on the floor of the grove. It was never a big fire, only enough to do what had to be done. I remember a day's end, the western sky an orange glow, the fire's embers starting to die down, my dad was being bothered by a fly of some sort. It wouldn't leave him alone. He slapped at the fly. "Get out of here," he said, and slapped at the fly again. "If I got to, I'll get my gun and shoot you." I wondered was my dad a good enough shot to pick a fly out of the air with a .22? He never did get out his rifle. The image is: my father swatting at the fly; the grove; the dying of the light.

The Hay Stack

The stack of bales in our far west forty must have been an emblem of some sort. It was a great pile of hay, fifteen or twenty feet wide, fifteen or twenty feet high, almost an eighth of a mile long sometimes. Mostly the hay was alfalfa, the best kind, stacked like the best kind of firewood, oak. The hay stack was our message to winter: we are ready.

Yes, we put a lot of hay into our haymow–the rope and pulley system and the great hay knives lifted eight or ten bales at a time into the dark mow. Yet some winters a haymow full of hay is not enough. Some summers the hay field kept producing, four crops of it, once five, the final crop in late September. A prudent farmer doesn't leave good hay standing in the field.

It was large work, throwing bales off the flat rack onto the pile of hay and stacking them, higher and higher, as high as the sun, hay dust clinging to sweat, sweat running in your eyes, stinging, burning summer heat and the smell of alfalfa.

A fellow doesn't grumble stacking bales outside when a breeze blows his way: it is always worse in the heat of a haymow where it's dark and humid and so close you get claustrophobic, you kind of panic and you can't breathe.

We'd put the sharp, cut edge of the bales down to the earth, knowing at the start the bottom layer always takes up some moisture and would likely be spoiled. The cut edge was always more square, solid, firmer. Then we'd crisscross bales in layers, fifteen or twenty layers, bales laid over each other and interlocked to keep the pile held together. How good the hay pile stands, that's how good your sons are. Have to shore up a leaning pile right out there in the open where the neighbors could see? Not if my dad had anything to say about it.

On Saturdays in winter, I might be sent out to that hay pile in the west forty to bring some feed up for the cattle. I'd start moving bales, carrying them from the hay pile, stacking them on the flat rack. And then–despite the 20-degree temperature, despite the blinding whiteness of snow stretching into the distance–all of a sudden I'm caught in my summer work. An intensity of alfalfa in the fresh winter air. A sear of deep, pulsing greenness. The smell of hay, a summer's day. Suddenly the Saturday in January was not quite so cold, the day's work not quite so long. You'd stand there wasting the moment, transported.

West Edge

A ditch ran along the west edge of our half section. The gravel road there had been re-made, as I remember, and a new fence line had to be put in. My father and I were at work on the fence, using the hydraulic post driver on the front of the Farmall "M" to set creosoted wood posts into the ground in a straight line half a mile long. I remember the feel of the sun, the wind in the hairs of my arms, the sound the post driver made–HUNGK, HUNGK, HUNGK. We used the Ford tractor to stretch woven wire taut along the posts, then drove in staples to hold the fencing in place. We had to set a strand or two of barb wire above the woven wire.

You don't notice how much you notice. In my image of this, the sun is eternally at 11:00 a.m., the sky is clear, there is a breeze. The edge of the field where we're setting the fence seems bare–much of the ditch had been scraped to black dirt. At the northeastern corner of the farm there was still some of the succulent grass we called "pull-aparts." There was the sharp grass we called "saw grass" and I cut my finger. I remember the keenness of that cut, the sting of it, the raw tear in the fabric of flesh. It's 11:00 a.m. on a blue sky Iowa day, I'm bleeding, and there's a lot of fence left to build.

Christmas Bicycle

That same year we got our first bicycle for Christmas we got a record player too. The winter had not yet been tough. A memory of the sun was still in my eyes as I stepped into the dimness of the house. "Well?" someone said. Well what? It took a moment for my eyes to adjust, then I saw the record player in its big blond cabinet. There was only one record with it, Hank Williams' hit songs. "Good-bye, Joe, we gotta go," he sang. Over and over. And there, near the record player, stood a bicycle.

We learned to ride bicycle that Christmas Day. We bundled ourselves lightly, those with legs long enough to reach the ground, and we took the new bike outside. There was snow on the ground around the house but when you've got a new bike and you're a farm kid who has never seen anything quite so shiny, who has never had anything so red and bright and wonderful, you don't care if it's winter, you don't care if you turn blue riding and riding until you've learned to stop the wobbling. We tramped out a track in the snow around the house. We weaved and wobbled our way, each of us, learning to ride.

I am the oldest, so I go first. That's just how it is, a family of nine kids, someone has to go first, it might as well be me. I climb on the bicycle and wheel away and I don't even make it to the corner of the house before I have snow up my nose. I pick myself up and pick up the bike and I climb back on. You ride the horse that threw you. The two oldest girls, Kack and Nancy, and my next brother, Flip, all wait their turns. "Hurry up, Tom!" they say impatiently.

There were rules; they were never spoken but they were very clear: you got to circle the house once on the track we had tramped out, then it was the next person's turn, in order of age. You stayed on the track around the house and didn't go free-lancing cross country. You didn't whine or cry out when you fell. And you didn't dally-oof around picking yourself up, there were others waiting.

The oldest four of Bill and Oma Montag's kids learned to ride bike in the snow that Christmas day in the 1950s. Inside, Hank Williams was singing away–"Good bye, Joe," again and again. We would work the grooves almost all the way through that thick, black piece of vinyl, playing it over and over. Hank Williams might have been dead already, I don't know, I haven't done the math.

Done with riding bike, we might have come back into the house, the two oldest boys, the two oldest girls, smug and swaggering and shining because we had a bicycle and we could ride it. No one could take what we knew from us. We didn't have a lot of money that Christmas, but it sure seemed like we had everything we'd ever need.

Our mother might have made hot chocolate for us when we came back in, blue and cold and laughing. Maybe we sat at the table at the end of the long kitchen, sat there back under the stairs, beyond the wood stove. We might have had our hot chocolate and laughed some more and congratulated ourselves on how fortunate we were–a new bike, learning to ride, a record player, and Hank Williams yodeling his way into the rest of our lives.

The Sunday Bicycle Ride

It would be a Sunday in spring. We'd have been cooped up all winter in farmhouse and schoolroom. Like horses in the barn, we'd be wanting to get out in the warm, bright air, to get out and run, to kick up our heels at the front edge of a new season.

We'd gather in the farmyard on our bikes, as many of us as wanted to ride the four miles of gravel road around the section of land our farm was part of. Someone would run into the house and yell to our parents "We're going!" and we'd be headed west down our gravel road.

It was exuberance; it was never a race. The road might still be soft in places. Our tires left tracks at times. The air of a Sunday afternoon in April or May would be warming, starting to shimmer. There was a country muskiness all around–the smell of decaying vegetation, good black dirt, moisture, a world all primed for another turn of the seasons.

We raced along to the west but we didn't race. On our left we passed the house of a man who worked for the Andersons. His wife made rag rugs, which were amazing for a young mind to contemplate: you'd take her a big box of rags and get back a fine, thick rug. The stretch between rag and rug was so great I could not imagine the transformation. I thought of these neighbors as "poor folks," for once when we were butchering chickens the Missus took home a bag of chicken feet for supper. She also kept guinea hens running around her yard. We might have bantam roosters loose in ours, but guinea hens?

Modern parents might wonder about the wisdom of sending four or five youngsters off down the road by themselves. What about automobile traffic? someone might worry. What about strangers? This was rural Iowa, remember, the 1950s. There were no strangers, or darn few. There was not much traffic on those gravel roads and even in spring you'd see the dust cloud coming a long ways off. We'd wheel to the very edge of the road, we'd stand straddling our bikes, and we'd let pass the farmer on his Sunday drive or the family coming home from chicken dinner at gramma's. No one was ever driving very fast. When you have nowhere to go, there's no need to hurry. You might as well enjoy the going.

We would turn right at the first cross road west of us three quarters of a mile. We'd turn right, which was north. Along our right-hand side the first half mile after we turned was our own farmland, forty acres of hay perhaps and then forty acres where we might put soybeans this year. On our left we passed what I remember as the Haywood place. In my memory there is a hill behind their house, the farmyard sets at a hilly angle. Perhaps there is a hill in my memory because I thought the Haywoods were hillbillies. I thought perhaps they didn't quite understand our rules. Not that we were ever the arbiters of proper middle western behavior, mind you. What did we know? There were evergreens around the Haywood house, close in. I liked the look of that house and yard. The Mister, I think, was one of those farmers who liked to cool off with a beer in Curlew whenever the day got too hot for farming.

At the half mile mark, close to where I think the Haywood house stood, a fence line divided our half section from the neighbor's. Later we farmed that ground, too, both those half sections, helping my mom's youngest brother Larry get a start in farming. The next year Larry farmed the adjoining land himself.

We made another right turn at the first crossroad to the north. Running the length of a mile headed east now there was not much to notice, only the homestead of Blaine Drown. Curlew was set down at the very end of that mile. Here we came past the Little League field first; it was green even early in spring. Across the street stood the school where I attended kindergarten back when six weeks in spring might be enough of that.

The whole quarter mile of Curlew's main street was paved, as was a three-mile stretch heading east from Curlew to the state highway. Paved roads. I might have thought paved roads were pretty cosmopolitan, if I'd known then what cosmopolitan was. We didn't see many paved roads; instead it was miles and miles of gravel roads in an endless grid across the countryside.

Often we'd stop for an ice cream cone at the cafe in Curlew. I'd hold the coins to pay for them in my upturned, sweaty palm and the owner of the cafe would count out what he needed. He was tall, stooped, and somewhat balding, grandfatherly in his manner. He had to bend to take the money from me. His wife wore her white hair in a bun at the back of her head. She wore a long, white apron as she waited on customers. She always wore a mild, wan smile as she pushed the scoop of ice cream into a cone.

By the time we crossed the railroad tracks and were headed south out of Curlew, we were just a mile or so from home. The home stretch. We passed the Gaddis farmstead on our right, where later Uncle Larry and his family would live.

It was a long, last mile from Curlew home, a bellyful of ice cream cone not withstanding. Our legs pumped and those fat bike tires crunched on stones. This stretch of gravel might be rougher than most, for it led straight into town and the constant traffic on any softness would soon turn one bump in the surface into several evenly spaced bumps, like a washboard. These rattled your teeth when you were riding in a car, and they certainly got your attention on a bicycle. You didn't want to head into a run of them at an angle; you needed to take them straight on, as farm boys took the rest of life, straight on, win, lose, or draw.

We always said "turn a mile south of Curlew," but we knew the corner was really only three quarters of a mile south of the train tracks. Here we turned right, headed west again, raced towards home, our tired legs pumping, all of us wanting to be the first to run into the house and yell "We're home!" The screen door slammed behind us as we came into the house, each of us, bamm, bamm, bamm, bamm, bamm, "We're home!"

The Sunday Afternoon

There was no hour ever longer than 3:30-4:30 p.m. summer Sunday afternoons, the farm, Curlew, Iowa, the 1950s. The afternoon buzzed and time stood still. We would have been to church in the morning and would be feeling saved, but to what end? By 3:30 p.m. those Sundays the earth had stopped its spinning. The sun stood still. The birds would not sing. Everything was s l o w motion. It was like being dead only you were still warm and breathing, awfully warm.

We were farm kids so we were used to an endless round of chores and tasks. A lazy Sunday afternoon left us feeling like we were slogging through some pretty deep mud, slippery-slow-going, and you'd wonder why, and what to do. I'd stand in the yard and throw a stone out onto the driveway just to see the spit of dust dancing on an unreliable breeze. I'd find myself a place under a cottonwood tree and let life fill me like a fly buzzing in a fruit jar. Zzzz, Zzz, Zzz. The moment was almost electric, but nothing happened. I had fallen head-long into the big emptiness of Sunday afternoon.

"Boys, chores," dad would say later, pulling us out of that hole in time and we'd get to doing chores–cattle, hogs, chickens. Someone would have to milk ol' Bossie. Chores were a sacred ritual, re-enacted twice a day, morning and evening, rain or shine, workdays and Sundays. If you raised animals for slaughter, you could never go far from home. Those animals would be butchered, sure, but you had responsibilities to them in the meantime.

Chores done, maybe we'd scratch out a fire pit in the gravel of the farm yard, in the coolness of the long shadows. We'd make a fire big enough to roast hot dogs for a bunch of growing farm kids. I'd sharpen a stick, drive a hot dog lengthwise onto it, and take my sweet time getting it cooked just so. There'd be a picnic table in the yard with chips or potato salad, and jello. Maybe green beans. We'd have Kool-Aid or milk or—on very rare and special occasions—a bottle of soda. I liked a strawberry flavor that fizzed up my nose, or Royal Crown Cola. My folks would be out there in the yard with us, they'd be sitting in their chairs side by side listening for the crickets, waiting for the eastern sky to start to darken. Something—a certain intensity of chirping, a certain blue royalness of sky—something signalled it was time to get out the bag of marshmallows. The fire would have come to embers, the wind would have cooled, we'd each pop a marshmallow onto a stick and roast it. The rule was you could roast as many as you wanted, within reason, but you had to eat them. You couldn't roast one for someone else unless you'd asked if he wanted it.

Maybe it was the sugar rush that set us to playing hide-and-seek in the growing darkness. Ninety-eight, ninety-nine, one hundred, ready or not, here I come. We ran and hid and laughed and shouted and the embers of the fire died to dim coals and the longest day of the week was coming to its end.

Always we were sent into the house with instructions to clean the sweet stickiness of marshmallow off our chins, off our hands, and to get to bed. Almost always we did as we were told.

A little later we'd hear the screen door slam shut as

our parents came into the house. "Let's get to bed, Ma," my dad might say. "It's another week coming."

My Curlew

Curlew is dead center in the northwestern quarter of Iowa. It is not far from nowhere, admittedly. When I was growing up, the town's most remarkable feature was the short strip of pavement that constituted Main Street. Memory tells me the quarter mile of concrete had been poured sometime in the 1950s; the history book says the year was 1953. I was going on six years of age. I remember the ferris wheel of celebration. Pouring Main Street must have been an act of incredible optimism for a grey little farm town where the light always seemed heavy with dust. We were a long ways from anywhere, but we always knew who we were, and that was enough most days, though sometimes you wanted to get away from Curlew, to find something more. Sometimes you got restless.

Back then, Curlew was approached by gravel road from three directions—from the south, the west, the north. Three miles of pavement heading east joined Curlew's slab of main street with a U.S. highway, supposedly the first cement road in Iowa; we'd take it north to Emmetsburg for groceries. How do you prove it was the first cement road? How do you prove anything you remember being told as a child? The highway to Emmetsburg was only about eighteen feet wide and it had curbs running all the way along each edge of it, curbs instead of shoulders. Cars had been narrower back when the road was built. Things then were keenly black and white, or at least more reliably grey. The curbing had been intended to control the run-off of rain, I think.

Train tracks came through town. Indeed it was reportedly a railroad man with a sporting bent who named the village; his name was Whitehead, the year was 1882, and he was president of the Des Moines and Fort Dodge Railway. All set in a row along these tracks: Curlew and Mallard and Plover, he named them.

Approaching the village from the south, as we would when coming to town from the farm, on the left just before crossing the tracks there was a small stock yard. The fellow there bought our hogs. The operation was pretty nondescript–grey, worn, weathered. Stock pens kept one farmer's hogs separated from another's. There was a scale large enough to weigh a truckload of hogs. A small heated shed for an office. The owner I remember as just the sort of greasy, bald-headed, cigar-chomping kind of fellow you'd expect to find buying hogs in a place like Curlew. We'd stand in his office while he wrote out a check to my dad. I always noticed a powerful smell of LP gas anytime I entered, as if there was a leak in the line feeding the gas-burning heater. I noticed that smell, mixed with the smell of hogs, and I'd see tacked overhead on one of the rafters a color picture of a naked woman, sitting wrapped somehow in a kind of chiffon fabric, holding her breasts and beckoning with her eyes. I'd stand there and sneak a look at her, trying to understand what she represented. Sometimes consciousness surprises you like mirrors in a funhouse.

Across the tracks from the stockyard, butt up against the rails, there stood the depot with its large black letters on a white background: CURLEW. There were no pictures of naked women in the depot. The whole place was stark and sparely furnished, as if the building, the village, the era were all at the very edge of despair and no one could afford to invest anything more in them. The air inside the depot had a stale, dusty taste. I remember a smell of creosote.

The Curlew grain elevator was also to the left, with grain bins along the tracks. We hauled a lot of grain to Curlew in those years. For a while my mother worked there testing the moisture content of grain for the government. Nobody said it but everybody knew it: "Government don't want to be paying farmers for no goddamn water."

The owner of the elevator was involved in Little League in Curlew. I remember he drove a '59 Ford that would–at the touch of a button–fold up its hard-top roof into the trunk and become a convertible. My buddy who lived in town, Bryan Wilson, used to mow lawns in summer for a little income and he told me of mowing near this fellow's back yard. Out back of the house the fellow's wife was stretched out on a lounge chair with no blouse or bra–her pale breasts were turned to the Iowa sun, the sun was kissing her rosy nipples. My buddy said: "I'd mow and I'd look. It was Mow, Mow, Look, Look. Look, Mow, Look. It took me all morning to finish that one simple job."

On the right hand side as you approached from the south, also set alongside the railroad tracks, squatted Curlew's lumberyard. We sometimes unloaded boxcars of cement for the lumberyard, 96 pound bag after 96 pound bag, my father and I and my brother. My dad carried two at a time, and when I got a little older, so did I. "Portland Cement," the bags would say, and I'd long to be in Portland, I didn't know if it was Maine or Oregon, and I didn't care. Instead, I was in a hot, stuffy boxcar with sweat pouring off me. The metal of the boxcar was hot enough it burned the touch.

A street ran in front of the lumberyard; just across it, in an old square house, lived the fellow who owned the radio/TV repair shop in Curlew. He was a brother of the fellow who owned the grocery store and the one who owned the gas station and garage. He may have sold a few TVs in his shop, and a few radios, but mostly repaired them. Actually I never saw him do much of anything, but then farm kids wouldn't think you did much of anything unless you worked on a farm. He sold BBs in his radio/TV repair shop—don't ask me why—and from the time we were old enough to have BB guns, that's where we bought our BBs. He also shot black powder pistols and rifles in competition and had a place in his basement where a hole opened in the foundation and a tunnel lined with fifty gallon barrels ran out under the lawn. He'd be able to attach a target to a cord and move it the prescribed distance out into the tunnel; he'd take his target practice that way. The earth at the end of the tunnel was all the backstop he needed.

Half a block from this fellow's house was where my parents had lived for a year or part of a year their first or second season farming the place at Curlew. There had been a fire out at the farm and the house was being repaired. As a youngster I remember thinking the house they'd stayed at in town looked like "a poor man's house." Whatever that was. As if I'd seen enough of the world back then to be able to make that kind of judgment.

Across the concrete slab of Main Street from the office and scale belonging to the grain elevator stood another big square house, white. That's where my buddy Bryan lived. We attended school together, St. Mary's in Mallard, we were two thirds of the Three Musketeers. The third was our friend named Greg from Mallard.

Bryan and I drifted apart after I went off to high school in Sioux City, and then to college. Bryan entered the Sea Bees during the Vietnam War, enlisted for a second tour of duty, died in Vietnam building a bridge. I knew his brother, David, too; his sister was deaf and I suppose there was a "Deaf Child in Area" sign posted on the streets near their house. After Bryan died, his father–who'd worked for the elevator in Curlew–somehow veered headlong into the path of an oncoming semi. Some said it was to end the misery he felt at his loss; some said it was a heart attack.

On the left side of the block just north of Bryan's house, just north of the grain elevator, stood a building that housed a tavern; it had originally been a hardware store, a hotel before that. I was still in bib overalls when my dad sent me into that tavern to get him a six pack of Hamm's–"The Beer Refreshing"–while he attended to business at the grain elevator. It seemed just so natural, the way the fellow packaged the beer in a brown paper bag, tucked it in the crook of his arm, and walked with me back out to the car parked in front of his place, handing the beer over to my father and talking with him a bit–corn, cattle, the prospect of rain. It didn't seem at all unusual to me to be an eight-year-old farm kid ordering a six pack of beer and saying it was for my father.

North of the tavern on the same side of the street the cafe sagged with the weight of its years; this was where we'd stop to get ice cream cones those Sundays we rode our bikes "around the block," as we called the four miles surrounding our section of land. Later, when the cafe closed, a writer from the Des Moines paper poked fun at Curlew. He had stopped at the cafe to get a cup of coffee and was told–when someone finally answered the door–that if he wanted coffee he'd have to go across the street to the post office. Getting a cup of coffee at the post office and not the building marked CAFE seemed funny to him. To the rest of us it was real life, grim and serious and ours every day. It's easy to make fun when you don't come back to face it day after day. It's harder to poke fun when you live it, your own town, your tether.

An empty lot opened up next to the cafe. North beyond that stood the telephone office. As a very young fellow I sat with family and friends on benches in that empty lot at dusk, and we watched movies projected onto the white clapboard wall of the telephone building. Sitting out upon a summer's evening seeing a movie projected onto a wall–that was what we knew, we didn't have a movie house, we didn't know the difference.

Gertie was the telephone operator. She was a spinster, I guess, and I guess she was brittle the way we thought spinsters got back then. The telephone office also served as her home. The switchboard was within arm's reach of her bed in the one room apartment. Gertie had assistants, yes, but the history book says "Gertie was the faithful one at the board day after day." Those were the days of hand crank telephones. If someone on our party line wanted to call us, they'd ring two shorts and a long; or Gertie would, for calls not originating on our line. You'd ring the operator, you'd say "Gertie, give me Blaine Drown." Gertie would say "Blaine and his wife have gone to Emmetsburg. They should be back about 9:00 p.m. Why don't you try then." I presume she knew all the gossip of the area.

North beyond the telephone office was Squeek's store. You'd probably call it a "general store" today. Back then it was the grocery store in Curlew and we'd shop there for some few items. Our main grocery shopping we did at Ted's Super Valu in Emmetsburg. Squeek's was a long, narrow, two-story, wooden building. Squeek and his family lived in the apartment over the store. Entrance to their apartment was gained by way of an outside stairway, one awfully narrow and rickety as I remember. I'm glad I didn't live up there.

I think Squeek was called Squeek because his voice broke into squeaks sometimes as he talked; yet sometimes I thought it was because he talked out the side of his mouth like a weasel. On account of the way he talked, I always counted my changed pretty carefully stepping out of the store into the bright sunlight. Of course, this is just a child's sense of the world, and Squeek isn't here to defend himself.

On the right-hand side of main street in the block north of Bryan's house, the first building held the Curlew post office. The building itself had once been the Easton Hotel, something of a grand place. The owners of the hotel also ran the post office in Curlew for a long while, that's how the post office ended up in a hotel. Of course later when the cafe across the street closed up, it became a coffee shop too. The postmaster would sort mail until he had a customer wanting coffee and a sweet roll. He'd work behind the counter in the coffee shop dishing up pie or would sell you stamps at the window in the post office–which was it that you wanted? Only ignorant people will see something in this to poke fun at.

The first door north of the post office was another tavern, you needed two, even in Iowa, even in a town of 100 souls. All that dusty Iowa wind made a fellow thirsty, the thick light, all those grey Republican years. The tavern was dark with a beery smell. The sun would not penetrate very far into the room's interior; the old farmers who sat there hour after hour didn't want to be reminded that time was a-wastin'. A few fellows might be gathered around a table playing cards. There was always a checkerboard set up; the men playing checkers had grey in their hair, beer on their breaths, and watery eyes, their hands were thick slabs reaching to move a piece on the board.

Some excitement happened in Curlew just in front of that tavern. I wasn't around to see it, but you hear the talk. Seems a man and a woman had been drinking, what we called a binge back then. We had those back then. Seems they'd run out of anything to drink at home so they drove to town to get more. The man went into the tavern. The woman stayed in the car. She was entirely naked. Entirely naked women didn't go unnoticed for long in Curlew. "Clip, clip, look, look," as my friend Bryan would say. Nothing ever came of the naked woman on Main Street, as we didn't have a constable as fast as our rumors, except it gave school boys something further to ponder there at the edge of their confusion.

How mundane the world is. Next door to where the naked woman sat in her car, a feed store. We only occasionally did business there; most of our feed we bought from a Moorman's feed salesman and it was delivered straight to the farm. I remember the windows at the front of the store let in way more light than you'd need when buying feed supplement for cattle, but I'm supposing the building was recycled from some earlier use–a dry goods store perhaps. An old building in a small community spirals through its list of usefulness.

Almost across the street from Squeek's store was the cream-colored brick building that Squeek's brother used for his TV repair shop, the place we bought our BBs. It had once been Curlew's bank, I think. Even in the 1950s it had been an awful long time since Curlew had a bank. I remember once seeing a calendar the Curlew bank had issued in 1913. I remember hearing about the bank robbery, which had taken place in 1921. A witness said the robbers came out of the bank so calm and they drove away so slowly he didn't realize the bank had been robbed. The clerk was locked in a back room. The long arm of the law nabbed the robbers in Omaha shortly afterwards. The bank closed a few years later when the cashier was caught embezzling. It never reopened. Now the building was a TV repair shop and it smelled of dust baked in the sun and gun oil, for I think the owner spent time there cleaning his black powder guns as well as working on TVs.

It seems there was a vacant lot north of the TV repair shop, fronting on the cross street. North across that street, kitty-corner from Squeek's, was a big stone building, a "garage" we called it, where another of Squeek's brothers, Eddie, maybe, worked on cars. There was a gas pump out front, back in the days when you only needed one pump. There was a soda machine out front, too, back in the days when the only soda you really needed was a Royal Crown Cola, cold and sweet and wet; or maybe strawberry. The bottles hung upright in a rack; each was held in place by the lip at the top of the neck. You put your coin in the slot and you slid the bottle you wanted to buy over to a mechanism that released it, ten cents. In an instant the glass of the bottle was coated with moisture as if it were a dewy night. Maybe there was orange soda in the machine, too, and grape, but it was hard to chose anything else when you had Royal Crown.

The walls of the garage were made of worked stones thick enough for a fortress. The windows of the building were small, compared to the building's size. The interior of the place was dark; lights came down from the ceiling and could be placed as needed under the hood of a car, up under near the bell of a transmission, whatever. This was a working man's building. Here was the constant smell of 10-W-30 mixed with soil, a grimy layer underfoot. On one of the work benches here, back in those dark and troubling 1950s, I found a magazine with pictures of men and women doing things with each other that I had never yet imagined. More of that confusion. Your breath catches and you say to yourself: "Would you look at that!"

I suppose there were a few houses between Eddie's garage and the big, square, brick public school building at the edge of town. There must have been houses there, for I don't remember any gap. Across the street from Eddie's there must have been a vacant lot full of green, scruffy trees, and some quonset buildings used for storing corn.

The school in Curlew is where I first kissed a girl who

was not my sister. A big kid gave me a dime to do it. A dime was a lot of money; it would buy two Big Boogie candy bars or a bottle of Royal Crown. We were in the gymnasium. Did I have to run her down to catch her? I think so. Who was she?

The school stayed open long enough for me to attend kindergarten there, back in the days when six weeks of kindergarten was all a young fellow got. I used to have a picture of me, taken my very first day of school. I'm standing at the corner of our farmhouse, in front of the oil tank, I'm wearing a light jacket, heavy shoes, brand new overalls, I've got a bag of school supplies to take with me, the smell of spring fills the air, the smell of new clothes. It was the first day of the rest of my life. The school building stood empty for a while after it closed, until it was bought by some "Holy Roller" religious outfit (that's what we called them) for use as a training center for missionaries. Good German Catholic farm boys who wouldn't know the difference between God touching them and a case of indigestion, you might imagine we did not have much use for Holy Rollers. Everyone is narrow-minded about something, we were narrow-minded about having fits when you are talking to God.

Across main street to the west of the school—on the extreme northeast corner of the very same section of land our farm was part of—lay the baseball diamond. This is where we played Little League. The ball field and playground had belonged to the school, I think, but it also served as Curlew's park. It was here kids would run and climb and jump, run the baselines, scoop up grounders, stretch singles into doubles or get cut down trying.

The rest of Curlew was residential. Population: 100. In addition to Main Street, two other streets, both of them gravel, ran north and south through town. Four cross streets ran east and west, plus there was the pavement along the north edge of town rolling east towards some real highway three miles distant, the thread of a connection to something big and bright and better, the hell away from Curlew, if you were getting itchy, if it was time to be going. The wind couldn't beat some people out of town, it couldn't blow some others away.

The Journey:

Into Curlew,
Tuesday, October 24, 2000, Afternoon

At the crossroad just north of the Rush Lake Cemetery there used to stand a little decrepit house where a woman lived "in sin" with a man not her husband. I had always tried to imagine what living in sin would be. You could tell by looking they didn't have much, so I figured the wages of sin were pretty low. The house is gone now. The trees that surrounded it, gone.

The Lesleins' house remains. It looks well-cared for. The mailbox still says "Lesleins–Leonard and Mary."

A sad version of a pre-fab house stands where the Andersons had lived; some grove remains around it, some steel bins. The barn and all the outbuildings I remember, gone.

At the corner north of Andersons' I turn west, to my home, to what remains of it now–one steel bin, some grove, and a whole lot of desolation. I promise myself that I will come back out here and walk this piece of ground, that I will touch the cottonwoods still standing where they had shaded us at play fifty years ago.

To the west, at the edge of one of the fields we had worked, there is a corn crib. I don't remember a corn crib there. It was put up since we moved away and already it has fallen into decay.

Where Anderson's hired man lived, that house is in as good a shape of any of the places I've seen around here. Someone prospers there. He probably doesn't farm for a living.

The fence I remember helping my dad put up at the far western limit of our farm? The fence is gone, the field runs right out to the power poles at the edge of the ditch.

There is no hill at the farmstead I remember as the Haywood place. There is plenty of grove remaining, with bee hives; plenty of cattle at the small, hipped barn.

As I drive east on the road along the north side of our section, I swear it, I see another red-tailed hawk. "Curlew," the sign says, still a quarter mile from the edge of town. "Home," it should also say.

The Curlew school has been torn down. In the park, the screen backstop at the ball diamond is still there. Seagren's garage is boarded up and looks as if it hasn't been used in a long time. The TV repair shop operated by his brother is still solid, a cream brick building. Across the street, Squeek's store is gone. So is Gertie's telephone office, replaced by a brick building more optimistic than Curlew's circumstances seem to warrant. Joe Wilson's house remains, though it has aged. Curlew is smaller than I remember. There are bare patches where once there were houses. Other houses, still standing, are obviously abandoned.

A Short, Irregular History of Curlew, Iowa

There is always a history book someplace that reports more than you'll ever remember. There are always people who love the place more than you've loved it: they've stayed. They've stayed and they've recorded all they can of life, in some meagre script, to the best of their abilities. Pieces glitter like jewels. Some of it fits the story you want to tell.

There is always some irregular history somewhere and for Curlew it can be found in a book put together to celebrate the town's centennial: *Our Centennial 1884-1984: Memories of Yesterday, Hopes for Tomorrow*. The book committee was: Alene Seagren, Edra Lowman, Doris Johnson, Sylvia Lund, Verna Bohn, Alice Bohn, and Lu Etta Seagren. A lot of other Curlew residents and former residents also contributed to the Centennial book. Thanks go to all those who save history for the rest of us; their work shapes our sense of where we've been. I was ignorant of much of Curlew's history as I was growing up. I am fortunate to be able to engage it now.

Shall we imagine blue sky that day? The day when Lawrence and Bridget Guggerty submitted the plat for the Guggerty Addition in Curlew to the Palo Alto County Recorder, Thomas Walsh. The date was May 27, 1884. The time: 9:00 a.m. Bridget had to sign her mark, an X.

Surveyor James Carss certified that "the annexed Plat of Guggerty's Addition to the Town of Curlew Section 10 T. 94 R. 33 is correct and made from data of actual survey." The addition quadrupled Curlew's size.

The first settlers had come to Palo Alto County in 1855, along the east bank of the Des Moines River where West Bend stands today. They had the Civil War ahead of them still; they had a land to tame, a wild, bucking kind of land, with wind. They had children to produce, strapping children. Full of hope, they sent a generation marching off into its unknown future.

When mail service started in the county in 1858, we're told "the mail would be put in a big milk pan and settlers would come and go through it, picking out their own." Can you imagine making the long trek for mail and finding nothing waiting for you in the pan, no word from the loved ones you'd left behind, that loneliness?

In those early years, "the winters were hard, cold, and then the blizzards were not fit for man nor beast."

A great number of settlers started coming to Rush Lake township (which Curlew sits within) in 1869, and more the next spring: Grier and Sanford, Sanders and Schuler, Tressler and Lacey. In 1871, Stebbins and Gross and Elson, George White, Joseph Fisk. In 1872, Fred Cross, D.M. Wilcox.

The grasshoppers were "a fearful pest in 1873 and later years." The hoppers were a foot thick on the water, the story goes, with more of them coming over the banks like a waterfall. You see them coming, you go after them with the backside of a scoop shovel, even as you know it's a futile gesture. But you've got to do something.

S.A. Easton owned the first hotel, sold it to Melvin Fisk and built a competing establishment across the street at the corner of Second and Main. In those bright and hopeful years, the dust never settled on Main Street between Fisk's Hotel and Easton's.

H.B. Jones was Curlew's doctor in 1882.

A.P. Roberts was operating a bank in Curlew by 1893.

The 1908-1909 Iowa State *Gazetteer* business directory compiled this information about Curlew:

Population: 275.

Baptist, Christian, and Methodist Churches.

Western Union.

Telephone connection.

Drugstore, hardware store, and bank.

Curlew Band–Clay Wiley, mgr.

Easton's hotel, grain dealers, dressmakers, masons.

T.E. Keiser ran the restaurant.

The Lund brothers sold hay.

Rush Lake Creamery.

The Seagren brothers were blacksmiths.

Barber, buttermaker, drayman.

Tiederman Elevator Co.

George Tressler, carpenter.

Butcher and painter.

General stores, lumberyard, real estate.

We learn, later, that you'd get a sack of candy at Whitmer's General Store when you paid your bill. Turner's Butcher Shop had an ice house out back; Woodman Hall, meeting place for the Woodman & Royal Neighbor Lodges, was over the butcher shop and was the scene of a variety of amusements–a winter lyceum, dances, box socials. The Odd Fellows met above Hatch's Hardware Store. "Sockeye" Griffin had a team and wagon freight business, he also did harness and shoe repair. A barbershop was run by Lee Leary until he went to Montana in 1923. Mrs. H.B. Ward "*always* had her wash out every week *before* anyone else in town." Mrs. Tom Carroll was known to everybody as "Mrs. Carl"–must have been an Irish pronunciation.

Churches

The Baptist Church in Curlew is said to have started as the Colidge Street Church in 1873. By 1875 it was called The First Baptist Church of Rush Lake. "The years brought a succession of pastors to minister in the church," we're told. "Abundant blessings were received in the evangelistic and revival services." Members built "the first First Baptist Church" in 1892. Around 1895, the building "was also being used by a Christian Church Group." The old church was remodeled in 1949 and served until 1980. Ground-breaking for the current building was held June 1, 1980. "What a joyful day it was." It is this building that currently stands as the only church in Curlew.

The first services by a Methodist minister in the territory that is now the town of Curlew were conducted by A.J. Beebe, in August and September, 1879. "He was minister of the Ruthven Methodist Church, which at that time extended as far south as the present town of Mallard. The early pastors worked in a sparsely settled community and over a large territory."

On October 9, 1920, the Methodist Church in Curlew was struck by lightning and burned to the ground. One assumes this was an accident and *not* God's way of saying he was displeased with these Methodists. A new church was built. In 1977, a third building opened for services; this last church is gone now, having been moved lock-stock-and-barrel to Emmetsburg.

Monica Cullen High Remembers Curlew

"The snow was at the gable end of the house on that April 3, 1881," the day Susie Agatha Easton was born on a farm a mile north of Curlew. Susie's father, S.A. Easton, was of Scotch-Welsh background; her mother, Ellen

Cadden, was Irish. Both of Susie's parents had been born in Ontario, Canada; they moved to Gouverneur, New York, after their marriage in 1874, moved to the farm north of Curlew in 1879, moved into Curlew in 1883.

Monica Cullen High is Susie Easton's daughter. Monica also tells us:

The first boy born in Curlew was Albert Arthur Easton, born May 1, 1884, in the Curlew bandstand. The family was using the bandstand for a residence until their house could be built. Albert was called "Stub." He served in the Navy for four years and was honorably discharged in 1905 "following some guard duty after the earthquake in California."

Ethel Glyne Easton was born May 6, 1888; she worked as a bank teller at Curlew's Citizens Savings Bank and was locked in the vault during a holdup.

Of the hotel the Eastons owned, Monica remembers:

"There was magic in the 12-foot ceilings in the ground floor rooms (with room for a very tall Christmas tree). Nine-foot ceilings in the upstairs rooms, and three stairways."

"Roomy closets, a swinging door and serving pass through from large kitchen to large dining room."

"A cistern pump and sink in the kitchen."

Space on the ground floor "was later rented out as the Curlew Post Office, which made it handy for the then resident postmaster, Nellie Easton."

There was "an ingenious fire escape for the second floor rooms... a thick rope attached to the window sill of each room, to be dropped outside the window for a quick escape in an emergency. Large knots were placed strategically to assist in the trip down."

At one time there were three pianos in the Easton Hotel. One of them had been bought from the W.W. Kimball Piano Company for $275 and had been paid for as follows: "One horse–$130; one White sewing machine– $30; one organ–$25; for a total $185, and the balance in monthly payments."

"I do have a vivid picture of all those oil lamps, with chimneys waiting to be cleaned by the girl who was helping my grandmother and attending the Curlew school."

A duplex outhouse was located behind the hotel. Years later, when the outhouse was torn down, Monica says, "I was fortunate to be remembered by one of the demolishers with a picture frame made from the salvage. My appreciation to Mr. Oral Headrick."

Monica herself had been born December 30, 1912. Her father, John Cullen, kept telling her mother to wait another day before going to Fort Dodge to have the baby. Monica indicates that, though her mother waited, the baby didn't. "Dr. E.D. Beatty from Mallard was there for the surprise arrival in the apartment of the building just south of the hardware store." The child's name had already been chosen, but it had to be changed from John Keith to Monica.

Monica remembers movies during the summer, shown between the bank and the drug store, the screen on the bank wall, "the projector grinding away back of the plank seating."

"Surely no one ever dared pray for rain during the movie season," she says.

She remembers that Saturdays were shipping days for the livestock buyer, her father. The freight train stopped to load livestock headed for the Chicago stockyards. "Saturdays were special for me, too," Monica says. "For three years, ages 10 to 13, I had a paper business– *Minneapolis Tribune* and *Chicago Herald* and *Examiner.*" The conductor on the freight brought the papers for her and she'd sell them over the weekend.

She reports that news of the Armistice of November

11, 1918, reached Curlew through its telephone operator, Anna Flaherty. Anna made it down the steps and back through the alley to the fire bell in record time, to ring out the good news, Monica says, but in the excitement she was "not exactly dressed for the occasion."

Some Town Council Business

In May, 1905, "it seemed that every meeting [of the town council] had something to do with building good sidewalks and crossings. Men of the community each worked on roads as needed, this was their duty and all complied."

In October, 1905, a committee of three went "to see carpenter Tressler about building a jail." In March, 1906, "a bill for $22.25 for carpenter work on the jail was allowed," then in September the council paid F.E. Seagren $15.00 "for building the cage in the jail."

In July, 1912, an ordinance was passed limiting the speed of motor vehicles to a prudent 15 m.p.h.

In a special election on November 3, 1922, the ladies in town voted 26-0 for Curlew to erect a municipal electric light plant. The men voted 37 for, 1 against. Total cost to bring the Electrical Light and Power Co. into Curlew–$3500. (You have to wonder, don't you, who voted against electricity?)

Sunday Afternoon Swim

It was Sunday afternoon, August 16, 1912. John Compton, 16, and his friend Maynard Cottington, also 16, hiked away from Curlew to check out the ditch being dug a mile south of town and a mile and a half to the west. A dredge crew member named Frank was out at the ditch when the boys arrived; Frank had been left to watch the equipment over the weekend.

Frank and John decided to go swimming in the ditch.

The water was twelve feet deep. Maynard didn't swim and would stay on the bank. John jumped in but soon yelled that he had cramps and needed help. Frank and Maynard thought he was kidding. John called for help a second time. Frank jumped into the ditch, Maynard jumped in too, clothes and all. All three boys went down together. Frank managed to pull himself to the surface and get to the bank of the ditch. John and Maynard failed to surface again.

Frank summoned helped. A general ring on the Curlew and Ayrshire phone lines brought 200 friends and neighbors to help retrieve the bodies. Vern Lyons' horse rake was dragged through the ditch. The lifeless bodies were retrieved on the first pass.

Can you imagine the uneasiness of the crowd, then the gasp as the dead boys were pulled clear of the water? A light had dimmed. The future would never be the same.

After a double service at the Rush Lake Cemetery, John Compton and Maynard Cottington were buried side by side.

Leaving Sweet Illinois

Arthur and Pearl Bohn farmed for several years in Champaign County, Illinois. "Their home was near a woods," we're told, "and picking wild flowers was one of the quiet joys of life." A creek ran through the woods, there was no bridge, and it was necessary to ford the stream when crossing it.

"Farm rent was very high in Illinois," the story continues, and after two years of drought the Bohns "decided to join the westward movement." They visited Iowa and North Dakota and decided that northwest Iowa was where they would settle. They rented a farm near Curlew.

It was February, 1915. A fond farewell in Illinois. The

day was warm, the birds were singing, the children didn't need coats as they played outside.

Art left by train ahead of everyone else so he'd be in Curlew when his family and livestock and machinery and furniture arrived. It took several days for the rest of the Bohn family and the two train cars carrying the family's possessions to come. When the train stopped at the depot in Curlew, the day was cold and snowy, nothing at all like the Illinois they'd left behind. Like any pioneer wife might have, perhaps Pearl Bohn, looking out the train window at the cold Iowa landscape, whispered under her breath: "Dear Lord Jesus, what have we done?"

In 1919, the Bohns bought a farm a mile north and three-quarters of a mile west of Curlew. The place was considered "one big cockleburr patch," yet "with hard work and perseverance" it became one of the better farms around.

In 1936, Art and Pearl Bohn retired from farming and moved into Curlew. Art continued to manage the Shipping Association as he had before retirement, he served on the telephone board, and he was mayor for several years.

His son, Russell, would be mayor of Curlew, too, more than half a century later.

The School

In 1915, women teachers in Curlew could not marry during the term of their school contracts; they could not keep company with men; they had to stay at home between 8:00 p.m. and 6:00 a.m. unless they were attending a school function; they could not loiter downtown in an ice cream store; they could not leave Curlew without the permission of the chairman of the school board; they could not ride in a carriage or automobile with a man who was not father or brother; they could not smoke cigarettes, could not dress in bright colors, nor could they dye their hair ("under no circumstances"); they had to wear at least two petticoats; and their dresses were to be no shorter than two inches above the ankle. In addition, to keep the school room neat and clean, they had to: sweep the floor once daily; scrub the floor at least once a week with hot soapy water; clean the blackboards at least once a day; and start the fire at 7:00 a.m. so the room would be warm by 8:00 a.m.

"Lloyd Seagren, while attending high school, was elected secretary to the school board and remained faithfully fulfilling that position until the school closed, serving 50 continuous years."

Hap Clausen died August 6, 1983 at age 93. He had been the school custodian in Curlew for many years, when Curlew had a school. He coached a girls' basketball team into the state tournament in 1945 when there were only a dozen students in the high school and only five high school girls were suiting up; Hap had to recruit a sixth grader to round out the the six-girl starting team; his three substitute players were also sixth graders. It was the war years and coaches were in short supply. It was a very small school and girls were in short supply, too. Folks think Hap is probably the only school custodian ever to coach a team into the state tournament. In later years, Hap "especially enjoyed the young and many sought out his advice and judgment." He is buried in the Rush Lake Cemetery, alongside his wife, Wilhelminia.

1953. Class photo. My friend Bryan Wilson stares into the camera. I didn't know he was my friend yet. His eyes are dark, deep inside. Has he seen the pain his eyes promise, has he seen death yet? There are seven girls in Bryan's class, eleven boys. I am not one of them. Mrs. Reinders, the teacher, stands to Bryan's right, our left, certain that this moment has been preserved forever.

Nicknames

There were nicknames in Curlew, lots of them: Skin Dennis and Huck Drown; Spider Hatch and Crunch Brumm; Hook Scott and Peanut Martin; Cob Hill and Nasty Face Smith; Toad Drown, Coop Schuler, and Compy Compton; Lefty Lowman and Sockeye Griffin; Stretch Nielsen and Toots Gates; Nub Gates, Happy Clausen, Goof Brechler; Rooster Ward and Snail O'Connor; Cotton Boyd and Loots Mammon; Tom Boy Wellar, Puffy Boyd, and Puffy Bower; Bony Lowman; Sour Puss Ward; Poodle Smith; Bizz Boyd and Duff Boyd and Ping Pong Fosnot.

On October 26, 1921, the *Emmetsburg Democrat* reported that "Tub King, Spot and Speck Leary, Spider Hatch and Butch Turner attended the football game at Pocahontas Sunday."

Gertrude Baker Remembers

"My mother used to send me to Whitmer's Store or to Turner's Meat Market.... I had to hang on tight to the money for if I dropped it down in the crack of the wooden walks, it would roll. One time I was sent to Turner's for some meat. Mother always told me what change I would get. This time I was supposed to get a dime and a nickel. Mr. Turner did not have a dime so he gave me three nickels. So I told him that was not right and I would not go home. I just stood there so he had to go out and get a dime."

The Winter of 1936

Albert Seagren remembers the winter of 1936. There was snow and wind "until it was impossible to get into town with a car."

"We didn't have a train for several weeks and coal ran out at the elevator and the lumberyard. The coal at the school was sold out by the sack and the school was closed for about three weeks."

"Dad asked me to stay up and keep a fire going in the store one night when it was 36 below zero. Melvin Fisk stayed up quite a while with me and we kept the stove red hot, but it was still cold in the store... During the night we heard a noise and pop bottles were freezing and the caps were hitting the ceiling."

"The roads were blocked so that many farmers cut across fields and came down the railroad tracks to get to town."

"It was in the winter of 1936 that a farmer lost a cow. He found it in his haymow. The snow had gotten deep enough for the cow to walk into the haymow."

Two Women, Farming

They were farming three miles west of Curlew on the 165 acres they'd been renting the ten years previous. They had been farming together for twenty years, when our story is told. We have a photo: they are standing at the end of a cornfield. To me they look as much like man and wife as any farm couple can.

Vera Booth is in a white, sleeveless dress that comes down to mid-calf. She is white-haired, robust, smiling. Her left hand is extended upward towards the tassle-tops of the tall corn, a gesture that seems flamboyant compared to the rest of the severity. Elsie Howard stands to Vera's left and a little behind, but pushed up close. Elsie is wearing bib overalls, legs cuffed at the bottom; a dark work shirt, long-sleeved, buttoned at the wrist. Her arms are held stiffly downward. Elsie wears glasses, her hair looks unkempt, a little wind-blown, she is a little rumpled, her face is creased with years, it is caught in the grimace of a farmer who is clearly uncomfortable with the attention he is getting.

"Oh it always seemed natural for me to farm," Elsie says. Her voice, as I imagine it, crackles like my grandmother's. "I liked it when I was a girl, when my father used to give me a little piece of land to use for my own crops."

When she finished school, Elsie says, "I couldn't think of any occupation I'd like better than farming. So I asked Vera to help me, and we've been at it ever since."

Vera does the housework, the washing and ironing, the cooking, and she looks after the sheep and horses, cows, ducks, and chickens. Elsie plants the crops, cultivates them, and brings in the harvest at the end of the season. In the busiest times Vera puts on overalls and goes out to the fields to help.

The women own a blind horse they harness for work if the tractor gets out of order.

Elsie goes to the fields at 5:00 a.m. to get after the weeds. "Lots of people tell me I shouldn't worry about keeping the weeds down on a farm we just rent, but as long as I'm farming I want to make a good job of it."

The winters aren't lonely, the women claim, they have plenty to keep them busy; and when they don't, Vera reads and plays her 200-year-old violin, Elsie listens to the radio.

"I guess our hobby is dancing," one of the women says. "We don't have much time for it in summer, but later in the fall we go to dances at Curlew and around at the neighbors."

They have traveled, including a trip to the Chicago Fair in 1933.

They shy away from the idea of retiring. "But if the day ever comes," they say, "we won't move to town. When you've lived on a farm all your life, well–it just seems natural to stick it out, that's all."

The Telephone Company

Telephone service had come to Curlew as early as 1898. The switchboard was located first downstairs in Rawson's

Drugstore, and later was moved upstairs, then after that to an apartment in the Fisk Hotel.

A schoolhouse was moved into Curlew to serve as a cafe but that business failed. The phone company bought the building, added an apartment for the head operator to live in, and moved in the switchboard.

When he was only in ninth grade, Lloyd Seagren was asked to take over as general manager for the phone service. He continued with the company until 1964.

Gertie Fisher was the secretary and treasurer for the phone company all those years she was employed there, and she was "the faithful one at the switchboard day after day."

Alene Seagren records this tribute: "Gertie, as we all know her, a friend to all. She worked for Curlew Telephone Company for nearly 40 years. A faithful employee giving all she had to her job. It was not an eight hour day, as she lived in the same room, so was on call nights. She would go out of her way to help people. She came to the window of our upstairs apartment several times to tell us we had a call from our son who was in the service."

Bert & Oral Headrick

Oral Headrick was orphaned by the time he was two and a half years old. He'd been born in Warren County, Iowa, and lived there with aunts and uncles until he was twelve, when he moved to Laurens and stayed with another uncle, Aultie Allen.

When he was twenty-one, Oral met Bertha Flier, who at the time was living three miles west and a quarter mile north of Curlew. Bert and Oral married in 1934. "This was during the depression," we're reminded. Oral worked on a farm "for fifty cents a day and did all the work on the farm at that time as the owner of the farm was travelling around selling Wind Blown Light Plants."

Soon enough, wanting to get into the hauling business, Oral bought a truck. Bert and Oral moved into Curlew then, in September, 1934, and started out living in a room at the old Fisk Hotel. "The people in Curlew were friendly," we're told, "so it didn't take long to get acquainted."

Oral started talking to farmers. "When the phone would ring and someone was calling for him to haul something, we would both hold our breath, thinking maybe we'll make it yet," Bert remembers.

"It was hard work," she says, "because there were no portable elevators, no hoists on the trucks. You shoveled the grain on and you shoveled it off. Ear corn isn't easy to shovel."

"I guess the thing I hated the most was hauling coal," she says. "At that time there were many country schools and lots of homes that burned coal. Many Sunday afternoons, or evenings, Oral and I would be on a coal car, throwing coal onto the truck, then hauling it out in the country and throwing it into a little window in a shed at a schoolhouse, or a little basement window. And these were the good old days. Ha."

Bert and Oral had one son, Gerald, born July 5, 1942. Gerald, who suffers from cerebral palsy, lived with his parents until 1980, when he moved into Handicapped Village in Sheldon, Iowa.

Oral stayed in the trucking business until 1973, when he retired from it for health reasons. His hauling business had been a success "thanks to all his good customers and friends."

"We have never been sorry we came here," says Bert.

Hollywood Calls

That little blonde girl you would have encountered in

the Easton Drug Store in the 1930s and 1940s would have been Jane Easton. Jane lived in Curlew with two aunts, Ethel and Nellie. Ethel ran the drugstore; Nellie, of course, was Curlew's Postmaster. Jane attended school in Curlew through the eighth grade.

After graduation from high school, Jane Easton took a position in Chicago as secretary to the vice president of a large wholesale firm. She also studied voice and for a time was featured singer in the Freddy Nagel band, singing in "many of the nation's swankiest and best known entertainment spots."

After a time, Jane moved to Hollywood where she had parts in several movies, including "Las Vegas Story" and "Two Tickets to Broadway." Later Jane moved to New York to further her career; yet that's where her story ends for us, abruptly.

The Post Office

Winona Loomis, a later postmaster, preserves the names of Curlew's earlier postmasters: Harriet A. Tressler 1883-1886; Samuel Easton 1886-1887; Joseph H. Christy 1887-1889; Frank Lacey 1889-1893; Samuel Easton 1893-1897; A.A. Easton 1897-1901; Henry Wiley 1901-1908; H.D. Bennett 1908-1912; Nellie Easton 1912-1955; Ellen Brumm 1955-1957; Elmer Brumm 1957-1981. (Elmer Brumm is the fellow who ran the coffee shop alongside the postal window. I think we called him Red Brumm.)

We're told that the first rural route in Palo Alto County came out of Curlew in 1902, twenty six miles long, traveled by the first rural route carrier in the county, Oscar J. Gates, who used a horse and cart to deliver his route. Do you suppose, making his long, dusty rounds, do you suppose Oscar ever once thought he was making history?

In December, 1904, a second Curlew rural route was

established, twenty six miles. Susie A. Easton was the carrier. She used a horse and cart and she served until her marriage to John Cullen in 1909. There is a photo preserved of Miss Easton standing alongside the Easton Hotel holding her horse's head, bridle in her left hand, her right hand cocked behind her back. Miss Easton is wearing a fey cap. Her face is set and she does not reveal a bit of what she is thinking. A girl perhaps ten years old is partly hidden in the buggy the horse is hitched to. A dignified man in a hat sits on a bench along the sidewalk, off to Miss Easton's right, our left. Visible through the horse's legs, a somewhat younger fellow is sprawled in the dirt of the street, nonchalantly surveying the scene to the west, as if laying about in the dirt is an everyday occupation, yes, I'm comfortable, thank you very much. A decorative ornament is captured in the photo, where one of the hotel's beams shows to the exterior; it was carefully carved in the days when every detail was important.

During Nellie Easton's tenure as postmaster, the mail went out on the evening train, delivered to the depot by Sockeye Griffin. If additional mail needed to go after Sockeye had left for the depot, Nellie would deliver it to the train station herself. She became "a familiar sight standing on the platform at the depot."

"Naturally there was no beauty shop in town for the ladies at this time," Winona Loomis records. "Bertha Headrick would go up to the Post Office and fix Nellie's hair. Often in the middle of getting her hair done, Nellie would jump up to wait on a customer."

Curlew Citizen Asphyxiated

Francis "Sockeye" Griffin of Curlew died upon a Saturday night in 1946, asphyxiated by a defective oil-burning stove. Sockeye had been born in Ireland in 1882; he relocated with his family to Sinco, Ontario, Canada, in

1887; and in 1891 he came to Curlew. As a young man, he'd spent several years in Montana. When he returned to Curlew, he established a dray line for some years and a harness shop and shoe repair business. In the last years before his death, he also served as Curlew's street commissioner.

"His body was discovered early Saturday morning," we're told, "by Doug Bennett, a neighbor who investigated when he failed to see any activity around the Griffin home." Bennett looked through the window into the one-room house and saw Sockeye's liefeless body. Bennett and a couple friends entered the house together.

"The heater was still going," it is said, "as was a kerosene lamp. No inquest was held."

The deceased left two sisters: one in Graettinger, Iowa; the other of Curlew; and two brothers: one of View, Montana; the other of Sioux Falls, South Dakota.

"Mr. Griffin was a familiar character, both at Curlew and in Emmetsburg," we're told. "He was an obliging neighbor and friend, was always ready to give a helping hand and will be greatly missed not only by his relatives, but by the entire community in which he lived."

That Johnson Boy

Jerry Lee Johnson, born May 19, 1941, arrived three months premature. "The only food that Jerry could eat," we're told, "was mashed bananas." Those were the war years, bananas were scarce, "but the neighboring grocery stores saved their bananas for him."

When Jerry was four years old, he tried to stop the power take-off to the elevator while his father was putting corn in the crib. Jerry escaped with only an arm broken.

When he was five years old, Jerry put his hand in the gears of a corn sheller. His only brother, Dick Johnson, thirteen years older than Jerry, rushed him to the nearest doctor who wanted to amputate. "Dick would not allow this," and took Jerry to Emmetsburg where Dr. Brereton saved the hand.

One time when a team of horses was hitched to the manure spreader, Jerry climbed up on the seat and yelled out "Get up." Away went the horses, through the grove, barely missing the trees, no damage to the wagon, no injuries this time to Jerry.

Jerry and his cousin, Gary Lowman, liked to hitch a wagon behind the pony and go for a ride. "They wrecked three or four wagons a year doing this," we're told.

After he graduated from high school, Jerry drove school bus for four years, without record of any incidents that we know of. Later he would drive Curlew's Rural Route delivering mail, a modern-day Oscar J. Gates.

Squeek's Store

The general store in Curlew had been built in 1896 by H.C. Wiley. Wiley operated it for twelve years; in the span from 1908 to 1926 the store was owned in succession by a fellow named Lienert, then by McBride & Ayres, by W.H. Wilcox, then by L.J. Dickersen, by Henry Elder, and then by Fred Seagren & G.A. Thompson. Squeek Seagren took over in 1926 and ran the store continuously until he sold out in 1971.

In 1926, we're told, Squeek's stock of goods "was much more dry goods than groceries—yard goods, underwear of all kinds, gloves and mittens, overalls, work shirts, shoes and overshoes, besides dishes and other items used in the home."

In 1940, Squeek added a locker plant with 120 lockers, in the back of the store and added a meat saw and grinder, too. "This," it is said, "added a great deal of work—cutting meat, wrapping it, freezing and storing it, and taking care of the lockers." Squeek didn't do any butchering himself;

that was done on the farm by others. Anyone who wished to have a piece of meat smoked had to take it to Emmetsburg or Laurens.

Mr. and Mrs. Fuller bought the store from Squeek in 1971 and kept it in business for two years as Geila's Grocery, until the building ended as many buildings do, "burned to the ground."

Curlew Residents Build, Pay For New Grocery Store

On March 17, 1974, the *Des Moines Register* reported:

Small town cooperation has scored again. A new grocery store will open its doors in Curlew Monday–a store built and paid for by the 110 residents of this Palo Alto County community.

The town had been without a grocery store since Geila's Grocery was destroyed by fire almost a year ago.

"The idea for another store kept kind of brewing all summer long," explained Mrs. Gwenna Appel, 41, who will operate the store with Mrs. Dick Johnson....

Mrs. Appel said the townspeople sold shares to finance the $8,000 construction of a new building on the site of the old store....

The construction work–except the block laying–was a community project.

"One day we had 16 people on the roof putting shingles on," Mrs. Appel said....

Unlike many grocery stores, Mrs. Appel reports, The Curlew Pantry is paneled and carpeted.

"We're real uptown," she said.

The Lumber Business

In 1941, Jim Ausland bought the Royal Lumber Company's holdings in Curlew. With shortages during World War II, Ausland found it difficult to get lumber to replace what he'd sold, so he went to northern Minnesota and bought some standing timber. He hired a crew to cut the trees and saw them into boards and dimension lumber. Les Shellabarger went up to oversee the milling of the wood and to get the lumber shipped to Curlew.

Those living in Curlew during the fall of 1943, we're told, "will remember the three-cornered stacks of lumber piled in vacant lots all over town." The green wood was being air-dried.

Ausland Lumber Co. went out-of-business in 1978 when Jim Ausland sold his stock to lumberyards in surrounding communities and sold his buildings to Dick and Jerry Johnson for storage of farm equipment.

"Before the doors closed on 37 years of business," we read, Ausland spent a nostalgic morning with old friends "as they flocked to the office bearing coffee and goodies and best wishes" for his happy retirement.

Where But Curlew?

A March day. The Iowa winds. The driver finishes delivering groceries to the Curlew Pantry. He catches his money pouch on the door handle of his truck. The pouch goes flying. "Needless to say with a high wind as Iowa can and does have occasionally," so we're told, the money and checks from the pouch go flying too.

It is $1250 flying on the March wind, high in the trees, behind stumps, over beyond the brush. The truck driver is a little frantic, only two hands and all that money gone off like wild birds. The folks who've been drinking coffee at the Pantry come running outside, they begin grabbing at any $1.00, $5.00, or $10.00 bill they can get, they search for more. What they gather right away they give to the driver right away. People continue to pick up money around Curlew for several days afterward, some of it found quite a distance away.

In the end, $1,219 of the lost money is recovered and

returned. "Where but in a small rural town could such a thing happen," the truck driver says.

It's obvious: in Curlew, what's yours is yours.

A Century Farm

In 1881, Fred Henniges of Dubuque, Iowa, purchased a farm a mile and a half south of Curlew. Henniges had a daughter, Minnie, who married Fred Leslein in 1911, in Dubuque; this young couple moved to Curlew to run the farm. Fred and Minnie were blessed with two sons, Albert and Leonard. When Fred and Minnie retired from farming, Leonard and his wife, Mary, soon took over the operation of the home place. In 1981 the Fred Leslein family farm became a "Century Farm."

The Railroad

Between 1882 and 1981, four railroad companies operated on the tracks running through Curlew: the Des Moines and Fort Dodge Railroad; the Chicago, Rock Island & Pacific Railroad; the Minneapolis & St. Louis Railroad, and the Chicago and North Western Railway. For a while, Nels Anderson was the railroad section boss. His sons were Willard and Edwin. Eddie Anderson was our neighbor. Passenger service to Curlew was discontinued in 1948, the same year that diesel locomotives replaced steam power on the line. Freight service was discontinued in 1971 when the Curlew depot was closed. The rail line through Curlew was abandoned in 1981 and the tracks dismantled the following year.

The Barrel of Appels

"Once upon a time way back when, the Otto Appel tree brought forth twin sons, Hans and Henry, born October 30, 1927, to immigrant parents from Denmark." Neither boy could speak English when he started school, "pity the poor teacher."

In 1951, Hans Appel married Gwenna May Grossnickle of Laurens, Iowa. "Five children were added to the family tree," we're told, "and they all turned out to be good, delicious Appels."

In 1955, the Appels moved from a farm near Graettinger to one at the southeast corner of Curlew. In January, 1956, Hans was sworn in as a city councilman and served as councilman or mayor for at least thirty-five years. Why did he keep getting reelected? One citizen explained it to Hans: "Well, Curlew is a pretty nice place and we don't need much leadership and you're as close to nothing as we can get."

The Appels kept dairy cows and hogs. When the wind was in the right direction, the neighbors would say they could smell the Appels' prosperity. In 1964, the haymow of the cow barn collapsed. People uptown in Curlew could hear the timbers cracking. Hans got the cows out before any were killed.

Another time a blizzard knocked out electricity for three days. Cows had to be milked by hand. Neighbors came to the rescue, yet "the morning milking was hardly done before the evening one had to begin."

Gwenna helped operate the Curlew Pantry for a few years. Both Appels were active in the anti-nuclear movement, in the Peace and Justice group, and in most community affairs.

In 1984, the Appels could report that they were "just now reclaiming the railroad track that runs through the farm. One hundred years ago it came through here and now most every trace of it is gone."

"What will the next hundred years have in store for us?" they wonder.

And What of the Next Hundred Years?

What will the next hundred years have in store for Curlew, the Appels wonder. And who shall record those years so well as the Centennial Committee remembered the first hundred?

We tend to forget that all history is local history at some point. We fail to attend to current events as they come rushing past us because none of them tap us on the shoulder and say "Watch this, it's going to be important." You just don't know.

Some will say a community begins to disintegrate when its school closes or when its general store shuts its doors, when the post office leaves. I say a community is doomed when it loses its memory, when there is no one to say: this is who we were, this is how we got here, this is where we've come from.

Memory is a terrible thing, two-edged like a sword. One edge is the truth, the other is a lie that lets us think of the past as the good old days. Fortunately, some of Curlew's past has been preserved for us in the Centennial book, there is much more than I could possibly report, one hundred and twenty pages of family histories, more of photographs, memories. Hardships and sadnesses are recalled: we can take pride in being true survivors. We can see that we've endured, eternal as the dust, the wind.

The challenge that remains–for Curlew, for any community, for all of us–is this: to record the next hundred years for those to follow. So that someday when someone comes asking about where he came from, he can find some answers. Will anyone do this for him? You hope so.

The Journey:

Curlew to Emmetsburg, Iowa, Tuesday, October 24, 2000, Afternoon

As I leave Curlew, I am swallowing back my sadness. I could choke on it.

Heading east on the paved road I pass the gravel pit at Graff's. We used to ice skate there, we'd play hockey. There is a house at the edge of the water now. This used to be scruffy cow pasture, now it looks almost like a park.

Why, you can see the elevator at Mallard as you come east from Curlew. I'd never noticed that when I lived here. It looks like you could damn near throw a stone from Curlew to Mallard. Was the world ever this small?

Where I think Namers used to live, only a corn crib in the middle of a field.

Along the highway heading north towards Emmetsburg, I see the place we called "Bimbo's." All that remains is a scraggly grove of trees and a couple structures collapsed in on themselves. "Bimbo, Bimbo, where you gonna go-li-o? Bimbo, Bimbo, what you gonna do-li-o?" I hear my brother Randy sing. Randy has been dead a long time.

I come into Emmetsburg with a heart full of emptiness. So much seems to have been lost.

Emmetsburg,
Tuesday, October 24, 2000, Afternoon

Peggy Osterman meets me at the door of the Queen Marie Bed & Breakfast where I shall be lodging. She is middle-aged, short hair tightly curled, glasses, a ready smile. "Sign in, sign our book," she encourages.

I know she has moved here from California. "How did you end up here, at the Queen Marie in Emmetsburg?" I ask.

"This place was advertised for sale in a Los Angeles paper," Peggy says. "My husband, Paul, saw the ad, thought we should buy it. It was time for a career change."

"Are you originally from California?"

"No," Peggy says, "originally I'm from Ohio but we moved to California when I was ten years old, so I went to school out there, went to college there."

Her husband, Paul, is originally from Wausau, Wisconsin. He worked for Rockwell in California. Peggy was a school teacher and then she worked for Rockwell too.

In the hallway upstairs, you see a commendation for Paul from the President, thanking him for his participation on the team that got Apollo 11 to the moon and back. You see a photograph of Peggy standing in front of a B-1 bomber with its crew; another photo, Paul with another crew and bomber.

Emmetsburg,
Tuesday, October 24, 2000, Late Afternoon

Where I remember the old Emmetsburg Hospital standing, air.

The Iowa Trust and Savings Bank—where my parents did business all those years—it has a new brick building in a new location, made to look like a colonial mansion. In the original bank building? "Antiques & Collectibles."

In the Kenmore building where Dr. Hyde had practiced, now there's a Pizza Ranch, a costume shop, a real estate office, and the McNally abstract office, "family-owned since 1924."

I stop for supper at the Sum Hing Chinese restaurant. My fortune cookie says "What Goes Around Comes Around." I get rained on as I walk back to my room.

Part Two

The Journey:

Emmetsburg,
Wednesday, October 25, 2000, Breakfast

Paul Osterman brings me coffee. Then he brings muffins and toast. Peggy brings the egg and cheese bake in a round ceramic dish. There is salsa for the eggs. There is butter and three kinds of jam, there are two kinds of juice–orange and cran-apple. There is plenty of coffee, and there is talk–Paul and Peggy have asked if they can join me at the table.

Peggy says a son studied engineering and Japanese in college and took a job in Japan. He married a Japanese girl. The couple has since moved back to the United States– Waukesha, Wisconsin.

"Our most famous guest here was Willard Scott," Paul says. "The college brought him in. He sat here in the afternoon having snacks with us 'til nearly six o'clock. He looked at his watch and said 'Oh, my, I should change my clothes. Well, these look good enough' and he didn't change his clothes. He had another snack and waited to be picked up. He gave a talk at a dinner up at the college and when he got back here he said 'Do you have any snacks?' We sat at the kitchen table and he had snacks and talked 'til midnight. He sure liked to eat and talk."

Emmetsburg to Curlew,
Wednesday, October 25, 2000, Morning

It is aggressively overcast.

I am headed south, back to Curlew. The west branch of the Des Moines River looks pretty much the same to me as it ever did, except the water seems low. Some things don't change. It had been another dry summer, with rain at just the right times to produce good crops.

"Bimbo, Bimbo," I hear my dead brother sing. A red-tailed hawk takes flight.

At the "Curlew Baptist Church, 3 miles" corner, I turn west. Soon another red-tail is marking my way.

Curlew,
Wednesday, October 25, 2000, Morning

I can tell by the way my Aunt Pat looks at me when she answers the door she doesn't have the least clue who I am. I introduce myself. "Oh, Tom," she says, and she hugs me, then puts my beard in the bowl of her hands, "I haven't seen you in this."

"Larry went to Ayshire to have a cup of coffee," Pat says. "He should be back any time." She brews a pot of coffee for us and we talk of children and she talks of grandchildren and now even one great grandchild. I tell her that I'm back tromping the old ground, to see what remains.

"There's so much gone," Pat says. "There are a lot of places that used to have farmsteads on them. Now there is nothing left. If you don't remember them, you'd never know there had been a house there. And you start to forget. Pretty soon it will all be erased. They call it progress."

"Some day this place will look like South Dakota," she adds. She waves her hands out towards the emptiness. "Some of these farmers plow farther and farther out into the ditch now that we have no fencelines. It looks like greed to me."

My Uncle Larry arrives home. "Hey, how are you?" I say. I can tell by the way he responds he doesn't recognize me either. At that moment he is so intensely Allen. "This fellow stopped in with some questions," Pat tells him. He looks quizzical. I introduce myself.

I tell Pat and Larry I'd stopped at the Rush Lake Cemetery. "Why should I know the name Backstrom?" I ask.

"Dean Backstrom rented the farm your folks lived on, once they'd moved." Pat says. "There was a problem with the gas to the furnace in the basement. Dean went down to investigate. The gas exploded and he was killed."

"Burned his lungs and he died at the hospital," Larry adds.

I talk some more about Curlew. "All but one of the buildings is gone from that block of Main Street," I say.

"Squeek's store burned down," Pat says. "Some people in town built the cinder block building that's on the site and some women tried to run it as a grocery store for a while, but you know small groceries can't make it. Everything costs them more. So now it's a community center. It used to be open 24 hours a day. There's a pool table in there, a big coffee pot. Some kids came in and tore the place up, so now it's locked. It's open for senior citizen get-togethers and family reunions."

Larry: "That section of land your dad farmed half of, and I farmed the other half–Mrs. Spies died and the section was broke up and sold off, some of it to one farmer, some of it to another, and the heirs still own part of it."

"The fence is gone that marked the half section," I say, "there, right at the Haywoods' place."

"That's wasn't Haywoods," Larry says, "that was

Bowers. Haywoods was another mile to the west."
Memory plays its cruel tricks.

The Farmstead at Curlew

A mile south and a quarter mile west of Curlew. That's what we told the truck drivers delivering feed or coming to pickup livestock. That was the way all of us talked about location in rural Iowa during the 1950s. A mile-square grid of gravel roads marked all that part of the state. Many of the farms were half-sections; two half-sections made a mile square. The landscape had a uniform and featureless roll and sometimes it was difficult to determine why house, barn, and outbuildings had been set down one place rather than another. I'd always thought of the land as flat, but I had not yet seen flatness. Why our farmstead had been plunked where it was I don't know, yet there it was–a mile and a quarter mile from Curlew, a long ways from anywhere.

It was a big white house on the place, longer than it was wide. There was a porch along the side of it to the road, high enough off the ground that our dog Tippy whelped way back under it one summer and my brother Flip had to crawl underneath and bring out the pups one at a time. Their eyes were barely opened.

There was a big window looking out across the porch into the yard from the dining room. I put a golf ball through that window once, the glass shattering out onto the porch. I had been bouncing the golf ball on the floor of the dining room. My mother said: "Thomas, don't be doing that in here, you'll break a window." Then she and my father had gone off shopping. Of course I kept bouncing the golf ball in the house; of course it went through the window.

The way onto the porch from inside the house came off the living room but we didn't use that door much. Actually we didn't use the porch much; when we did, we came onto it mostly by way of a set of steps rising from the front yard.

We entered the house at the south end, off a slab of cement my dad had poured in front of the place one summer day. I remember helping him work it to a flat surface; I was so proud to be helping. My dad was pleased to have concrete to walk on when going out to the car, instead of spring mud, summer dust, the snow of winter. A doorway and steps down to the cellar beneath the house stood beside the door into the house. It was a cellar, not a basement: the floor of it was concrete, yeah, sure, but the place was dark, the field stone foundation exposed; there were spider webs in the corners and crawly things in the rafters overhead. It was down there we did the laundry in a big old wringer washer. One morning to help my mother I went down before school to wring out a load of laundry and get it on the line in the yard and I ran my hand into the wringer all the way up to my forearm. Fortunately, I was a pretty stoic about my predicament. I turned off the machine, snapped the wringer loose, and pulled my hand back out the way it had gone in. I got the basket of clothes put out on the line and was ready for school on time. I didn't tell anyone what I'd done. You don't like to broadcast your stupidity.

One small distinctive feature of the farmyard–a little east of the house, near where the car was usually parked, there was a slab of concrete with an old faded red-handled pump on it. You'd pump, then pump it again and soon you'd have a stream of clean, cold water filling your enameled tin cup.

Like the road and the driveway, the farmyard east of the house and south of the barn was plain raw gravel. There was a remnant of old sidewalk running from the corner of the concrete slab my father had poured out to a two-seater outhouse thirty feet or so to the north. We stacked wood between the concrete slab and the pump, along part of the sidewalk. We used that wood in a pot belly stove. I remember many a winter evening getting up from my spot on the floor in front of the TV, bare-footed, running the length of the sidewalk to the outhouse through the snow, then stopping at the wood pile for an armload of oak. Do you suppose I was too young to understand that a fellow shouldn't run around outside in the snow with no shoes on? Do you also suppose that God takes care of fools and farm kids?

My father had built a swing set so the first eight of his nine kids could all swing together at the same time. It stood on the patch of lawn in front of the sidewalk leading to the outhouse. We could all be swinging west to east side by side, all but my youngest brother, Randy. If Randy timed it properly with his nearest sibling, which would be Hank, he could swing south to north, the ropes of his swing tied to the crossbeam at the end of the swingset. Sometimes we did that, all of us, just to see if we could. People who drove into our yard were astonished by the size of our swing set. Some of them, too, I suppose, were astonished by the size of the family.

There was yard around the house, real lawn on the south side, the north side, and at the back where the grass gave way to our grove of trees. The grass closest to the road was often greyish, dusted when passing cars kicked up a roiling haze off the gravel. My mother's clothes line was in the yard on the north side of the house and sometimes clothes drying there got dusted by passing traffic as well. Dust was a fact of life, like Republicans.

A fence beyond the clothes line marked the north edge of the lawn. The fence sagged: farm kids climbed on it and leaned back hanging off; we generally treated it the way town kids might treat a jungle gym. One year I wanted to plant watermelons along that fence line. My father said, "Son, watermelon will never grow there." I said, "Dad, how do you know?" He said, "Soil's packed too hard. Go ahead, try. You'll find out for yourself." I tried it. Tell you what: watermelon won't grow along that fence line.

To the north of the fence two massive cottonwoods loomed. Cottonwoods whisper to each other all day and all the night and the sound of their conversation was a constant chatter through our lives. Rittle, rattle, you'd hear the leaves. In the shade of those trees my father would dump a truckload of sand at the beginning of summer, every summer. Kids in town might get a full sand box to play in, we got a dump truck load. Eventually the great hump of sand would be leveled to a huge smoothness by our play. My sisters might lay boards out to mark the walls of a house and the rooms in it. My brothers and I might use a little baling twine and clothes pins stuck in the sand to mark the edges of imagined fields.

Just beyond the sand pile stood the old chicken house. It was white, long and narrow, and it ran east to west. Inside there were roosts along the north wall, an aisleway where farm boys fed and watered the chickens, and nesting boxes on the south wall where the chickens laid their eggs, or were supposed to. If you don't already know how much manure a few hundred chickens can make during the course of a year, you don't want to know, trust me. You don't want to know how long it takes to scoop a manure spreader steaming full of the pungent stuff. And the first load only starts the task. Hauling manure was a good winter job, the stink held low by the cold.

Kitty-corner northeast of the chicken house, set back from it far enough a tractor could pass between them, was our machine shed. It was here we kept our equipment protected from the elements–the baler, for sure; the side rake, corn picker, cultivator, whatever fit. This was another oblong building, white, running east to west; it was longer and wider and taller than the chicken house. The inside of it seemed especially dark in summer as you came in out of full sun. There was a smell of old straw, of grease and baler twine, of time–the way time leaves its trace of scent. Wide sliding doors opened on the front of the machine shed and these gave room enough to get big pieces of equipment in and out.

Behind the machine shed, between the machine shed and the cattle yard to the north of it, lay the rock pile, pretty unremarkable except for its size. It was longer than the machine shed. Some places weeds and scruffy trees were growing up through it, but mostly it was rocks brought in off our fields, great rocks and modest ones, grey rocks and red ones, speckled and nondescript, rocks soaking up heat in the summer and giving it back when the weather turned cold. "Randy, why are you sleeping on the rock pile?" my mother asked my brother. "It's warm," Randy said. The west end of the rock pile was the east edge of our grove.

If the machine shed was to your left and you were looking north, you were standing at the gateway to a cattle yard. A big white barn stood just to your right. We milked several cows in that barn when I was very young, barely old enough to help. We separated the cream to send to Mallard for butter. Milking stanchions, some rooms for storing feed, and space to shelter cows from summer sun and winter's winds–these were on the first floor of the barn, along with the smell of hay and a kind of cool darkness that summer never could quite get hold of. The haymow made up the entire second level of the barn. At any season it smelled rich with the fullness of alfalfa, even when it was empty awaiting another season. To get into the haymow, you climbed a ladder from the lower level; it didn't seem like a big deal then, but this must have been dangerous for small farm boys. We were oblivious to most danger, or else we took it in stride as part of farm life. Or else God takes good care of fools and farm kids.

Once I was throwing a baseball up against the front of the barn, playing catch with myself. I'd throw the ball high against the wall, then catch it like it was a pop fly. My parents had come out of the house to the car. They were going to town for groceries. "Don't be doing that, Tom," my mother warned. "You'll break a window." They drove off to Emmetsburg. I kept tossing the baseball high up against the front wall of the barn. Of course I broke a window.

If you stand in the gateway between the machine shed and the barn and look north across the cattle yard to the windbreak of young trees along the north edge of the cattle yard, about directly center in the field of vision will be the farm's true working well. A neighbor in the well business had drilled it for us.

Standing on the other side of the barn, the east side, you'd often enough be standing in muck in the cow yard between the barn and a big old circular stock tank. I'm not going to say the tank was big enough to swim in, but sometimes we kept fish there the whole summer–it was ten or twelve feet across and three feet deep and, as fences cut right through the center of it from several directions, the tank served cattle in a couple of pens at once.

It was here, between the water tank and the barn, that I saw a cow go down from bloat. My father attempted to relieve the extreme pressure of the bloating with a butcher knife. The effort resulted in a snapped knife blade and failure. The tightly drawn skin was tougher than sharpened steel. The cow died an awful death, just that quick and unprepared.

If you were standing in the center of the water tank looking east, you'd be looking down a fence line on the north side of which there was a pen where we fattened beef cattle; on the south side, a white, wooden corn crib. When I was young we maintained a "straw shed" in the center of the cattle pen, to shade and shelter the cattle. The straw shed was the size and shape of a hog house or other outbuilding but instead of being made of wood and therefore somewhat permanent, it was constructed mostly of woven wire fencing and straw. Every year after harvesting oats, before we baled any of the straw, we gathered enough of it loose on flat racks and pitched it atop the woven wire roof of the straw shed and between the fencing where walls were formed. It was a day's work pitching enough straw to refurbish the old shed for another year. The fencing made a space wide enough for a wall of straw a foot and a half or two feet thick. This was cheap shelter using local material.

The white wooden corn crib off the southeastern arc of the water tank stood far enough away to leave a lane adequate for a tractor and wagon to pass through. The crib was composed of two separate parts for storing ear corn, with slats spaced far enough apart that the corn had a chance to give up its moisture and dry out; between the cribs where the ear corn was stored there was an alley wide enough–again the common measure–to drive a tractor and wagon through. Above this, bins for storing oats and soy beans. An elevator nearly always poked up into the cupola from the east side, used for moving corn or beans or oats from a wagon up into the crib and bins. Where the grain ended up was determined by a spout in the cupola at the end of the elevator. A farm kid felt like a man as he climbed the elevator into the cupola to adjust the spout from one bin to another.

Set off from the southwest corner of the corn crib, with its door to the west end and with space enough between it and the cow yard along the barn, there was an old red shed. We called it the milk house. When I was very young and my father was milking cows, this is where the cream was separated from the rest of the milk fluid; I have a memory of spring water flowing in the milk house, enough to cool milk cans set into a concrete tank. Yet I am romanticizing: the water came from the well, from a hydrant, out the end of a hose. In later years the milk house might have more properly been called a tool shed, but force of habit wouldn't let us do that. Some things persist, in spite of logic. The one thing about people that shouldn't surprise us is that they act like people. Habits are habitual, you just might not see it. Yet–also because we are human–we're always surprised that we're surprised.

If you stood at the south end of the corn crib and walked due south about twenty paces, you'd end just about directly in front of the hog house. It ran east to west, the hog house did, it was longer than it was wide, and it opened on its south side to a couple concrete "feed floors" where we fattened pigs for slaughter. Pigs have a smell all their own, as the neighbor of any pig farmer can tell you. Even a blind man knows a pig farm. In reasonable doses, it's a good smell, though it seems a bit acrid and harsh to the newcomer.

As you walked south along the fence of the feed floors,

a feed shed would be at your immediate right hand. There were three rooms in the shed; two held different kinds of ground feed and between them we kept bags of feed supplement waiting to be mixed into the next load of corn we ground. The feed shed in full summer sun had its own distinct set of smells, as one might imagine. Flies would buzz desperately in the window panes, trapped in sweltering heat. Of course, the feed shed was the popular place on the farm for mice and rats, and was popular, too, with our horde of farm cats. The only place a farm cat might rather be was in the barn, within striking distance of a shot of milk straight into the mouth straight from the cow's teat, a straight white line, sping.

There stood a 200-gallon tank of gasoline about equidistant from the front of the hog house and the front door of our house and equidistant from the front of the barn and the driveway into our graveled farmyard, set just slightly east of the line between the barn and the drive. The tank rested atop a rack five feet high, beneath the shade of some scrubby, weedy tree; I'd like to say it was box elder. This was the gasoline we put into our tractors: its road use taxes had been refunded. We appreciated the shade of the tree protecting us from the five or seven minutes of high sun when we filled a tractor with fuel.

If you stood in our driveway and looked east along the road you would see more of the usual middle western icons. There was a round steel bin we put shelled corn into for long-term storage. There was a chicken house with doors wide enough to drive a combine through; it had started its existence as a more usual building but we split it lengthwise, pulled the two halves thirty or forty feet apart, and added roof and walls and big, big doors to fill the gap. It would house a thousand chickens, which–if you don't know–is more than enough chickens. The stupidity of chickens reaches critical mass whenever 200 or more of them are gathered in one place, so you can imagine the trouble in this chicken house. To say nothing of finding a possum in one of the egg boxes before school one morning, with nothing but a feed shovel to beat at it with, and a young man's astonishment when—returning with something more deadly—the possum has vanished. I thought I had knocked it unconscious. So *that's* what they mean by "playing possum."

To the east of the chicken house there was another wooden corn crib. This one, too, had spaces between the slats, to allow the corn to dry. The two halves of it were set only far enough apart that a man could just barely walk the tunnel of darkness between them. The story often told was of me, barely two years old, crawling back into the cool darkness of that corn crib for a two hour nap while my frantic parents searched for me all over the farmyard.

I learned early that the roof of the crib was much too slippery for shoes with cheap synthetic soles. If you were going to walk the elevator up to the opening in the roof of this corn crib to readjust the spout, you had better have good shoes. One slip, and you'd fall—it seemed like—a thousand feet to the ground. One scare was enough.

East of the corn crib was another driveway into the farmyard. Two round steel mesh corn cribs stood to the east of that, cribs my brother Flip and I helped our father erect. These were pre-formed pieces locked together with bolts. Flip and I walked two by fours stood on edge through the steel mesh as we bolted our way to the top of the crib. We must have been 11 and 8 years old, or 12 and 9, when we walked the narrow edge of that lumber, putting the roof into place thirty feet in the air. I wasn't afraid of such heights then, nor of such a narrow beam of walkway.

Directly north of the round cribs, across a driveway

and patch of weeds where we kept farm equipment that was not being used, there was another cattle lot, a feed floor, we called it, where we fattened beef cattle for slaughter. It was behind and to the east of the hog house. It was the edge of the farmstead, bordering a field deep with the best soil in Iowa, the field ran all the way to the cross road a quarter mile distant. It would be a cornfield. In the long light of autumn, I would be disobedient once more, running a horse the length of the corn stubble after I'd been told not to. I would come back to the farmyard afterwards, and take my punishment like a man.

The Farmhouse at Curlew

Set fairly square to the world, it was a big, drafty farmhouse on the place at Curlew. There was a porch on the south side of it, overlooking a patch of grass, the ditch, the gravel of our own country road. It was the 1950s, we were Catholic and Democratic among Protestant Republicans and we were never much for porch-sitting.

The door we used most of the time came into the house on the east end, into what you'd call a "mud room." Maybe we called it "the entryway." We always kept a garbage pail out there, a five-gallon bucket that collected kitchen scraps for the hogs. One wall of the entryway was wide enough for our freezer. We hung coats and caps on the opposite wall, and beneath them along the baseboard we set the rubber boots meant to keep spring mud off our farm shoes. Even when we buckled them all the way to the top, somehow those boots never seemed to do as much good as they promised.

We had a baby sitter once who in a moment of anger dragged one of my brothers out to the garbage pail in the entryway and tried pushing his head down into the pail. She might have been angry, but then we were angrier, all of us kids. When our mother got home, she took us upstairs to put us to bed while my father took the baby sitter home. The four oldest of us set our mother at the edge of a bed, we corralled her and told her how it was. We gave her the facts of the case, we said this just wouldn't do, we said yes we should be punished when we do something wrong but putting a kid's head in the garbage pail was never justified.

Next day our mother talked to that woman. She never baby-sat for us again. Her ears are probably still ringing.

From the entryway you stepped into the long, narrow kitchen of the old farmhouse. The floor was tiled with linoleum squares, white and grey, and three black ones. Along the north wall there were cupboards and a long counter, and a sink at the window where my sisters did dishes every night after supper. At the west end of the counter, another window, then the doorway and stairs to the second floor. Along the south wall, a doorway to the dining room; to the right of that sat the cook stove like a fat aunt, then a wood-burning stove, and finally a doorway to the living room. Under the stairs at the far end of the kitchen were benches and a table built into the little alcove; there was a small window there in the west wall, too, or a picture of the sunset through our grove of trees, no it was a window.

We had a refrigerator, a Shelvador, but I have no recollection of where it stood. Perhaps it was on the west wall of the entryway, close to the kitchen door, perhaps not. I have no image of it at all.

One day my mother was at the cookstove making pancakes on the griddle for all of us, a great pile of them. Hot grease sizzled and sang on the griddle. Pancakes are magic to a six-year-old. I pulled a chair over close to the stove and climbed up to get a better view. I was shirtless for the summer day. "Get down, son, you're going to get burned," my mother warned. I didn't listen very well even back then and I didn't get down. Not until the lip of the griddle had burned a smart red slash across my belly. "That's how you learn," my mother said.

The wood-burning stove in the kitchen was no country decor option taken from some pretty magazine. We needed it in that big, drafty house. To heat that part of the house, we had to keep the pot-belly stove burning, which meant running out to the wood pile every so often for an armload of oak, and cleaning ashes out at the bottom of the stove and collecting them in an old bushel basket we kept by the chimney. We dumped the ashes on Saturdays, out in the grove to the west of the house.

At the foot of the stairs, where morning light would stream through the window at the end of the counter, almost directly in front of the wood-burning stove, my brother Flip threw a temper tantrum once. He was perhaps four-years-old, he was unhappy about something, he threw himself onto the floor there, kicked his legs and whined and cried. He kicked and whined and cried and kicked. The rest of us kids went outside to get away from the irritation of it and our mother came, too, I think. My brother was kicking and crying on the cold tile floor, we were out playing in the bright sunshine. Eventually every tantrum empties out like a bucket slopped to the hogs. Flip saw his efforts had come to nothing, he was left out of the fun, his tantrum-throwing days had come to an end. That's how you learn.

As one entered the dining room from the kitchen, a big oil-burning stove was immediately to the right, in the corner of the room. This stove and the pot-belly wood-burner in the kitchen provided all the heat we had. Registers in the floor allowed heat to rise to the bedrooms on the second floor. When it was fired up, the oil-burning stove got plenty hot. Once I melted several crayons by holding the end of each against the stove, watching color run down the hot surface until the liquified crayon fried entirely. The colors were beautiful as they melted and flowed but all of them ended about the same color brown. You may imagine correctly my parents were none too happy.

It was kitty-corner across the dining room from the stove, in the opposite corner I'm saying, that I once thought I'd seen a wild creature cowering. It was Easter morning and I had risen early and sneaked downstairs in the dim light to see what candies the Easter bunny had left in our baskets. I saw the pile of fur hunched into the corner, a wild thing with no place to hide. "Mom, Dad," I shouted from the bottom of the stairs, being sure to keep my bare feet up off the first floor, "there's some animal in the dining room. It's dark and furry and hiding in the corner."

One imagines my father and mother getting out of bed—way earlier than they'd planned—to come downstairs and investigate. "Son, it's one of your sisters' fur muffs," my dad said. "It's no wild animal, it's just a muff. Go back to bed." As he crawled back into bed himself, I suppose my father should have muttered: "That boy's going to be a poet, he's got imagination but he's no damn good for anything."

The table in the dining room stood in front of the window. We ate there once we'd grown too many and too big for the area under the stairs at the end of the kitchen. We played cards at the dining room table, too, Sunday afternoons in winter—Pinochle and Five Hundred, all of us. My sister Colleen could make a Nine Diamonds bid in Five Hundred when she was four-years-old, no help from anybody. I was always jealous of the way she could see to the essence of things so easily.

It was at the dining room table I edited and published a few issues of a family newspaper. I don't remember the name of it, perhaps *The Curlew Chronicle* or some such. Each copy was handwritten in farm boy scrawl, the circulation was eleven copies, the editions were few.

Curlew:Home

There was a phonograph in the corner of the dining room, close to the archway into the living room, the cabinet a fake blonde color. We listened to Hank Williams on it. We listened to a little forty-five that was a dramatic rendition of Tom Sawyer, we listened until we knew the story by heart. Any one of us could recite it word for word, and sometimes we did, each of us taking a part. "Hello. My name is Ralph Gerardo and this is the story of Tom Sawyer."

"Tom Sawyer, you come white-wash this fence," his Aunt Polly called out every time.

I was only about ten years old when my parents invested money they didn't have to buy books we couldn't afford–the Encyclopedia Britannica, a set of The Books of Knowledge, and a ten volume science encyclopedia. These filled three shelves of a book case in the living room–if all of them were ever on the shelves at the same time. Most often, several volumes were not in the book case but were being read. Many a Sunday evening in winter would find us sprawled across the living room floor, each with a book spread open in front of him or her, each of us discovering worlds far beyond the one our gravel roads marked out for us. It was a great wide world out there, and these books gave us a glimpse of it. It cost my parents dearly to buy them, a whole year's earnings off the farm, maybe, yet the books showed their value every day: a farm kid could receive no greater gift.

A big stuffed chair at the corner of the living room nearly blocked the doorway out onto the front porch. Our mother would collapse into the big stuffed chair at the end of her long, hard days–a farm to help with, nine children to raise. We worried for her, the wear and tear. Many a night while Dad was still in the fields we spied down through the register in the floor of the bedroom above, to make sure that Mom was okay. Whenever she told us to take our fighting out behind the barn where she couldn't hear it, we did; even so, nine children constantly underfoot wears a woman out.

Our television sat at the west end of the living room, between the two windows in that wall. The first television my parents bought stayed in our house only an hour or so, long enough for us to see "Hop-a-long Cassidy" and to begin hoping we'd see many more such adventures. That first set gave out right away and it took some enormous days to get it replaced. I saw parts of the 1952 Republican National Convention on television, amazed that something happening so far away could be brought so close. I remember seeing Edward R. Murrow gravely indict Wisconsin's Senator Joe McCarthy, the beginning of the end of the McCarthy era. I had no idea then how courageous Murrow was. I remember that my mother woke us in the middle of the night to come downstairs and watch John Fitzgerald Kennedy win the 1960 Democratic nomination for President: Catholic farm kids in grey, Republican Iowa screamed with joy.

One evening, sprawled in front of the TV doing schoolwork, the nine of us kids ate all the ten dozen donuts and long johns my mother had made that very afternoon. We were growing, hungry farm kids after all. It was only a baker's dozen for each of us.

Upstairs were the bedrooms and the bathroom. The stairs themselves would seem large to a small boy; the risers were cut for a man's step. There was a small landing about halfway up, with a turn ninety degrees to the left. Near the top of the stairs, a window to the west.

I stood on that landing when I was two and a half years old. I couldn't go back upstairs because my mother was calling me. I didn't want to go down the stairs because

I was on my way to the hospital to have my tonsils taken out. This is my very first memory.

The landing itself was dark and I stood in the darkness and I was afraid. There was a pool of light at the bottom of the stairs, warm and comforting, bathing the floor at the end of the kitchen, yet I could not move towards it. I held a small cloth sack containing my pajamas and some underwear. "Tom, come on," my mother called. Life might be a great, wide adventure, but having my tonsils out wasn't supposed to be part of it. "Come on, son, we've got to be going," my mother called again from the light.

I remember the smell of ether in the hospital. I remember being very afraid. I remember being strapped onto a cart and wheeled down the hall. I watched my parents stop at a doorway; they were coming no farther with me. That would just not do. "I want to hold my daddy's hand," I said. "Do you know your numbers?" someone asked. My father was holding my hand then. The mask was a darkness over my nose and mouth. "Yes," I mumbled. "One..." The ether. Then nothing, an emptiness.

It took me years to realize it had not been my father's hand I'd been holding going into surgery. I felt a sense of betrayal at this recognition, yet I couldn't figure exactly who had betrayed me. My parents excluded at the doorway? The kind nurse who cupped the scared boy's hand into hers?

Afterwards, while I was recovering in the hospital, it was ice cream for breakfast and ice cream for dinner and ice cream for supper too. Or I suppose it might have been sherbet.

I could not know any of this as I stood on the landing of the stairs beforehand, transfixed, unable to go back up the stairs in retreat, unable to go down the stairs towards some perilous future.

Ever after it seemed as if a ghost lived on the landing. My world had changed irrevocably.

All our bedrooms were on the second floor, off a central hallway–three bedrooms for the nine kids (when finally there were nine of us), another bedroom for my parents. The bathroom–with tub, toilet, and sink–was at the far end of the hallway.

We had not always had plumbing in the house. There were some years of running barefoot in the darkness to the outhouse. I was perhaps five when the bathroom was installed, the space cut out of two adjoining bedrooms at the east end of the house, one of them mine and Flip's, the other my parents'. While the bathroom was being constructed, I woke during the middle of the night; I lay in my bed looking through the studs of a wall being framed in; I thought I saw ghosts moving in there. My breath caught in my throat. I couldn't let them hear me or they'd find me. I had to hold my breath. Shapes materialized and evaporated. I couldn't catch my breath.

Eventually, of course, the farm boy went back to sleep, snug and safe in the house that held him fourteen years.

My Parents

I don't remember my father smiling much, yet I don't remember him not smiling. I remember his look of determination. A steadiness of gaze, a set to his chin, the lean of his shoulders forward, into it.

He was a surprisingly young man when I knew him first–in his twenties. Thin, yet muscled for his honorable profession. He was not a tall man–perhaps 5'10"–but seemed taller than any farmer in the neighborhood. His skin in season would be tanned and weathered, the hair of his arms turned golden. Through the years the knuckles of his fingers deformed with work. His eyes were steady blue like an Iowa wind.

He knew farming, of course; he could husband the seasons. We raised beef and hogs and chickens; and for a while we even had sheep. Early on we milked cows and sold the cream for butter; later we kept only one milk cow, enough milk for nine kids. In the fields he rotated corn and soybeans and oats and alfalfa. Once there was sorghum. I remember sugar cane. My father was a good farmer but that does not mean farming was good. I remember our feed salesman stopping while we were baling hay; he told my father the price of hogs had jumped slightly. We shut down our baling operation, loaded a truckful of hogs and took them to market. The line between making it and not making it was a few cents per pound and my father knew where the line was.

The beef he raised was recognized as superior by the cattle buyers in the area and our animals always seemed to do just a little bit better in the auction ring.

I must have been ten or eleven years old. We were at the auction barn, far up in the cheap seats–my father, my sisters, and two of my brothers, eight children in all, set in a row from youngest to eldest next to my dad. My mother and the baby were at home. Our cattle came into the ring. "This fine bunch belongs to Bill Montag," the auctioneer said. "Bill is here today and it looks like he's got his family with him."

We puffed with pride. All eyes were on us. "We left the little ones to home," my dad called out to the auctioneer. He meant, I think, that we'd brought only the fully finished steers to the sale barn. Everyone in the sale barn, however, might have wondered just how many more little ones–children–there could be yet. My father is not one to explain himself further.

A farmer doesn't suffer fools gladly, at least my father didn't. The tax assessor was making small talk: "Think it'll rain?"

"It'll be a hell of a long dry spell if it don't," my father said.

My father rented the farm at Curlew from late in 1947 'til the mid-1960s when we bought the farm near Dows. The people he rented from at Curlew were the same people he banked with. Having one set of hands taking money out of your pockets is always preferable to having two sets of fingers going through everything. (Actually my dad and the landlord and the banker had a good relationship overall. It got to the point if my dad needed to borrow money to buy feeder cattle, he'd write the check for the cattle, fill out the loan application when he got home, and mail it off to the bank. The bank would cover the check and loan him the money. When you told people you were Bill Montag's boy, you got some respect.)

I saw a check for $10,000 once, made out to my dad, after he'd sold cattle. The sight of that much money kind of took my breath away. My dad let me hold the check for a few minutes. I handed it back to him. "Yeah, that's about how long I get to hold onto it, too, son," he said. He took the money to the bank to pay off a loan, or part of one.

I earned seventy-five cents an hour walking bean fields back in those days so when my father hired on at $4.00 an hour to do some carpentry at the auction barn in Humboldt, Iowa, we thought the money train had just pulled in. Not many people were getting $4.00 an hour back then, at least not people we knew. Dad had to drive 45 minutes each way back and forth, which seemed only a small inconvenience for the big money. Dad helped build new stock pens, loading docks, and shelter barns using green wood and big nails.

Dad didn't drink but occasionally, he was a Montag. Three or four times a year, though, he and my mother might go off dancing at the Ridato, a pavilion some fifteen miles south of us. He might have a whisky or two, listening and dancing and listening, and on very rare occasion might have more than that and not be able to get up for milking the next morning. My mother would say "Get the chores done, boys, Dad's sick." Which condition was some cause of concern for us, for our dad was *never* sick. We figured it must be *really* bad. One time the only thing he could stomach all the next day was a few nibbles of oyster crackers, that's what we called them. That's like being on death's door.

My father set high expectations but he was never harsh. Mostly he communicated what he expected of us by his example, because he never said much. "Kinda crooked, isn't it?" might be all you'd hear about it and you'd know you hadn't done it right yet. The lines of his fields were clean and straight, his fences were taut, his beef cattle and his hogs were premium. How could we strive for less?

When I wonder where I got my rebel streak I remind myself that my father, quiet as he was, was Catholic in Protestant farm country, he was Democrat in those grey Republican years. He could detect a load of bullshit before it ever came off the truck, and there were plenty of fellows peddling it–feed salesmen, county agents, even a farmer down the road maybe. "I don't think so," my dad would say and the sale was doomed; might as well pack it up right now. A cloud of dust like a rooster tail and the fellow would be headed off to try his luck with some other farmer. Sometimes the neighbor might ask the salesman "How many did Bill Montag buy?"

My father was one of seventeen children. His was the large Catholic farm family. When they retired from farming Grandpa and Grandma Montag bought a house in West Bend. I remember standing in their living room watching it snow on television; television was very new at that point and I had never seen one before. It seemed so strange. My grandmother's name seemed stranger–Luna. Grandfather's name was Henry, he was tall and lean and a little stooped by the time I knew him. Sixteen of Henry and Luna's children survived to adulthood. My father was about the middle of the pack. The farm my grandparents owned had a small creek running through it. Water. In Iowa! A field with stones and sun and the run of water in a brook crossing it. Grandfather helped my dad put the shed onto the back of our barn at Curlew, something like a lean-to, but better quality; it was shelter for our cattle. My grandfather moved like my father, only slower and more methodical, much slower and more methodical than the farm boy at his heels; he knew what he was doing so he didn't have to hurry. I got nails for him, I held the other end of 2x4s for him while he nailed them into place, I watched him and my father work and I might have wondered what is this strand that connects parent and child. I might have wondered then, I wonder now: what is this strand that connects grandfather and grandson across an eon. Later, after Henry and Luna died, the family argued about the farm. Siblings stopped talking to one another. The large family was at odds with itself. I took away this, a belated gift from my grandparents, I guess: don't ever argue about money with family; give up desire, let go, do not wish to have.

My dad and all his siblings were bright kids. One or other of them won the county-wide spelling contest, including my dad. I know that Pa didn't finish high school, yet I don't know many men, even today, who read as much as my father does. Reading was important to him.

My father fought in Europe during World War II. He told only a few war stories. He did what he had to do and saw nothing glorious in it. He was never good at killing things.

Once his detachment stole some old hens from a convent in Germany; they cooked those chickens for two days, and cooked them some more, and still could not get the meat tender enough to chew. They had to throw that supper away.

My father had carried the detachment's radio on his back for the greatest part of the day. Then a fellow relieved him of the burden. Minutes later a sniper's bullet cut through the radio and cut through the soldier carrying it, killing the man. My father never said "That could have been me" but we knew that could have been him and if it had been him my brothers and sisters and I would not have been born. Life is like a game of pinball, ka-ching, ka-ching, ka-ching.

My parents knew each other as children. My father was eight years older than my mother. At some point, seeing my mother, my father thought, Who would marry *her*? My mother saw my dad playing baseball at the Catholic school playground. She was standing behind home plate, holding onto the backstop, when my father came up to bat. "That's who I'm going to marry," she said to herself. My father's jeans had holes at the knees. "If I was married to him," my mother thought, "I'd patch those jeans."

My mother was twelfth out of thirteen children in a good Methodist family. One of her brothers was killed as a youngster, run over by my grandfather's truck as Grandpa backed out of his yard. Grandpa Allen died young—my mother was only eighteen years old at the time.

This is how I explain all my double first cousins: two of my mom's brothers married two of my dad's sisters. This was small town Iowa, a long time ago, large families are going to do that. So I have more than twenty relatives I'm cousin to through my father and through my mother both. Some folks might think all those cousins would look like brothers and sisters. I have to say this: there is strong family resemblance.

If my dad's family could be described as well-behaved and maybe sometimes prim German Catholics, I'd have to characterize my mother's family, the Allens, as Scottish outlaws. Sometimes they acted like they were running from the law, or wanted to be. Where someone from my dad's family might try to swindle you or would cook the books where he worked, an Allen would haul a load of somebody else's beef to New York City and sell it out of the back of his semi on some street corner. It was a matter of style, and the Allens had their own, ragged and rough, and they could take some pretty good hits as well as hand them out. Uncle Les, when he was hit by lightning, was too bull-headed to die of it. His toughness wasn't just bluff.

I remember a Sunday at my Gramma's house in West Bend. Gramma lived in that big old square white house in the middle of the big lot in the shadow of the elevator. When all her sons and her three daughters came home and brought wives or husbands and children with them, the crowd spilled out into the shade of the side yard where there was a breeze. Some of those Allen boys had been in the Navy during the war and had learned to carry a flask of whisky in the back pocket. The Navy took your farm boys and sent you back drunkards, I think. Sometimes the whisky got to talking and the talk and the sun got to working and once one of the smaller brothers-in-law went after one of the bigger uncles with a sand shovel. You wonder how many years of needling by some bully the fellow was reacting to.

My gramma was quicker than she looked, and sturdy, and she took hold of that sand shovel, she took it away and set it up against the corner of the house. "That's enough of that," she said, and it was. We got to eating in the shade of the big old cottonwood, a cooling breeze came blowing through, the tenseness of the world dissipated, but the ten-year-old always remembers the argument about to be settled with the business end of a sand shovel.

Gramma's family had been to South Dakota homesteading at some point, but they had recognized quickly that South Dakota is no place to try farming for a living, and had returned to the comparative lushness of Iowa.

We always used to say there had been an Indian in the blanket on my mother's side of the family–the high cheek bones, the skin tone–and near as my mother ever figured she was 1/64th Indian. Didn't know where, didn't know when, didn't know how. If we look far enough, we'll see that there's a little Indian in all of us, I think.

Gramma talked a little funny but we didn't know it; we talked the same way. She said crick for creek, she said rench for rinse, she said zink for sink. Did she ever say "Use some crick water to rench those dishes in the zink?" No, but that's how she talked.

My mother told of playing basketball when she was in high school, and I think I've seen a photograph of her in a grey and modest uniform. That was in the days when there were boys' rules and girls' rules: the girls didn't run up and down the court but kept three offensive players on one end of the floor, three defensive players on the other end. I think my mother played defense. She was an Allen and didn't have much problem getting in somebody's face.

My mother also had a role in one of the high school plays. She was some kind of Hawaiian hula-hula princess and she wasn't embarrassed being silly in front of a lot of people she didn't know. A Montag couldn't do that. My mother knew little of the proper shame I thought dad's family kept around for just such occasions.

My mother always had health problems, it seemed. When she was pregnant with me, her doctors thought she might die of whatever toxicity developed. They told her another pregnancy would likely kill her. I was the first of nine children born to my parents, all of them healthy and squalling. Except Henry who was several weeks premature and was kept in an incubator. And Randy, the right side of whose body was always a little larger than the left. High blood pressure was a problem for my mother, fainting spells, she had a kidney removed, had a hysterectomy by the time she was thirty years old. As a child I often feared my mother wouldn't live to see her next birthday, or mine, yet the birthdays have kept rolling past.

Sometimes after we'd been put to bed for the night Mom collapsed. We'd be looking down to the living room through the hot air register in the bedroom floor and see her sprawled out down there, then one of us would go running outside to find dad. "Mom's fainted again!" we'd shout to him. He'd come up to the house and help her get into her favorite soft chair, he'd send us back to bed and go back to his chores. The doctors were doing for her what they knew how to do, which didn't seem like enough.

Sometimes we'd peek down through the register and see her crying and wonder at that–why was she crying? After all, she had nine wonderful children. We were wonderful children, weren't we? You had to get a little older and have a little more experience of the world to recognize exactly how much stress nine kids create as they shout and fight and carry on, with never a moment's silence, never a moment's peace, always babies to watch, laundry to do, vegetables to put by, dishes piling up, another meal to prepare, and then to help in the fields.

My mother's pride is that we were well-behaved and that we obeyed her. For the most part we obeyed her. When we didn't, she knew she could always say "Thomas, come here," and I would. I was running away from home, angry. I had everything important wrapped in a handkerchief and tied to a stick over my shoulder. I was four years old. I was headed off down the gravel road. My mother stood at the end of the drive and said "Thomas, come here," and I trudged back. Right here is where a poet learns that words have power, right where "Thomas, come here" works at one's soul.

It always seemed to me that my mother was an equal partner with my father. There was enough work to be done that they didn't have time for chauvinism. My mother raised the babies, sure, but she drove tractor, planted corn, baled hay. She fed chickens and hogs and cattle. Life was hard enough for both of them. They were like two horses in harness, to move the wagon both of them had to pull, and both of them did.

True, my mother did the most discipline. My father wasn't as good at holding the line as my mother was. We got spankings when we deserved them, not often, but often enough we were well-behaved. We knew how to work. You could hear the neighbors say "Those Montag kids know how to work." Even today it's a lucky employer who has got one of us on the payroll. Across the board, without fail, I think all of us still give a full day's work for a day's pay. There's nothing like being raised on a farm by hard-working parents to help you learn there are no free rides, you get what you earn. If you don't put seed in the soil in spring time, you are not going to reap any harvest in fall. If you don't cultivate those rows in June, the weeds instead of the crops will draw up the moisture. If you don't bale hay in July, what are you going to feed the cattle in December?

None of this had to be said. It was lived. My parents were the kind of adults they wished us to become. Do your work, pay your bills, take care of one another.

My Father, Water-Witching

He never speaks of it unless I ask, and even when I ask my father doesn't say much. He acts like it was something every farmer needed to know. He learned it from his father like it was milking a cow or planting corn. My father could witch for water.

He wasn't a water-witch. You would never say that. I don't remember people coming to get him when they needed to find water. Yet when we had to locate a water line that ran across the farm yard so we could attach another line to it, my father took a piece of no. 9 wire, bent it to a point and a curve to each hand, and he walked across the yard towards the hog house until the tip of the wire shoved downward suddenly.

It was there–where the ground had tugged so sharply at the wire–that my father had us dig. And it was there– four feet deep–that we found the water line.

When we needed to dig a new well on the place, we hired a local well-digger to do the job, but it was my father who told him where to dig. He had witched about the farm yard and had found the earth tugged the strongest in the grove of trees north of the barn, beyond the cattle yard. He found a spot he thought there was water–200 feet down, he'd said. The trees there were part of the windbreak along the north edge of the farmyard. We'd had to tear open a hole in the fence to get the well drilling rig in place. The drill went down to 202 feet and hit water.

We got a cement truck in close enough to pour the concrete walls for housing the pump. The structure looked like nothing more than a hump of earth with a trap door opening to the underworld.

If one listened carefully while playing in the yard or filling a tractor with gasoline, he could hear the pump running. That hum in the background was certainty, security. An assurance, like knowing my father could find water any time he had to.

The Journey:

Curlew, Wednesday,
October 25, 2000, Morning and Afternoon

Now I am walking south out of Curlew towards the farmstead I grew up on. The road is paved. When I was young it had been washboard gravel. Now the concrete is worn smooth where the snow plow has scraped it.

A pickup comes up from behind, slows to a stop beside me. A very old man says "You exercising?" "Yeah, I'm exercising," I reply, and the fellow drives off. I wonder, could that have been Len Leslein–the nose, the eyes? The pickup goes on down the road, turns into Leslein's farm yard. Must have been, I think.

Where I turn west towards the old farmstead, there are deer tracks in the soft gravel of the side road. The ditches now are wider than those I remember.

I remember my mother saying that when Bankers' Life foreclosed and got the farm, they had bragged it was the richest section of farmland in Iowa. Later, when the Spies owned it, my parents rented it, the end of summer, 1947. I would be born two weeks after the agreement was signed.

A cock pheasant takes
SUDDEN
flight from the ditch to my left.

Now I am standing at the driveway leading into the

piece of ground that had been our farmstead. This feels like a sacred moment, holy in a quiet way. Wind in the big pine tree near the driveway makes the farmstead sound like a cemetery. The pine is twice as tall as I remember, twice as big around. I can see that it has put on good new growth again this year. I step onto sacred ground.

Now I am standing on a patch of grass and thistles that is distinctly greener than the rest of the ground. This is where the house stood. Only the greenness and the thistles give hint that stories have been erased here.

Oh, the big old cottonwoods. Two of them. They are broken here, they are hollow there, they are not long for this world. Both of them lean to the east under the insistence of the Iowa wind, they lean farther to the east than I remember.

Only half an hour ago, Pat Allen told me: "I remember your mother always said when she died she wanted to be buried in one of those big cottonwood trees. She loved those trees." They are old friends of mine, too.

The machine shed is gone, of course, and the rocks that had been piled behind it are gone too. Should I imagine those rocks were dumped into the hole of the house's cellar, pushed in there as fill?

Yesterday when I came past the farmstead, I'd thought only part of the grove north of the farmstead was still standing; now I recognize it is all here, the grove never extended any farther to the east than that. Everything seems smaller than it used to be. The world has shrunk. From here I can see the pile of golden corn heaped on the ground at Mallard, it shines. Perhaps the world has changed because now I cast my eyes to the far horizon sometimes instead at the ground beneath my feet. Or perhaps there is so much I've forgotten and now I'm relearning some of it.

The wind moans in the big pine. I'll say it again: the farm yard sounds like a cemetery.

Where the barn used to stand, corn grew there this season, it has been harvested, the ground has been worked.

Some few leaves remain on the trees at the northwestern edge of the grove: there is still a mulberry tree or two left here, I think. Small consolation. I stand for a moment in my sadness, then climb the ditch from the grove, out to the surface of the road, and I leave the old farm yard behind.

Deer tracks lead the way west. Several sets of them, some old, some fresh. It's as if the gravel road has become a deer trail. A set of tracks suddenly veers off into a field at a driveway. Other tracks leave the road farther on, and you know those deer had to jump the rare fence if they were to enter the field. A fence! Make note of that. Farther on, tracks come out of the ditch from the left.

The wind wants to blow the sky blue. Pieces of the sky crack open, yet the grey overcast predominates and there is haze in all directions. I hear the whrrr of truck tires on the concrete road behind me half a mile. There is enough wind that I keep thinking a car is coming up behind me; I turn and see only emptiness.

Okay, I ask myself, all those people in the Rush Lake Cemetery, what did they die for? What did they achieve? What mark have they left? How do we know they've been here? What did they do that matters?

I have to laugh at myself. It's still always more questions than answers, isn't it?

I pass the decaying corn crib I hadn't recognized yesterday; it stands near where we always stacked our bale pile. Across the road where Anderson's hired man had lived, there is still a Moorman feed sign attached to the fence, greatly rusted. Just barely legible: "Edwin N. Anderson." Now a small patch of sky above me is resolutely blue and a line of scrubby trees breaks the wind.

Another cock pheasant takes flight. It moves from left to right. On the strength of its sound alone, I think, it gains altitude, it sets its wings, it glides nearly the full beauty of a quarter mile. Perhaps I exaggerate, yet only slightly. Lock that arc of flight into the mind's eye: it is reason to live and let live.

I remind myself: don't ask too many questions you don't answer. Yet I protest my own admonition: what if the answers to some questions have been lost, what if God only knows? In the search for home, I'm thinking there are always more questions than answers. So—patience. The world will reveal itself.

I am standing in a patch of full sun; the wind is warm; the air tastes like I am 12 years old, playing in front of the landlord's cottage, Lake Okoboji, August 15th, some summer an awfully long time ago. Then I turn north and walk on my shadow.

Wind through the wires at one of the power poles makes a sound like a computer modem dialing up. It is a harsh alien sound set against that of wind smoothing grasses in the ditch.

"All you can do is watch for signs," I say. "The world will reveal itself."

Remnants of orchard at the place I mis-remembered as the Haywoods'. It was the Bowers back then, and it still is. All the beehives—you have to scramble to make a living here, I think. The barn needs repainting. A hog feeder rusts. A shed sinks back to earth. A tank for watering cattle is rusted so badly that its other side is showing through.

I hear a jet overhead. This is the land most Americans only fly over. They know very little of it. Meat comes wrapped in cellophane, grain comes puffed in cardboard boxes, don't bother us with the details. As I clear the grove at the Bower farm yard, I see a red-tailed hawk flap lazily, as if to confirm the truth of my observation.

I hear a sound behind me, like a dog following. I turn to look: it is nothing but the past. The past is a dog following, with its tail between its legs. Yesterday is so much smoke. All we get is a whiff of what is gone. So much is gone.

I step onto the driveway to what had been our northwestern forty; a rock and a post mark the divide between the half sections. The fence line between the parcels exists now only in memory. In some places I can discern where fence had been, in other places the fence line is being farmed. Here is the forty where I plowed the beans under, here is where I cut my hand on the rough saw grass. A pair of crows lift in front of me–caugh, caw, caw, augh, one of them says. Their blackness shines. They work their way away and another pair follows behind. One crow lands on a power pole and scolds me sharply for a minute, then–it is as powerless as I am to change things– it moves on. Listening carefully I notice now that the sky is all of a sudden full of the sound of unhappy crows.

There are more deer tracks in the soft road. I don't remember ever seeing deer tracks anywhere near the farm when I was a child. It is a different world now, scruffier and rough, and it has deer in it.

Another crow. Close. Haugh! it says. Haugh! Ha!

I turn the corner and head east, the final mile back to Curlew ahead of me, the fourth leg of my square walk. It is 12:30 p.m. How long have I been at this? An hour and a half? Longer? Almost two hours, perhaps.

Beer cans in Iowa, about four of them discarded per country mile.

A spit of rain, a passing darkness.

Grass grows into the edge of the road from the ditch. The fields encroach on the ditch. With time enough, the earth will take back our roads. And surely the earth has time enough. Our ways will be erased entirely, the wind will remain, rain will resculpt the land. Perhaps we are only a momentary blip in the course of evolution, perhaps we are an experiment gone awry. Perhaps our history is only a few motes dancing in sunlight.

I have to breathe deep and swallow back my fundamental loneliness in the face of such a thought. Yet no sooner do I think it darkly than the sun comes out. There are no accidents. Everything means *something*, whether I'm prepared to decipher it or not.

The railroad has been gone from Curlew a very long time, that is obvious. From the northwest I sight down the line that had been the tracks, the tracks are only memory. I sight down the line all the way to Mallard, no obstructions, no promises.

All of a sudden I am standing again on the ball diamond where I had played Little League. In the field to the south, a cock pheasant calls again and again and again. I see it rise and settle on the field at the west edge of Curlew. Quickly it disappears from sight on the worked land. My friend says a pheasant could hide on a pool table.

The wind hums through the wire of the backstop behind home plate. "Hey batta batta," it would say if it could.

In town now, I walk two blocks, the length of Fourth Street, and pass two abandoned houses. On the fence of a property at the east edge of Curlew someone has hung out a yellow diamond of a sign: "Dead End." This morning Pat Allen had said it was just recently there have been any kids in Curlew. "For so long, we were without any children in town, and now there are sixteen of them. When the new minister moved in, he brought five right there."

Ambling, investigating, I find that as many as six houses appear to be abandoned. The elevator at Curlew is closed down, sheet metal is peeling off the structure. The lumberyard is closed up. The telephone company has a fine brick building, where Gertie's switchboard had been housed, yet there are no windows, it looks like a bunker built against adversity. Here is the post office, there a beauty parlor. A trucking company is headquartered in the building that used to house the elevator's office. And there, square and sturdy, sits the First Baptist Church.

Are there other reasons to come to Curlew?

West of Curlew,
Wednesday, October 25, 2000, Afternoon

The Haywoods' place had been fixed so firmly in my memory. Now I know that what I remembered as Haywoods' was actually Bowers'. If you can't trust memory, what can you trust?

I drive out two miles west of Curlew and a little south to the place the Haywoods had actually lived. Now there are only three steel bins remaining and a small barn. Yet there is something to memory: the rise of hill I remembered, there is a rise of hill to the ground here, behind where the house would be if it were still standing. All the trees are gone, every one. The sky kisses the scar of what is left.

There is a red-tailed hawk here, too.

A Day in the Farm Boy's Life

Every day was the same. No two days were alike. We'd rise early for chores, always. We'd be out the door by 6:00 a.m., my father, my brother Flip, and I. Usually my father milked the one old cow we kept after we got out of the business of milking cows. We milked that old girl by hand. Some days I had to milk; it was a warm, reassuring sound, the stream of milk hitting the bottom of the bucket. I'd have the milk pail between my knees; I'd be sitting on a little T-shaped stool with my head into the side of the cow, the end of her tail pinched between my left knee and her back leg, so she couldn't slap me; I'd be pulling milk out of her–ssping, ssping, ssping into the bucket. Milking is a ritual you don't mess with, done morning and night, the cow as willing to give the milk as you are ready to take it, ssping, ssping, ssping.

While my father milked the old cow, Flip and I had cattle and hogs to feed and water and the chickens to take care of. The cattle and the hogs, especially the hogs, were creatures deserving respect and even some amount of affection. They were being raised for slaughter, you never forgot that. They *were* going to be meat on the table. Animal and farmer were part of the great cosmic dance. The animals would be slaughtered, that's life. There is death rolled up in life, entwined in every fiber of it. It was our task to see that the animals were well cared for while they were ours, that they died quick and clean when they died by our hand. If we were angels, we wouldn't have to eat. We have these animal bodies, however; we evolved as omnivores, I do eat meat.

On spring mornings we were as frisky going at chores as the young cattle out in the feedlots: they'd run and kick their back legs up. The smell of a new season, of moist, dark soil, of ditches dreaming green grass. It made me want to kick up my own heels. The promise of everything, spread out before us as the sun came up to warm the air after the hard Iowa winter. The clean smell of the air in spite of grey drabness across the landscape. Doing chores in spring, you could believe anything was possible. You were certain you'd find your way across the ol' rock pile to become something other than Iowa farm boy.

In summer, chores were almost an afterthought. We were so busy then with field work—cultivating the corn and beans, baling hay, taking in the oats when they turned, baling straw. Chores were book ends at the beginning and the far end of some long stretches of other work. Sometimes Flip had to do the chores alone if Dad and I were late in the field, sometimes mom and the girls helped him. The girls never milked the cow. Milking works the muscles in both forearms and if you aren't in shape for the repetition of squeeze and pull, squeeze and pull soon the muscles get to burning from wrist to elbow. Squeeze and pull. My father would be out in the green summer fields until the shadows grew long and the sun flushed with desire in the western sky.

Autumn was always a sad season for me. We might take animals to slaughter in autumn; we'd bring the crops in. We'd strip the land. The world was baring itself, exposed, open. Something had ended. Death was marching, we could hear the drummer drumming. The coolness of the morning air as you stepped outside for chores on a fall morning, the bite of it, the tang–such reminded us of the ceaseless tromp tromp tromp of things, the endless cycle of life and death and life.

Winter chores. Ah, winter. When you least wanted to be out doing chores, the animals needed you the most. You had to make sure they had feed, that their water was not frozen over. You hated the cold and snow as you stepped out, your breath against the dark air, yet you enjoyed your toughness. If I can do this, you thought, I can do anything. The snow would be white, the day would be grey, the chores would seem an endless tromp tromp tromp.

I have said little of chickens, little of the chicken chores. The chicken is God's dumbest creation. By the time he got to making chickens, obviously he'd used up all the brains. Chickens could cluck, generally they could find the box in which to lay their eggs, they could find a place to roost for the night, and that, folks, is all the bragging you can do about chickens.

There was a cycle to chickens. We'd be taking eggs from the hens in the hen house on a spring morning, at the same time we were filling the little water jars and feed pans for fuzzy yellow chicks in the brooder house. The chicks would have to be warmed by heat lamps. We'd hope the small birds wouldn't be scared by the sound of a spring storm or a dog's barking or the slam of a door–like all chickens, they had a knack for piling on top of one another in the corners and smothering each other. A dead chick was money wasted.

We'd start chicks in the brooder house each spring, we'd tend them carefully. The birds grew through the summer and by fall we'd use the new pullets they had become to replace some of our old hens. Come September, we'd check the old hens' bottoms–if you could fit three fingers of a child's hand between the bones there, that hen would be placed in a chicken coop for butchering. In with the new producer; out with the fagged out hen. Chickens don't know any better; God ran out of brains by the time he made them, remember. He created chickens for the eggs and for eatin' and not at all for intelligent conversation.

A farmer's life has a tromp tromp tromp to it. The farm boy's life did too. He did morning chores, he came into the house for breakfast. His mother and sisters had been making the meal–hot cereal or pancakes or some such, and it would be on the table, steaming. The girls would be dressed for school and after breakfast they'd have to do up the dishes and finish the beds while Flip and I changed out of our farm clothes into clean britches for school.

We'd go off for a day's classes at St. Mary's Grade School in Mallard. There was a year or two we got to ride school bus, I don't remember why. I do remember some big girl on the bus teasing my sister Kack. That girl was an eighth grader, I think her name was Sharon, she had a reputation for being tough. I was in third or fourth grade and had not yet met anything in the world I couldn't handle. I was wearing a pair of my clod hopper farm shoes and I kicked Sharon in the shins. I mean I kicked her in the shins good: you could hear the sound of it resonate in her bones; you could see her teeth wobble as she grimaced in pain. I said "I'll do it again if I have to." I think she understood you don't want to get into a shoving match with the devil. She didn't bother us again, ever. Nobody ever bothered us much.

For most of the years we were in grade school my parents had to drive us there every other week, the five miles to Mallard. The Joe Hoods lived west of us a mile or so and their daughter Jolene was in my class, so my mother and the Hoods would trade off hauling school kids–that's what they called it. To me it always seemed a little unfair for the Hoods—the week my mom drove, we took only one extra child; when the Hoods drove, they loaded in an extra four or five or six, however many were in school that year.

The morning rides were uneventful. Early on, we had a 1950 Ford sedan; then a 1954 model; then after 1958 we always had a station wagon. The Hoods had only a sedan: when it got to be six or seven kids in the car, we sat pretty close; and the older we got, the closer we sat.

Ah, school. Keeping farm kids corralled in stuffy classrooms is like keeping horses confined to the barn—they'd be busting full of energy trying to break themselves out.

St. Mary's School always had its own smell—unwashed farm kids was part of it, and library paste, that's what we called it, and the starched smell of the nuns. The smell of hot lunch being prepared in the basement. The smell of girls. Life pulses and throbs in a school, even an elementary school, even a Catholic elementary school, and the farm boy throbs with it. Who are these female creatures not your sisters and why do they act that way? The strange angles of them, how they are put together, those girls, but when you push one, she seems sturdy enough even if she's soft in places. An electric smell, as if God has just walked through the room, the molecules of the air seared by his very presence. The smell of unwashed farm kids, the untouched nuns, a thousand tingles growing up.

Readin' and 'ritin' and 'rithmetic and religion. We learned the basics—phonics, the Palmer method, multiplication tables, three-persons-in-one-God.

I learned to read on a little blue bench at the front of the classroom. Our benches were child-sized, tiny, with child-sized blue backs. At reading time we left our desks and went to the front of the room for our phonics lesson.

Every day we'd stare at the black squiggles on the white paper. We'd fidget on our little blue benches. I'd wonder what it was that Sister Damien was talking about because I couldn't see it. It sounded marvelous, but none of it was on the pages I had. My black marks didn't make that kind of sense. And we'd go up there another day, up to our little blue benches in front of the room. We'd wrestle again with those black marks. Then one day all of a sudden it was so obvious. "Oh my!" I said to myself, "this is something." Every black mark meant something and now I knew what they meant. "Oh my!" I said. "Nun, get out of my way!"

Anything you learn in school after you've learned to read is anticlimactic. You recognize you don't really need to go to school to learn, you could learn nearly everything you learn in school from books if you wished. Yet there are laws about such matters and I'm not sure my parents wanted to add "home schooling" to the endless run of tasks they had. So I stayed in school. The blue bench of phonics was behind me. Every book in the world was in front of me.

Fourth grade. A grey day. A nun had to teach our religion class because Mrs. Budd's husband wasn't Catholic, was that it? The nun is telling us about the ritual of Mass, about the consecration of the host, about the moment of transubstantiation, the instant when a mere wafer, just a piece of bread, becomes the body of Christ.

"If the priest fails to consecrate enough hosts for Communion at the point of consecration during Mass," says the nun, "can he go back and consecrate more of them later? Do you think so or not? Those who think not, stand up."

Nobody was standing up. Nobody in that grey world on that grey day in that grey instant was standing up for what was right and true. It was so obvious–the moment of consecration had passed, the ritual was bigger than one man's failure, one congregation's need. The priest could not go back to the consecration; to me it was plain and simple. Still not one of my classmates would stand.

My chair made an awful sound as I pushed it back. I stood. Alone. A whole classroom turned, their eyes full on me. Their silence like a weight, suspended. The stares– "Who does he think he is?" I was so alone.

Then–an eternity later–it must have been only a moment–after what seemed like an eternity–the sound of the nun's chair being pushed back. "I'm standing up with Tom," the nun said. "He is right."

Well, when you tell a fourth grade farm boy he's right and no one else has got it, you are planting the seed of rebellion. He'll start listening to his heart instead of believing everything he's told, won't he? He'll start examining the world around him with fresh eyes; he will begin to weigh truth on a whole new scale.

Some of those years in school I spent an awful lot of time out in the hallway with my slower classmates, helping them with their lessons. I carried a lot of crates of milk from the basement for morning break, I clapped a lot of erasers. I stoked coal in the furnace. And it seems like I spent a lot of time going to funerals at the church across the lawn; we helped to fill up the pews, which I suppose helped the deceased into heaven.

A bad teacher can destroy you as surely as a good teacher lifts you to the greatest heights. I cannot sing because the nun told me I cannot sing. She kept me in at recess as punishment for having a slow ear. When we went to a Catholic Youth Organization's eighth grade chorus competition our class was pitted against all the eighth grade classes in the region. To improve our chances, the nun told me to mouth the words, fer chrissakes. There I stood, on stage, mouthing the words, not a sound from me. That's like cheating, isn't it? Is the "good" in "good sister" entirely honorific, not descriptive?

One of my classmates decked that nun once when she got out of line with him. She tried to push him to the floor and he knocked her down. We all thought he'd get excommunicated for hitting a nun, but he only had to stay home from school a few days, that was all. A few years later the nun ended up taking some rest cure at one of those peaceful places in the country with tree-lined driveways, bars on the windows, and dull, glazed looks on the faces of the residents walking the grounds.

Eating hot lunch at the parochial grade school in Mallard I learned to hate asparagus and I have wasted half my life hating asparagus as a result. The cooks would get these large tin containers of creamed asparagus as "government surplus." They'd heat that stuff and serve it and call it asparagus and expect us to eat it. I learned to hate beets the same way. Often I took sustenance from plain bread and from the yellow cheese that was also government surplus.

School was school. You did what you had to 'til you could bust out for recess. There was a merry-go-round just north of the school building; it was small enough you could really get it flying 'round and 'round. Sometimes little kids wanted to ride fast with the big kids. No bawlin' if you fly off, we made them promise. Sometimes they fell off and really went flying. The nun at the window watching us just shook her head and turned away.

We had a good set of swings on the playground and we'd compete to see who could swing the highest. We'd swing up and up to see if we could alley-oop over the top, 360 degrees: none of us ever did, but we did get high enough the tension went out of the chains. We'd go crashing towards the ground until we were jerked to an immediate and complete stop just a foot or so from oblivion. Sometimes we'd swing as high as we could, then jump off like a soldier parachuting out of an airplane. Except we didn't have parachutes and sometimes we got hurt. The rule as I understood it was: you shouldn't cry unless you were bleeding pretty good. Little girls needed to stay away when we were jumping out of the swings: we always wanted to scare them by seeing how close we could come to hitting them. The bigger girls needed to stay away, too: we liked to land on them, the bigger ones who were getting soft in all the right places.

We played baseball on the diamond to the north of the merry-go-round. The edge of left field bordered the swing sets. We didn't often have enough kids to play a real game so we played work-up. You might start in the outfield or at second base or catcher. Three kids started off batting. "Outs" were made according to the usual rules, plus the second two batters had to drive home the first man on base or that would be an out. When one of the batters made an out, he went to right field, everyone else moved up a spot–second base to first base, the catcher got to bat. That's why it's called work-up.

Sometimes the pastor at St. Mary's, Father Pick, played ball with us. I'm not sure that he had ever played semi-professionally, but he talked like it. He had played enough that he'd once split the fingernail on the index finger of his throwing hand. It grew back shaped like a tent or the roof of a church. He had been playing catcher and a fast ball caught his finger and broke the nail. The finger healed funny. Forever afterward, he wanted to insist that the kid who was catching should fold the fingers of his throwing hand in towards the palm. "See this," he would say, holding up his hand, "this is what can happen." Good Catholic boys, already half-convinced we were going to burn in hell for our wild imaginings, we did what we were told.

When the last bell of the day had sounded and the school doors swung open wide, we boiled out of the building. Farm kids, set free. A great noise. The rush to the car. I was glad to be out of school. Yet I liked school. There were books in school. I could read. Sometimes the classroom seemed like a prison cell. Sometimes it seemed like an escape route. Books were friends; school was sometimes a bright light in a dark room.

When we got home we changed into our farm clothes. Before we went out to do the evening chores we'd get ourselves something to eat—a couple slices of bread with gramma's yellow mayonnaise (or we thought we were lucky if we got Miracle Whip); or a baloney sandwich; or a piece of chocolate cake with chocolate frosting. While Flip and I did chores, my sisters helped to fix supper. My dad always liked his steak very well done. He said he didn't like it to beller when he put his fork into it. Sometimes—during Lent, maybe—we'd have nothing more for supper than tomatoes and macaroni, or pancakes. Other times we might have pot roast with potatoes and carrots and onions and my mother's good gravy.

In the evening your parents would want you to do your homework, of course. You'd compromise with them and get to sprawl in front of the TV while pretending to work out math problems. Often you got a little snack of something before going upstairs to bed—a long john or piece of cake or scoop of ice cream. Sometimes you got to stay up later than you should, but not often, because next morning there would be chores bright and early, there would be another day of school, there would be the tromp tromp tromp of life marching its endless circle.

Reading While Doing Chores

One wonders how they put up with it: here's an Iowa farm, 360 acres of corn and beans and oats and hay ground, chickens and hogs and beef cattle, and an old milk cow. And the eldest son wants to *read* while he's doing chores.

Image: I've set a five-gallon pail under a hydrant and started the water running. It will take most of a minute, perhaps, to fill the pail. I reach into my back pocket and pull out a paperback, *The Kid Who Batted 1.000*. I read quickly while the bucket fills with water. Then I turn the hydrant off, put the book back into my pocket, carry the water to wherever it's needed. A few minutes later, another pail to fill, I read another page of my book, whichever book I'm reading.

The Kid Who Batted 1.000, as I remember, was about a farm boy whose special talent was being able to foul off any pitch thrown in his direction. The knack took him to the major leagues briefly, as a pinch hitter who was sent into the lineup when his team was desperate to get a runner on base. The kid would foul off pitches until the pitcher had thrown four balls and walked him. Every at bat he got walked–eventually.

His batting coach certainly didn't want to spoil the kid's ability to foul off pitches, yet took the time to show the young fellow how to hit one particular pitch over the left field fence. Of course this is how fiction goes: the last left field fence. Of course this is how fiction goes: the last time the kid bats in the major leagues he gets that one particular pitch he's learned to hit. Instead of fouling it off, to everyone's surprise he sends it over the home run fence. Then he retires from baseball and goes back to the farm.

The moral of the story, maybe, is that a little glory is okay, but you've got to help your dad on the farm. Heady stuff for a ten- or eleven-year-old farm boy, compelling enough that I kept the book in my back pocket while I did chores and read from it every chance I could.

It wasn't the only book I carried with me. There were others. There was one about a farm boy with a special knack for driving race cars. One called *Patches*, I think, about a pioneer youngster out on the plains, learning something on every page, of rattle snakes and horses and cutting hay.

The books transported me, took me off the farm, away from chores, from the smell of hogs, of chicken manure. When I'd stand at the gravel road in front of our farm house and look towards the horizon I could not see as far as I could see in my books. Reading saved me.

The Journey:

Mallard,
Wednesday, October 25, 2000, Afternoon

I am taking copies of books of my poems to the Public Library in Mallard. "I'd like to give copies of my books to the library," I say to the woman. "I grew up at Curlew and went to school at St. Mary's Grade School here in Mallard."

She looks up and smiles at me. Apparently she doesn't quite know what to make of a poet donating his books to her library, this likely doesn't happen often, and I don't quite know how to explain my intentions. She accepts the books anyway and thanks me.

I am back in my car parked on Main Street, working on my notes, and the woman comes out of the library. "Okay," she says to me, "may I ask you something?" There may be the flush of embarrassment in her face. "Are you related to the Montags around here, in West Bend?"

"Yes," I say. "I have a hundred and thirty-nine first cousins, I must still be related to some of them."

"My mother-in-law is related to the Montags," she says. "There's a lot of them."

She goes back to her work and I go back to making notes.

Mallard,
Wednesday, October 25, 2000, Afternoon

Johnson Brothers Beverages, Spencer, Iowa, was delivering beer to a bar down the street just a moment ago. Now the truck is pulled up in front of "Duck Stop." Same beer, different spigot.

Mallard still has train tracks coming right up to the grain elevator at the east edge of downtown. A great pile of corn on the ground rises beside the tracks, waiting to be loaded into boxcars and shipped out, to be made into something boxed in cardboard that people in New York and California will recognize.

All the houses around Mallard that I used to think were "rich people's houses"–well, they all look kind of shabby in the afternoon light.

Emmetsburg,
Wednesday, October 25, 2000, Evening

Supper at the Chinese restaurant in Emmetsburg. My fortune cookie: "You are heading in the right direction."

Emmetsburg,
Thursday, October 26, 2000, Middle of the Night

I'm awake at 2:30 a.m. wrestling with the obvious: you don't know until you know, and you can't know until you admit your ignorance. How could I have lived fourteen years in a place as uncomplicated as Curlew and not known something of its history? How can a fellow occupy a piece of ground and not want to know? I am no longer so cavalier in my ignorance, so when did I change, when did I start to see value in small human triumphs, the quiet virtues?

I toss and turn in bed, fumbling with such questions, thinking I may never get back to sleep. Perhaps I won't. I am coming to realize my task is not so much to write down what I find out as to find out what I don't know. It's an unsettling prospect, as if salt and pepper have been mixed and I must separate them.

I turn off the light and leave the task for later.

Lightning Strikes the Barn, I Think

If nothing else, the farm boy who will be a poet has got imagination.

How else to explain his going to sleep on a summer's night after a hard day's work, going to sleep to the sound of hogs out on the feed floor letting slam the covers on the hog feeders, a metallic p-bamm, p-bamm, p-bamm, going to sleep to the soothing sound of cattle bellering, low and constant as they will, going to sleep all the way to the edge of an Iowa farm boy dream, and then P-BAMM being rudely awakened as a thunderstorm breaks on top of us.

The bedroom I shared with my brother Flip was dark. I could hear my brother's steady breathing. My heart was racing. I got out of bed and stood at the window looking out into the farm yard. The pole light near our gasoline barrel created a circle of illumination almost large enough to touch the edge of the milk house. I heard the spatter of rain on gravel.

P-BAMM. There was another strike of lightning, extremely close, filling the air between house and barn with brilliance. Thunder followed immediately. I looked at the barn. I looked at where the lightning flash had touched the barn. I looked at where a trail of smoke seemed to pull away from the barn, a tendril in my mind's eye that curled like smoke. My eyes filled with an image of smoke and the afterimage of the lightning bolt.

"Dad!" I shouted. "Dad, the barn's on fire!"

My dad woke. My mother woke. All my brothers and sisters woke. Lights came on. The house filled with its usual confusion.

"I saw lightning strike the barn," I said. "The barn's on fire."

We could see the barn from windows in three different bedrooms. One by one I heard my family say "I don't see anything." There was the sound of wind, the sound of rain on gravel, the sound of brothers and sisters muttering and going back to their beds.

My father said "I don't think the barn's on fire, son. The flash of lightning played tricks with your eyes. Let's get back to bed."

Soon the darkness. My brother sleeping already. His breathing steadied. The p-bamm p-bamm p-bamm of my own heart still pounded. I heard the sound of rain on gravel. Darkness was filling the cracks of night. Soon sleep came for me.

I woke in the morning to blue sky. The barn was glorious white: it shimmered all lit in a new day. It was clearly a fine barn that had never caught fire, not the night before, not ever.

"Barn looks okay to me," I heard one of my sisters say. I did not look up from breakfast to see which one.

The Journey:

Emmetsburg,
Thursday, October 26, 2000, Morning

I slept late this morning, then instead of rising to write, I read. I read about following what develops instead of trying to create it or orchestrate it. I read about thinking long thoughts.

I had tossed and turned for much of the night–a welter of images creating a "Curlew stew" in my mind. I saw two women walking in Curlew yesterday, for the exercise. I saw a sheriff's deputy come through town as I stood at the edge of the park. A couple cars rolled along Main Street, a pickup truck. Two phone company employees stopped at the brick building downtown.

I saw cottonwoods where the farmstead had been, leaning so far back into yesterday they'll be gone soon. I saw corn ground where barn and hog house and feed shed had been, a patch of grass and thistle where the house had stood. I saw the good omen red-tailed hawk at every turn. The overcast sky cleared for awhile, then darkened. A spit of rain. The song of the wind in the trees of the grove at the farmstead. These are images that flashed at me in the night. These, and the images of all those abandoned houses in Curlew, left falling to rot. Even some of the houses still occupied seemed to be humped close to the earth.

Are these the images of desolation or of hope? Are desolation and hope the heads and tails of a single coin, flipped into the air? Am I waiting to call it? Will it come up desolation, or hope?

Emmetsburg,
Thursday, October 26, 2000, Morning

Over breakfast we talk of trains during the night and of the train we are hearing as we speak. Paul says he is on call as a grain inspector when box cars are being loaded. He wonders why he hasn't been called this past week. He says to Peggy: "When you answer the phone you should say 'Queen Marie Bed and Breakfast, Travel Service, and Grain Inspection'."

Afterwards, reading briefly before I start my day, I see this instruction: *amor fati*–love fate, accept what is.

I am off now, to see what *is*, today.

Between Emmetsburg and West Bend,
Thursday, October 26, 2000, Morning

A threesome of crows. Heavy grey skies. The land throbs like dull pain.

As I come upon the town of Cylinder, there is a red-tailed hawk. Where I turn south off Highway 18 towards West Bend, the driver of a Kerber feed truck waves to me as if I'm an old friend.

The train that left Emmetsburg just before I did beats me to the railroad crossing on Highway 15 west of Whittemore. I have to slow, then stop. I have to wait for the red light to stop its flashing.

Everything seems to be ahead of me today, but not by much.

West Bend,
Thursday, October 26, 2000, Morning

The idea is a cup of coffee at the Villager in downtown West Bend. I am waiting for the West Bend Library to open; I'll be leaving copies of my book there too. The Villager is a drug store that has a coffee counter; there are stools along the front of the counter, two old fellows are talking about exercise.

"If you walk every day," says one of them, "then you'll want to walk. If you start skipping days, then every day you'll find another excuse not to walk."

"I've got a Nordic Track," the other fellow says. "I try to get on it for twenty minutes every day." He's a big fellow with a wide smile and ears like scoop shovels.

"My daughter says it's all a matter of time management. If you want to do it, you'll get up half an hour earlier and you'll do it."

"You're a morning person, aren't you?" one of the fellows says to the woman behind the counter.

"No, I'm really not," she responds. "I get up at quarter of six every day but it's not because I like to."

"You've got to make breakfast for Tony?" one of the fellows asks.

"I'm not married to Tony," the woman says. "I don't make breakfast for Mark either. He eats a big meal at night and he's not hungry 'til noon the next day. I'm sure it's not good for him."

She moves down to the far end of the counter and talks with her friend. They talk about what to make for supper, they share a recipe. The two men say good-bye to each other. The wide-eared fellow who remains spins his seat towards me and says "You're not from around here, are you?"

"No," I say, "I'm not." Then I'm telling him who I am.

"I knew your dad when he was a youngster," the fellow says. "Henry was your grandfather then. That was a big family. You say your mother was an Allen? I knew the Allen boys, they were a raucous bunch. The one who worked at the auction barn in Humboldt was a big man like your granddad. One of them was a little fellow. He'd get lickered up at a dance here or there then he'd like to pick a fight. He didn't care how big the other fellow was. Those boys all died pretty young, didn't they?"

"All but Steve and Larry," I say. "Steve is out in Oregon. Larry was the youngest. He's still living over at Curlew."

"You must remember Jap and Ole," the fellow says. "They had the car dealership here."

"Yeah, I knew Jap and Ole," I say, and we are talking my family and his family and where I live and fishing in Wisconsin and fishing anywhere and he tells me a couple of years ago his daughter called him up from her home in West Des Moines and said "Dad, get your pole. I'm taking the day off work and I'm coming up. We're going bullhead fishing, you and I. I remember how much fun we used to have catching bullheads. I'm going to catch a mess of them and bring them back for my family."

When the big fellow gets up to leave we shake hands and say good-bye. As soon as he is out the door, the woman comes down the counter and asks "Would you like another cup of coffee?"

"We don't know who you are," she adds, "but when he started talking to you, we knew you were going to be here for awhile."

"You're a Montag?" one of them asks. I explain. "Do you have a brother Philip?" the woman behind the counter wants to know. "I went to second grade here in West Bend with a Philip Montag." I tell her I do have a brother Philip but none of us ever went to school in West Bend, we went to school in Mallard.

"I never knew there were Montags at Mallard," the other woman says. "My mother is from Mallard. I'll have to ask her about that."

"Did she go to the Catholic school?" I ask.

"No, she went to public school."

"My mother is related to the Montags," says the woman behind the counter.

The Montags are related to everybody, I say to myself. Everybody is related to everybody. I pay for my coffee and leave.

West Bend, The Grotto of the Redemption, Thursday, October 26, 2000, Noon

I walk past the pond towards the Grotto, the noon siren sounds. The siren is quite near, it is a HUGE honk. The geese on the pond take to the air at the sound of it, for short distances, they set down again on the water, they honk noisily among themselves. They must hear the siren every day and every day, I suppose, its hugeness surprises them.

⌒ ⌒

A bronze statue of Father Paul Dobberstein, the priest who created the Grotto, the priest who baptized me. The statue was created by Michael T. Montag of Omaha, Nebraska–9-13-92.

West Bend, Thursday, October 26, 2000, Afternoon

Leaving West Bend I stop at the cemetery at the west edge of town, out beyond the high school. I find my Uncle Les Allen's grave right away (1925-1985). He was struck by lightning and lived to tell about it. He's buried with his wife Socks (1929-1992). Her real name is Opal, that's what it says on the stone, but everybody knew her as Sally because when she first met Les she told him she was Sally, and the name stuck. I don't know why Les called her Socks. Buried with them, sons Gary (1952-1974), Jon (1955-1976), and Bobby Joe (1951-1951).

Nearby, the grave of my uncle Duane Allen, who died of leukemia (1926-1962); the other half of the stone, Mildred M., 1926-. Mildred has remarried and lives in Pocahontas, Iowa. I have not heard much of her or those cousins in thirty-five years.

Then I see it–the stone for Grandpa and Gramma Allen. Alvie C. 1892-1944. Ida M. 1898-1974. The stone is flanked by a pair of pine trees, humming, praying. There are two pots of silk flowers decorating the grave. There is no other stone in the cemetery guarded by pine trees the way Grandpa and Gramma's is. My parents, I think, are responsible for the flowers.

In an unused portion of the cemetery I see a threesome of crows set out in nearly a straight line twenty yards long. They point straight at me.

I find Grandpa and Gramma Montag's markers easily, too–Henry (1882-1956) and Luna (1884-1959). The gravestone is on my left, on my right a pair of red-tail hawks with the threesome of crows suddenly pestering them. For a moment one of the hawks is perfectly motionless on the wind, bright in the warm sun; eternity is an instant.

There are plenty of Montag graves here: John (1853-1933) and Katherine (1860-1944), my dad's grandparents. My mother says Katherine was "very German." John had been born in Germany and came to this country when he was four years old. He lived the early part of his life in southwestern Wisconsin near Dickeyville. He married there, had a son Charles. After his first wife died, John remarried Katherine Hinderman, now buried here beside him.

John and Katherine had seven children born to them in Wisconsin–Joe, Henry, William, Regina, Dora, Edward, and George. Henry would be my dad's father. Then, like many in those days, according to my Great Uncle Jap, "they decided to move to the Northwest Country" and they lived five years in Sac County, Iowa, where two more sons were born–Ferdinand and Adolph.

When the railroad laid tracks right through John's farm, he sold that land and moved to Palo Alto County, Iowa. His farm in Fern Valley Township near West Best consisted of 320 acres of "just as good a farm as can be found anywhere." It was on this farm that Uncle Jap was born in 1901. Was my Uncle Ole born here too? I don't know. I don't know exactly where Uncle Ole fits in.

John "was a man of his own mind," my Uncle Jap has written of his father. "Always kept up with the advancing age. When new improvements came into being, we were always ones to first take advantage of them."

When my mother was a little girl, she tells me, she stopped on her way home from school to talk with Katherine Montag every day. Then before she died Katherine told Jap's wife Miriam "when that little Allen girl gets married, you give her this quilt from me."

"Here I marry her grandson," Mom says, "and I get this prize quilt from Katherine and she has been dead a couple years."

Montag: William (1885-1926) and Eva (1890-1959), an uncle of my dad's, Raymond Montag's father.

Montag: James (1918-) and Dorothy (1924-), my great-uncle Joe's oldest boy.

Montag: George (1895-1967) and Izma (1901-1953), another of my father's uncles, the postmaster in West Bend for many years.

Schmalen: Peter J. (1896-1984) and Esther Montag Schmalen (1905-1992). Esther is one of my dad's sisters. I remember the smell of Pete's cigars at family reunions, the smoke of his cigars holding together the clamor in the church basement where we gathered and ate and talked. And talked.

Montag: Leo F. (1901-1987) and Miriam S. (1908-1969). Leo is Jap, my Great Uncle Jap. My parents don't know how or why he was called Jap. His wife Miriam died suddenly in 1969, of heart attack Jap has recorded. I always thought it was breast cancer. Her death seemed terribly unfair back then, and it still does.

Jap sold cars, Fords, about one hundred twenty-five new units a year and eighty-five used ones at the time he retired from the business in the early 1970s. He sold Fords to my parents, I remember him coming over to see us. His feet were as long as boards and if they didn't stick out the other side of his car when he turned to face the driver's door, I'd be surprised. He was tall and lean, taller than anyone I knew. And Jap could talk. I thought it was because he liked to; maybe he did, but years later my father told me Jap came for his visits when he wanted to collect some of the money my dad owed him. He'd stand and talk 'til he got paid. He'd talk through lunch and he'd talk through supper if he had to.

Wind and sun, and there are more graves here. Montag: John O. (1917-1999) and Mary A. (1920-), John was one of my dad's brothers. He farmed, yet I remember him on Sundays in a suit, white shirt, and tie. My sense that the Montags are a little better than other people? I might have gotten that from Uncle John's Sunday suit.

Wirtz: Alfred J. (1907-1989) and Marguerite Montag Wirtz (1910-). Marguerite is one of my dad's sisters. Al Wirtz had been born and raised in Argentina; he had been a gaucho on the pampas. Al had lost part of a finger, he talked about "phantom" pain, about the finger feeling so cold while it wasn't there, about how all of a sudden it felt very warm, as if a wolf had gulped it, and how it hadn't bothered him since.

Montag: Joseph (1881-1974) and Frances (1890-1986), the oldest of my dad's uncles.

Montag: Ferdinand (1897-1979) and Mary M. (1899-1996), another uncle of my dad's. No one but Jap was skinnier than Uncle Ferd; if Ferd turned sideways he disappeared, except for his mop of white hair, and even the wind couldn't find him.

Montag: Raymond V. (1917-) and Marguerite L. (1919-). Parents of Carol, Dorothy, Bernadette, Roger, Karen, Peter. Raymond would be Dad's cousin.

Why are the Rinks buried so close in among the Montags, I wonder. Oh, yes, Eva Montag, Raymond's mother, was a Rink.

Farther off, on a separate plot: Montag: George R. (1919-) and Minerva M. (1923-). George is one of my dad's brothers.

Other stones in the cemetery: Maxwells are relatives, yes. Alma Maxwell is Dad's mother's older sister. Sloans are relatives, of course. Elsewhere, those West Bend names: the Banwarts and Dorweilers and Bonnstetters.

Everywhere the wind, like a prayer.

I leave the cemetery, I drive on into afternoon.

Between West Bend and Mallard, Thursday, October 26, 2000, Afternoon

It is not often I see a crow perched on the peak of a roof. I see one here, between West Bend and Mallard. And all of a sudden, the afternoon brightens.

A Report Card, a Girl, and Chores

I was in seventh grade, or eighth. I was at the age when things start to get all mixed up–school and girls and everything a blur.

Image: we are in the parking lot of St. Mary's grade school in Mallard, we have piled into the car to go home. The car is crowded and Jolene is sitting on my lap. She has gotten an "A" in arithmetic. I have BOTH a "B" and a "D" on my report card for the subject and my mother wants to know why.

We always took Jolene to school and back, or rode with her parents back and forth. It was our week to drive. Jolene was in my grade. She was an only child. Because her parents had gone away for the day, she would be staying with us through supper.

Jolene was an only child and for no other reason than that we liked to think she was a little spoiled. As she sat on my lap in the car, however, it was clear she was not spoiled, but was a good specimen of a farmer's daughter, slender but sturdy, and soft in all the right places. Where can you put your hands that you won't be touching something you shouldn't? We must have been in eighth grade.

I was angry about the "D" in arithmetic. I did well in the subject. I got good grades on my tests. I participated in class. I just didn't do the stupid homework, okay? By the time I'd spent a couple hours after school doing farm chores, I didn't want to sit down and do a lot of math problems, so I didn't, not very often. I got the "B" for my work in class and on the tests, I got the "D" for my attitude about homework.

We got home from school, changed into our farm clothes, and went out to do chores. Jolene had brought old clothes along. When I went out, Jolene went with me.

Image: I've got two 5-gallon buckets of feed I need to carry across the yard to some hogs. "Here," I say to Jolene, "you bring this one." She was an only child and for no other reason I was thinking she was spoiled. Making her carry a big bucket of feed would get her unspoiled. Jolene was a trooper; she carried the feed.

When we got to the gate into the hog pen, either I set my bucket of feed down hard onto her foot, or she did. The rim at the bottom of the bucket banged hard on the nail of the big toe on her right foot. Eventually the toe nail would turn purple, then black, then it would come off the toe and a new nail would grow in. The moment it happened, Jolene was startled, she cried out "Oh!" and pulled back. The sharpness of the pain pooled a rush of tears in her eyes, but she wouldn't let them flow, she bit them back. I was impressed.

Later I showed her one of our electric fences. I said "It's not so bad" and took hold of the wire, the jolt of electricity coursing through my arm. It would have buckled my knees if I'd let it.

"Here, you try it," I said to Jolene. Sometimes children are so cruel.

A Big Farm Family

As my father was one of seventeen children in a Catholic farm family and my mother one of thirteen, it should come as no surprise my parents raised a large brood themselves. I am the eldest of nine, four boys and five girls. We were a pretty big farm family ourselves.

In order from oldest to youngest we were: Tom, Kack, Nancy, Flip, Mer, Diane, Weenie Pig, Hank, and Randy. Kack was Kathy. Flip was Philip, Jr. Mer was Marilyn. Weenie Pig was Colleen. Hank was Henry, named for my dad's father.

Back then it was clear that Kathy was sharp-tongued and observant, as the second oldest must be, the oldest daughter. When she saw something that was not quite right, her eyes could flash like flint striking steel, yet she had a sense of humor, too. She and Nancy were scrubbing the kitchen floor on a Saturday night; they had worked their way down to the west end of the kitchen so they were within view of the TV and could watch Tennessee Ernie Ford while they finished their work. Tennessee Ernie Ford said something that made my sisters laugh–something about "the liver went down the river" and Kack laughed and laughed. She laughed and scrubbed and laughed. And doubled over in pain. She'd laughed hard enough, apparently, to cause herself appendicitis, and my folks had to haul her off to the hospital for repair. My dad didn't think it was appendicitis, though, and wouldn't let the doctor cut on her. Dad was right. She soon recovered. Even today, "the liver went down the river" causes laughter, and then Kack might hold her hand to her side, low where that pain had been.

Nancy was no nonsense and determined, as hard a worker as Kack, a little more forgiving. She is the sibling who looks the most like me. Forty years later, at my daughter Jessica's wedding, Nancy and I stood side by side, cheek to cheek for the camera, to capture our resemblance. It was more than skin-deep. We didn't know way back then that I'd be a poet; nor did we know Nancy and her husband would produce a son who was soon a better poet than his uncle.

Flip was the farm boy, the one among us who understood a little more about the turn of seasons, the planting of crops, the tending of animals. When he and I had work to do together, he always got the dirty end of the job, because I was the oldest and he wasn't, that's just how it was. He accepted his lot stoically and kind of muttered under his breath. When he grew to manhood, Flip tried farming some few years during an unforgiving Republican economy–can you say Reagan–but he could not make a go of it and had to trade the brightness of the field for a dim factory job. Farm boys always seem to be good employees. They know what work is.

And Marilyn, ah Marilyn. She was always too little to go with the big kids when they went off to have fun, and too big to go with the little kids. She was stuck in the middle, neither fish nor fowl, and she could have resented that. She never did. She would smile and laugh and say "Oh, well" and that was all of it, no grudge, never a lingering disappointment, always the harmonizer.

A Big Farm Family

By the time they made Diane, they broke the mold. Diane couldn't do it the way everybody else did, what was the purpose of that? She might drive fast back and forth to school, once she was old enough to get her license, but she got there, what's the problem? Diane thought I was an awfully bossy big brother and was glad to see me go off boarding for high school in Sioux City. Everyone else might have cried as they said good-bye to me, Diane didn't. She said to herself, "Good, now maybe we can watch something on TV besides what Tom wants."

By the time you said "little sister" referring to Colleen, you meant little sister. She'd barely started school when I went off to Sioux City. I always thought she was the "smart one" in a family of smart ones–she played complex card games with adults before she ever started school, and won. She could pull the bones out of your argument if she wanted to and leave you stuttering; but she was sweet enough she didn't do that often.

Henry. A wiry child. His butch hair cut. Bronzed summer skin. His need always to know what was going on and how to do it. When it came to working the fields, Hank might have been second-string to Flip and me because of his age, but he was never second class. He was always a little sassy, as you probably need to be when you're riding so near the caboose. He was always a little more classy than the rest of us. He could keep his pants sharply creased.

Randy we called the Little White Angus Bull. Even when he was small, he seemed broad of shoulder, the full package. He didn't care how big you were, if he needed to take you down, he would try wrestling you to the ground and succeed enough to be encouraged. Randy is the heart torn out of us, killed driving truck before he turned twenty-one years of age, our long sadness all these years. My mother has never been the same. You can never lose a child and recover, you cannot choke back that much sadness.

Randy's Birth

It was July, a blue sky morning, sunlight tickling my nose.

Bert Headrick came driving into our farm yard. What did she want?

My parents weren't home. They'd gone off to the hospital. Mom was having another baby. Her ninth. Dad had taken her to Emmetsburg during the early morning hours. Flip and I had done the chores. We had not yet gone out to the fields. My sisters had made breakfast, now they were doing up the dishes and making beds.

I was ten years old. I was in charge. I walked up to Bert Headrick's car with a ten-year-old's sneer: "Yeah, what do you want?"

Bert got out of her car. "You've got a baby brother," she said. My dad had called her with the news, had asked that she come out to the farm to tell us.

"We've got a baby brother," I shouted.

Flip heard me. He was in the yard. My other brother and my sisters heard me, they were in the house. Henry was just a baby himself, and Colleen not much older. We were crowding each other with the news, talking and crying. Crying with joy–it was a blue, steaming July day kind of joy. An ecstacy of good news, the eight of us were now nine, things were closer to being even, four boys now, five girls.

We didn't know yet that we'd call our new brother Randy. We didn't know yet that we'd say he was our little white Angus bull of a brother. We didn't know that one side of his body was larger than the other, that one leg would grow longer, that sometime later doctors at the university hospital in Iowa City would work to even out his legs so he could walk normally. We didn't know yet that Randy would see no impediments in life, that there would be no obstacle he couldn't go over, under, around, or through, mostly through, mostly straight on through to the other side. We didn't know yet that he'd die twenty years later, driving semi.

For the moment we had a great piece of good news, we had more joy than the July morning could contain. Twenty years later it would be a large chunk of our hearts torn out when we heard the news of his death, when the bad news had sunk in, when we knew it had to be true. We wouldn't ever hear him laugh again; our sadness was huge as the sky.

We didn't know anything but bright July sunshine, a little breeze playing with us, tears of joy welled up in our eyes, our hearts busting—hooray, hooray, hooray!

First Born Responsibility

I was the first-born, the eldest. There were privileges and responsibilities to go with the rank; for instance, when my parents were away, I was "the boss."

And then when my parents came home, if one of my brothers or sisters had done something wrong, they got a spanking for it. And I got a spanking for letting them.

At one point I must have rebelled at the perceived unfairness of it. I remember running out behind the chicken house past the big buzz saw set up for cutting wood. By the position of the light I'm remembering, it must not have been noon yet. My mother followed me out there.

"Thomas, come here," she said. She said it again. I turned and went back with her. We were out behind the chicken house. She had the *good* yardstick from one of the lumber yards—not a flimsy little piece of pine an eighth of an inch thick, but wide, thick hardwood.

I don't remember the offense, I do remember how unfair it seemed: no other kids I knew got such spankings as I did when a brother or sister was naughty. I do remember sunlight reflecting off the shined steel of the buzz saw as I leaned into myself, taking the punishment. My mother broke that good, thick yardstick and I remember I was sorry she'd just ruined the best one we had.

Breaking My Sister's Collar Bone

I was not a violent child, really I wasn't. I was physical the way farm kids are, but not violent. Besides—how could I know that my sister was so fragile, that her collar bone would break so easily?

We were at my dad's parents' farm on a Sunday afternoon, I think. An uncle farmed it then; my grandparents had moved to town. Members of the family had not stopped talking to each other yet. We were there for a Sunday visit—uncles and cousins and what not.

The men clumped in the living room. The women were in the kitchen. The children were outside in the afternoon sun. We'd had our Sunday dinner.

There was a bicycle in the yard and my sister Nancy wanted to ride it. Nancy was two years younger than me, a little scrawny because she always ate the wings of the chicken, not the drumstick or the breast. Nancy wanted to ride the bike and I wanted to ride it too.

She was standing to the left side of the bicycle, one hand on each handlebar, standing in full sunlight; the sun gave her dark hair highlights of dancing color, her high cheekbones were tanned already. She looked like an Indian about to mount his pony.

I pushed at her. To take the bike away from Nancy, I pushed her, pushed her down. It wasn't any harder than

I'd ever pushed anyone else, no different than I myself had been pushed. Suddenly she let go of the handlebar in her right hand, went to her knees. She threw her left hand up to her right shoulder. Cried out. I took off riding the bicycle across the yard.

I don't think she told my parents about her sore shoulder until the next day or the day after, when it hadn't gotten any better. The doctor examined the shoulder, he put her arm in a sling. When he asked her how it happened, Nancy said I'd pushed her to get the bike.

When my mother got home from this trip to the doctor, she said "Thomas, you broke your sister's collar bone." My sister thought it was kind of funny she could say "My brother broke my shoulder;" I thought it was kind of funny the collar bone would snap so easy. The world was going to be more delicate than I had ever imagined.

The Journey:

Curlew,
Thursday, October 26, 2000, Afternoon

I stop at the Post Office in Curlew to buy some stamps and mail my postcards. Two women are talking as I walk in, one on each side of the counter, speaking of someone's illness. They cut short their conversation so I can do my business. The woman on my side of the counter leaves the Post Office. I put the stamps on my postcards, hand them to the woman who is Curlew's postmaster.

"And who are you?" she asks me, straight as an arrow. I explain. I tell her where I grew up. I tell her Larry Allen is my mom's brother.

"I know there are a lot of Montags over at West Bend," she says. "You're related to them?"

Later I will find out her name is Kathy Kramer. She tells me that she and her husband have a farm now two miles north of Curlew. They used to raise hogs but they don't any longer–"Who would ever have thought a farmer would have to give up raising hogs!" she exclaims. "You just can't compete with the corporations that own the big hog farms *and* the packing plants. What they don't make in one place they'll make up the other."

"We started farming in 1969," Kathy tells me. "The first combine we bought cost us $10,000. Now combines cost $250,000 and farmers are getting the same price for corn now as they did back then. How is that supposed to work out? The little farmer is going out of business, the big corporations are taking over, and nobody cares."

"People don't worry about what's happening out here to our farms," she says. "I tell them: some day all the little farms will be gone and the corporations will get what they want in the grocery stores, and then you'll worry. Then it will be too late. There's already a lot of farms gone. Look at all the empty groves. It's scary how much is disappearing."

"It's like we're being walked on," she says. "They just keep doing it and we keep letting them. How long can that go on?"

"I tell you," she says, "I have daughters who are only about thirty years old. They live in the city and already they've got more than we've ever had. I'm happy for them, don't get me wrong, but somehow it doesn't seem fair the farmer can't make a decent living."

"These small towns just keep getting smaller," she says.

"We're happy," she says. "You can't make enough money farming so somebody has to work in town. I've worked for the Post Office, I had my eye on this job but I worked as back-up postmaster here, Rural Route back-up in Emmetsburg, at the Post Office in Laurens and so on, until the Post Master job opened up here in Curlew."

"There is talk about privatizing the postal service," she says. "Right now Congress mandates that these small towns have post offices. If ever they were to give up that notion, a lot of the little post offices will close down."

"When a community loses its Post Office, that's the beginning of the end," I suggest.

"That's the beginning of the end," she says.

"The average age in Curlew," she says, "I swear the

average is in the 80s. The mayor is 93. You remember Russell Bohn? He's the mayor and he's 93 years old."

"We've got really old people and we've got a few young families who moved here because living is less expensive. There's really nobody between the old and the young."

I mention that I'd stopped at the Rush Lake Cemetery to take a look around. She tells me about a fellow who was bicycling through the area on his way to the start of a Bike Ride Across Iowa, that he'd camped for a night in the Rush Lake cemetery. "He set up his tent right in there with the tombstones," she says. "I find cemeteries a peaceful place, but I couldn't do that."

One of her daughters had taken care of the cemetery the summer after she graduated from high school, mowing and so on. "At first she didn't like being out there by herself," she says. "No, I find the cemetery to be a peaceful place." I don't tell her how much time I've spent wandering cemeteries.

"Yeah," she says as I'm preparing to leave the post office, "I saw you poking around town yesterday." Nothing goes unnoticed here.

Staying at Bryan Wilson's House

It was a pretty big deal for a farm kid who had never been anywhere: spending the night at a friend's house in town. Even if the town was Curlew. Even if the house was only a mile and a quarter away.

Bryan Wilson was one of my two best friends in grade school. The other was Greg Reinders from a farm just outside Mallard. Friendship is strange magic to start with, and friendship among children especially so. The flash of a thousand little nothings sustained us. Our relationship had already been cemented by the time we played Little League together. He was a better ball player than I ever was, and I wasn't jealous.

I was old enough to have a BB gun the first time I ever stayed overnight at Bryan's house. Bryan had a younger brother, David, and to some extent we excluded David from our play. Bryan had a deaf sister, too, Melissa. There were younger siblings.

The night I stayed at Bryan's house, his mother was doing laundry. I remember the smell of fresh laundry in the house. I remember the smell of supper on the stove, different from what I was used to. I remember country-western music on the record player, again and again, "I've got spurs that jingle, jangle, jingle." I remember Bryan's father teasing me, as he always would, good naturedly. I remember all the elbow room at the table.

I slept overnight at Bryan's house, but for some reason he and I went out to my family's farm in the morning before school. We might have had to help with chores. For sure we did battle with my brother, Flip. Bryan and I had a BB gun in our arsenal and Flip had clods of dried mud. We'd shoot BBs at Flip; Flip would throw clods of mud at us. Bryan had the best shot—just as Flip raised his arm to whip another hard clod in our direction, Bryan put a BB in the meat on the palm of Flip's hand. That stung his hand sharply and Flip dropped the clod immediately.

I remember the morning sun behind Flip as the BB hit his hand. I remember the clod of mud dropping to the ground. I remember the small puff of dust as it broke up on impact. I remember that we had to end the battle so we could go to school. Some things you cannot run from.

Soda

It would be a bright blue day in July. We would be celebrating the Fourth with a few firecrackers and snakes. Each of us would get a couple bottles of soda. That was our special treat, a couple bottles each on the Fourth of July and sometimes for a birthday, and that was all the soda we got in a year.

I remember the grass in the yard around the farmhouse was so intensely green. The strawberry soda was so red, it was redder than blood, more red than anything, and it fizzed up my nose.

We enjoyed the day away from the fields on the Fourth of July, if we were well enough along with our work. It was like Sunday, except we didn't have to go to church.

In anticipation, my mother would have cooled the bottles of soda in a tub of ice in the basement. By afternoon we luxuriated in our good fortune, we were rich as royalty–strawberry soda, the Fourth of July, and then we'd have the best fried chicken in the world for supper.

At one point my sister Marilyn asked our mother, "Mom, are we rich or are we poor?" The response: "Honey, if you have to ask, I suppose we're rich." We felt as wealthy as the Rockefellers: we had egg money to buy groceries with, we had the money we earned walking bean fields and baby-sitting to buy school clothes every September, we had soda on the Fourth of July.

Welcome Jones

I always associated the fellow's name with a tornado or one hell of a hail storm. Some kind of storm had ripped through, I remember. My parents and some of us kids piled into the '58 Ford station wagon to go out and survey the damage. The worst of the storm had been west of us, west and south. We headed west.

I remember seeing pellets of hail piled up in the roadside ditches like snow drifts. Disks of hail the size of thick onion slices.

Three or four miles to the west my father turned the car north at a cross road, and then I saw his name on the mail box–"Welcome Jones."

"Hey," I said. "Did you see that? That's a strange name."

One of my parents told us the story. "He was the thirteenth child in the family," my mom said, or my dad. "Just so the neighbors and everyone would know he was wanted, his parents called him Welcome Jones."

There's a name that means something.

It wasn't until much later I started to wonder what kind of world some of us are born into, what kind of hard times, to what kind of loving parents. Welcome Jones knows.

Iced Tea at the Neighbors

No one would remember why my brother Flip and I were at the Lesleins', I think it was the Lesleins', a quarter mile east of us and a half a mile south. It wasn't for shelling corn, I know. The angle of sun suggests it was summer. Perhaps we were walking Len's bean fields pulling cockleburrs and cutting out stalks of volunteer corn. That's probably it.

I think we were taking lunch at a table on the porch of the farmhouse, or in the kitchen. I think we must have lived by some rule that said you don't penetrate to the living room of your neighbor's houses when you worked for them, but instead you washed up in a dish pan in the yard; you took your meal in the shade of a tree or on the porch or–at most–in the kitchen; you used the outhouse rather than the indoor plumbing. This is my sense of things upon reflection; in those days we never spoke of the norms that bound us. We couldn't even see them.

We were taking some lunch, a noon meal perhaps, sandwiches and whatever, and the beverage we were offered was iced tea, unsweetened. Well, I never. Who'd ever had iced tea? Nobody at our house. It tasted like somebody had stuck weeds in a bucket of rain water for a month and then offered you the juice. My brother and I looked at each other across the corner of the table. Such a raw drink. A couple of farm innocents, weren't we? Who'd ever heard of such a thing?

The Journey:

Curlew,
Thursday, October 26, 2000, Afternoon

Now I am walking counterclockwise around the section of land I grew up on, I am heading west out of Curlew. Out in the country, I am six miles from Mallard yet I can see the heap of corn piled on the ground at the elevator there. It shines.

When I am northwest of the old farmstead I see that the trees where our farmhouse had been are just a wisp of smoke, a ghostly embodiment, a passing shadow. Everything happened there, and nothing happened. It's all gone and nothing is gone. It was not important; it was essential. Home is in your heart, you take it with you, you wear it like a stink.

A pang in my heart. I bow my head and say a prayer. It is a prayer of thanksgiving and prayer of hope. "This is good land," I pray, "these are good people. May they not be lost."

In the distance, silos thrust up their phallic potency. When all the silos are gone, will the land's fruitfulness have declined as well? Are the silos a symbol of the farmer's will? Will tearing down the silos be the same as giving up hope?

I think the loss of our farmstead at Curlew is not only a personal loss for me, it is the emblem of a loss for the community. Curlew is less because that farmhouse is gone.

I'm just south of the Bower farmstead now, heading south, and a pheasant comes up out of the field into the ditch well ahead of me. It's October 26, yet a grasshopper leaps in front of me; I see a beetle scurry across the road. Though I expect it to, the pheasant does not come back up as I pass the place it landed. It is learning to keep its head down.

Now I'm headed east, I'm west of the old farmstead and I think I see the West Bend elevator shining in the sun; it is like a giant cairn marking something sacred. I look again and the sun is off it, it is barely visible. When I look a third time, a moment later, it is gone entirely. Then just when I think I won't see it again today the sun paints it once more, and it glows. Follow the signs, it seems to say.

A single fence post stands at the edge of the fields to my left, fields that had been ours. The fence post marks where one crop ended and the next began, soy beans to the left of it, corn to the right. Is this what it comes to, a single fence post?

All the while I'm walking back towards Curlew now, the elevator at West Bend flashes on and off. It's there and it's not there. It lights up just often enough to make me think this land is real and permanent, not some wispy dream.

The Accident

The first thing you ought to learn is: never fool around with a piece of equipment you're not familiar with. I don't remember why we *ever* had an Allis Chalmers on the place, we were Farmall people, Farmalls and Fords, never Allis Chalmers. Yet there it was, orange as a warning sign. The tractor had a cultivator on it, so it must have been June.

My dad was sitting on the ground, his legs out in front of him; he was replacing shoes on the cultivator perhaps. A shoe for the cultivator is a piece of metal larger than a grown fellow's hand, shaped something like a bent arrowhead; as you headed down the rows of corn or beans the shoes tore out the weeds or threw dirt up to cover them.

I climbed onto the broad seat of the Allis Chalmers while my dad was working at the cultivator, I grabbed hold of the steering wheel and fell into a farm kid reverie, endless days in endless corn fields. I was pretending to steer the tractor into that future, I pulled a lever like I was shifting gears. The cultivator dropped suddenly to the ground, my dad's right hand pinned beneath one of the shoes. Moving the lever, I had released the hydraulic pressure holding the cultivator off the ground. Pressure gone, the cultivator slammed down.

I don't know how we got my dad's hand out from under the cultivator. To raise the equipment would require that the Allis Chalmers be running so it could generate some hydraulic pressure, but I remember those old tractors needing to be started with a hand crank and I don't think the typical nine-year-old farm kid could hand crank an Allis Chalmers to life. Perhaps the tractor had a battery and starter. Perhaps it had been running when I'd dropped the cultivator. I don't know. I only know what my dad's hand looked like afterwards, badly bruised with a large open scrape on the back of it. None of the bones were broken but his hand was sore.

Dad never did say much about the incident, only "You better be a lot more careful messing with stuff you don't know anything about." That's a good lesson to learn at an early age, before you start getting interested in girls. Yet maybe dropping a cultivator onto your dad's hand might not be the best way to learn it.

Shooting Out Headricks' Car Window

It must have been Christmas Day. I was probably a little irritated that Bert and Oral Headrick thought they could just drive out to our farm from Curlew and make themselves part of our celebration. I didn't care if they were related to my mother, it was *our* Christmas.

I shouldn't have been so selfish, I suppose. They were caring for a severely handicapped son, and doing a good job of it. So you should know they were saints, in a fashion, not villains. I was, nonetheless, irritated to see them, and though I didn't do it on purpose, I did put a hole in the window of the door on the passenger side of the Headricks' car.

They had pulled into the farmyard and parked in front of the house. Our mob of farm kids pell-melled out of the house and gathered 'round the car. We didn't think about it, but I'm sure we felt better having them surrounded; I did.

Bert opened the door on her side of the car. I wanted to show her my new BB gun. Flip had one just like it. We were armed and dangerous and PEWW the BB gun went off inches from the side window of the car and now there was a hole in the glass. PEWW, it was quick, the harm was done. Another hard lesson learned fast.

I don't remember what my parents said to the Headricks, but I do remember what they said to me. I've been awfully careful around guns ever since.

Getting My Leg Run Over

The dream of it was so vivid. I was riding on the Ford tractor. My mother was driving. We were headed west on the gravel road in front of the farmhouse. I was on the ditch side of the tractor, my butt against the fender of the big rear tire. I turned and watched the grass in the ditch dance by. The grass flowed past like a river.

Then I lost my balance and fell off the tractor. My head and chest and hips cleared the big turning tire, my legs did not. In my dream, the tractor ran over both my legs. I suppose it hurt but I woke up suddenly and felt nothing.

It is two or three mornings later. It is spring. The lane is full of great ruts of dried mud. In the cool morning light, my mother and I head out to the pasture to chase ol' Bessy up to the barn for milking. The morning air is suffused with gold leaf light. Ol' Bessy has an open ulcer on one of her hips. I am sure it is painful. We'll treat it again when we get her up to the barn, but for now Bessy doesn't want to move.

I hop off the tractor, come up behind the cow and slap her on the good hip. She heads toward the lane. Soon we are headed down the lane–Bessy, and me, and my mother following behind on the Ford tractor. Suddenly my foot is caught in a deep rut. I try to pull it out but the lips of the dried mud have caught hold of my heavy farm shoe.

I said *suddenly* my foot was caught in the rut. Faster than you can say suddenly I was caught and the front wheel of the Ford tractor was running up the back of my leg. I shouted, of course, but my mother had already started reacting and got the tractor stopped. The tire had come up the back of my leg nearly to my buttock. Much of the weight of the tractor was supported by the hardened mud I was caught in.

I was scared, I suppose. And my mother was scared, too, I imagine. She backed the tractor off the rut, freeing my leg. I pulled my foot loose from the clods of mud which held it.

I was looking down the lane, south, counting my blessing. Ol' Bessy was five or six feet in front of me. My mother was behind me on the tractor. In that instant my world stood still. I saw my dream of being run over. I felt a little numbness in my leg where the tractor tire had squeezed it. Nothing was broken, obviously; nothing was damaged permanently. Except a fellow's pride.

I worked my leg a couple of times, bending it at the knee, flexing it good. I yelled Yee-haw at the cow and started walking towards home again.

Allergy

It was a lovely kind of autumn day–blue sky so bright you could see everything, some breeze rustling the dried leaves of corn stalks and the weeds along the fence line. We had work to be doing out in one of the fields. It was handwork of some kind, I think, for we walked out to the field and we walked back. Maybe we were picking up ears of corn that had been dropped during harvest.

Walking back to the house that Saturday afternoon in October we came across stalk after stalk of milkweed. Their stiff pods were cracked open and the fluff was revealed. Silly farm kids, of course we didn't recognize that in releasing all the fluff from a milkweed pod we were seeding what we'd have to cut from next year's fields. Given the beauty of the milkweed fluff riding the spine of a blue autumn breeze, I'm not sure we would care. The whole way back from field to farmhouse, nearly half a mile, we stopped to open every dried pod and to play with the fluff.

It was warm enough that day I didn't need to wear a coat. I had on a long-sleeved sweat shirt and by the time we were halfway back I was itching under the sleeves. Dust coming off the corn stalks, I figured, the scratchy feel of the dried corn stalks was giving me a scratchiness under my sweat shirt, on my arms and now on my chest.

When I got back to the house, I took off my sweat shirt and saw the problem—welts raised everywhere, on my arms, on my chest, now on my legs and back. Hives of a sort, I guess, an allergic reaction. Near as anyone could tell, I was having a mild allergic reaction to the milkweed pods. Well, perhaps "mild" is too mild a word—the itching was intense. I used calamine lotion to soothe the itching somewhat and looked like a blotch-colored monster. I replenished the calamine on the hives several times. I thought maybe my plight would get me out of evening chores but that was a foolish hope, wasn't it, ain't nothing gonna get you out of chores.

I learned two things that day. First, that which is beautiful can hurt you. Second, you live with consequences. Good lessons for a farm boy just at the front edge of puberty.

Shelling Corn

"Tell the old men to stay the hell out of the way," I say to my father. I am young and cocky and full of myself. My brother and I are shoveling corn out of the crib into the conveyor that pulls the ears up to the corn sheller. The whole world rumbles and groans and squeaks around us—metal moving against metal—and the kernels of corn scream as they come off the cobs. I am frustrated that a neighbor come to help us shell corn has been getting in my way as I scoop. I am much too young to understand "pace" the way an old farmer does. My father doesn't say anything. He never says much. He doesn't feel he has to.

And although I don't see my father do anything to get her there, soon enough one of my sisters has brought a big pot of coffee out to the crib and the farmers collect around her filling their cups. Coffee steams. The sheller keeps running. My brother and I keep scooping corn and scooping corn and scooping corn—we are machines ourselves and we keep the conveyor full. We are young, muscular farm kids, busting full with the energy and promise of youth. The farmers stand in a bunch, watching us work; they sip their coffee. They are comfortable in the noise and they are comfortable not talking—for they are, after all, farmers.

Shelling corn is usually an all day job. Neighbors share the work—an old social habit, from the days of premechanized farming. The logic is simple: you help me with the work I cannot do alone, I will help you. It's like a barn-raising, but at a lesser scale. It is a way to share the burden, to spread the weight of some of the hardships of farm life; it is a way to be sociable; it is a way to get the work done with as much comradery as Iowa farmers could ever muster in the late 1950s, the early 1960s.

The shelling machine itself belongs to a fellow in town. He runs a small trucking company and this shelling business. It will be his trucks hauling the shelled corn away–taking it to bins at the corner of the farmyard or to the elevator along the train tracks in Curlew. He gets so much per bushel shelled and so much per bushel hauled.

The shelling machine itself is mounted on the frame of a truck. The cab of the truck is red, or used to be, a very faded red now, old truck red, don't you know. The sheller itself is bright, a fresh green. He has put a new shelling machine on an old truck chassis. Waste not, want not.

Always the sheller man arrives first, before the neighboring farmers. We have barely gotten our chores done when he pulls into the farmyard. Setting up the sheller and the conveyor is a ritual, easy and familiar when you've done it several times. The conveyor is in sections stacked along either side of the sheller on the truck. It takes two of us to hoist the eight-foot sections off the truck and carry them into position along the corn crib. We make short work of it, my father and I and my brother, working with the sheller man.

It is simple enough a task to fasten the sections together, to link the chains and drive bolts through the holes where parts connect. It is simple enough a task, but the sheller man always insists on doing this part of the job himself. A jammed or broken chain ruins not only a section of conveyor but could also end up damaging the shelling mechanism. A piece of broken metal run through the innards of the machine is much less forgiving than an ear of corn.

It doesn't take the sheller man long, then he has the conveyor set to go. In unison we start to move it into place—alongside the crib if we are going to work through openings on the outside. Sometimes we run the conveyor right through the center of the crib where a "tunnel" has been built in for just such a purpose.

Once the conveyor is set, the sheller man moves the truck with the sheller on it into place and levels it to make it sit square to the world. Then he starts his equipment running—slowly at first, then faster, then up to full operating speed. He wants to be sure the chain in the conveyor is not binding and the conveyor is set up straight; he watches carefully to catch sight of any link of chain or piece of wire that might have been left in the conveyor inadvertently. He listens carefully to the sound of the sheller itself. He "feels" the operation, and so do you—the equipment gives off an elemental rumbling vibration; if that vibration doesn't feel the way it should, you know something is wrong and needs to be made right before corn shelling actually begins.

To open a crib, we start at one end of it or the other. There are "doorways" built into the crib every sixteen or twenty feet along its length; these were closed up with slats of wood when the crib was filled with corn in the fall. Now we remove one slat and work a little corn out, then remove another slat, and then another. We are chipping a cavern into the great mass of corn, a cave, a hole gouged out of the solid yellowness of corn. We use a corn rake to work corn loose and into the conveyor. The corn rake is like a pitch fork, except the tines have been bent ninety degrees. The tines catch ears of corn—you work the rake back and forth to free the ears. The conveyor groans, it groans and squeaks, the corn sheller roars, hungry for a more steady diet of corn than we can give it as we work the first ears loose from the crib.

Initially all the work must be done from the outside of the crib. The full length of the corn rake is needed to chip away at the stock of corn. Now and again, a great avalanche comes tumbling down to the opening. You need to be alert, to get the corn rake out of the crib before the avalanche jams it in place. The cavern we've been creating collapses, ears of corn solidify into a great mass right in front of the opening, it's almost like starting over. We hollow out another cave at the opening, we create another avalanche of corn.

It is exciting to be the first one to crawl into the crib you've opened, exciting because it is dangerous. If you have misjudged the likelihood of another avalanche of corn, you could be crushed under the weight of it, caught between the force of corn and the unforgiving nature of the crib wall. Certainly you would never, you would not ever climb into a crib while there was still corn hung up overhead.

Once in the crib, the task is pretty clear—to rake corn towards the opening where someone else pulls it into the conveyor. Let me be clear: you rake corn and you rake corn and you rake corn. There is a reason farm kids are persistent and dogged and eternal. You rake corn and you rake corn and you'll do it tomorrow if you have to, and Wednesday too. You rake corn until the great mound of it has been reduced to a size that must be scooped over the opening of the crib and into the conveyor.

Ah, the poetry of scooping corn! The sheer blood rush of it, the physical pulse of motion, the clock work turn and return, the long muscles of one's back pulling and reaching and pulling. The slide of aluminum shovel over the wooden floor, under and into the corn, a little rock of the shovel to work corn loose, the turn and sweep and shove of it. Unless you've done physical labor and loved physical labor you cannot fully appreciate the joy of it, the intense physical release of it, the silver tingle and jangle and run of it, the animal part of you functioning fully, your heart pumping, your blood screaming yes, yes, yes.

Then soon enough we have to move to the next opening along the crib, start to gouge out the next cavern, pull down the next avalanche, climb into the crib again, rake corn and rake corn, shovel it. Life is an endless repetition of the same few elemental motions, like the circling of an electron around the nucleus of an atom.

Then it might be time for dinner. On the farm dinner is the noon meal. What you eat in the evening is supper.

Dinner is a big meal. Roast beef with carrots and potatoes and onions. Side dishes of corn, green beans. Maybe chicken and home-made noodles. Bread, always bread, always white. Pie or cobbler for dessert–apple or cherry probably. Afterwards the men will want to go outside to smoke–you never sit in a neighbor's parlor in your work clothes. The men would sit for a spell in the shade of one of the trees in the yard or on the tail gates of their pick-ups. They might go for a short walk to settle their dinner, out to see how the garden is doing, a neighborly gesture. Then–the noon hour ended–it is back to the business of shelling corn.

The afternoon looks very much like the morning did, except the sun is on your other shoulder. We might finish one crib and have to move the setup to another. My brother and I let the farmers do that work. This is a chance for us to stand up straight, stretch out our back muscles, which have been burning with the heat of the day or with the fury of the work.

One crib. Another. The noise. The corn dust. Sweat. My father's long strides take him across the afternoon. There may be a breakdown, which is time for us to catch our breath while it is being repaired. When we break open a nest of bumblebees that had been hidden in the corn, I work my shovel carefully to get the nest out of the crib, then toss it into the ditch along the gravel road in front of the farmstead. Someone pours gasoline onto the mass of nest and bees, which explodes into flame.

Afternoon's light lays longer on the land. Those farmers have to be getting home for chores. Day is nearly done. We have our own chores to be getting to. The sheller man shuts down his equipment for the day. Or maybe we have finished shelling corn before we've run out of afternoon and the conveyor gets taken apart and loaded onto the truck. Either way, the machine will be set up somewhere tomorrow, rumbling and groaning and creaking. If it is not at one of our cribs, it will be at one of the neighbors'. My brother and I will be expected to come scoop corn. We are good at it and all the neighbors know it.

The Journey:

Curlew,
Thursday, October 26, 2000, Afternoon

I have just entered Curlew after walking around our old section. I get off the road and walk a sidewalk along the lawn of the house where Bryan Wilson had lived, the right-hand side of Main Street. My face feels a little sunburned, my hair is wind-blown, I stink with sweat.

"Hey!" shouts a fellow from the other side of the street, "are you a Montag?"

"Yeah, I'm a Montag," I say.

He is coming at me from across the street, he's talking to me, "Which one are you?" he asks.

"I'm Tom, the oldest."

"Your dad was Phil. I'm Jerry Johnson. My brother Dick and I used to shell corn for your dad, and haul corn. The last time I saw you, you were a punk kid."

"Yeah, I was a punk kid," I say. "You're still in Curlew?"

"Yeah, I'm still here," he says. "The farthest I ever got was Emmetsburg."

Jerry Johnson and his brother Dick bought the Ausland Lumber Company buildings after Jim Ausland retired and ran a farm supply business out of them. The Johnsons were also involved in running the grocery store in Curlew for a while after Squeek's building burned down and the new cinderblock building had been put up. They ran the store for a while, then someone else ran it, then it went out of business, Johnson tells me.

"You just couldn't make it go," he explains as we walk north up Main Street. "You got charged more to get deliveries in here. Then they started bringing a bus in here to take people shopping in other towns. When the store closed, people complained. I tried to explain to them that if you want a store to stay in business, you have to give it your business. For some people, it just didn't sink in. The building is used for the community center now." He points off to the left, across the street.

Johnson makes his living as a rural postal carrier. He'd planned to get out of that line of work because his route hadn't been big enough to pay him full-time wages. "They promised they'd expand my route so I held on a while longer. They gave me a good part of the Mallard route and gave part of it to the fellow from Havelock, and eliminated the carrier who worked out of Mallard." Johnson has a hundred and four deliveries–"that's a big route"–and the other fellow has forty.

"Well," he says, "I better go in and talk to my wife. She runs the beauty parlor here." We're standing in front of the beauty parlor now.

"Good talking to you," I say.

"See you," he says.

Part Three

The Journey:

Curlew,
Friday, October 27, 2000, Morning

It is a chilly morning. Overcast. Clouds like lead balloons, like silver bullets, like the shine of my wife's grey hair. I have parked the car at the north end of Main Street in Curlew, across the street from where the school used to stand, when Curlew had a school, next to the old park where I had played Little League. I am ready for anything.

9:41 a.m. A Budweiser truck rolls through town from north to south. It slows but doesn't stop. What more can you expect these days, the taverns gone.

9:42 a.m. A tan-colored car comes into Curlew from the first farm north of town, driven by a white-haired old woman. I'll find out later she is Jerry Johnson's mother, I'll find out that back in 1948 when my parents rented the farm at Curlew her husband might have thought he would get to rent it and never quite figured out how my dad snuck in line ahead of him.

("It didn't hurt that we were Catholic," my mother remembers. "It didn't hurt that your dad had an account at the bank in Emmetsburg all those years before." My dad added: "It didn't hurt our name was Montag neither.")

The white-haired lady in Curlew whips her car across the oncoming lane and parks in front of the beauty parlor.

Slowly she gets out of the driver's seat, opens the back door of the sedan and sets a walker onto the surface of the street; very slowly she makes her way towards the door of the beauty parlor.

9:45 a.m. The white-haired lady, Mrs. Johnson, reaches the door of the beauty parlor.

9:47 a.m. A car comes through Curlew and takes the road straight out of town to the north.

9:49 a.m. A pickup coming from the east stops at the stop sign behind me, turns north, misses Curlew entirely.

9:50 a.m. Three blackbirds cross Main Street in formation. The flag in front of the Post Office flaps vigorously northwest to southeast. A block to the east of me, where the Methodist Church used to stand, there are five thousand blackbirds on the lawn, in the trees. They come together, they fly apart. A kind of love-making, a kind of communion and separation.

9:52 a.m. Two blocks to the east, a white station wagon heads north to the highway, turns left, turns right at the stop sign, goes north away from Curlew.

9:54 a.m. An orange pickup pulls away from the trucking company office and heads south. A white pick-up comes onto the street behind it, heads north. As the white pickup comes past me, a blue sedan meets it, keeps heading south, disappears over the rise of Main Street.

9:58 a.m. A woman walks east to west across Main Street, towards the community center.

10:00 a.m. The woman walks back across Main Street to the beauty parlor. Is she carrying a styrofoam cup? Coffee? I don't know that the community center is open.

10:04 a.m. A new red pickup heads south through Curlew from due north.

10:06 a.m. A woman comes out of the beauty parlor and gets into a maroon-colored car parked in front. She backs out of the stall and heads south. The sun finds a weak spot in the clouds and teases it. Behind me, a pick-up comes in from the east, stops, turns north.

10:09 a.m. A John Deere tractor with a loader pulls a hay rack heaped with dirt; it moves east to west behind me. The sound of the tractor resonates in the heavy morning air.

10:14 a.m. A pair of crows cross Main Street from west to east at the far south edge of town, near the hulking remains of the grain elevator.

10:18 a.m. A nondescript grey 4-wheel drive kind of vehicle—it's not a pickup but it's not exactly an Explorer either—comes into town from the north, parks in the drive of the white house on the southeast corner of 4th and Main. The fellow goes into the house. Another car parks in front of the beauty parlor and a women with a blue sweater gets out the driver's side. She helps an old woman out of the front seat on the other side of the car. The pair makes its slow way to the beauty parlor. The old woman is pushing a walker.

10:22 a.m. A jet rumbles overhead.

10:26 a.m. A green car comes in from the north, parks across Main Street from the white house at Fourth and Main. The driver goes into one of the quonset buildings there on the west side of the street.

In my rearview mirror I watch the same John Deere I'd seen earlier now going east for another load of dirt.

10:32 a.m. A white pickup crosses west to east behind me.

10:41 a.m. There has been a quiet spell, then suddenly all hell breaks loose. Relatively speaking. The woman with the tan car walks her walker to the street, puts the walker in the back seat of the car, climbs behind the steering wheel. A couple fellows come out of the quonset building and stand talking to one another. Then the fellow with the green car drives away. The other fellow gets into his pickup parked there and follows to the south. The woman with the tan car moves it less than half a block, gets out and walks V-E-R-Y S-L-O-W-L-Y without her walker to the mailbox in front of the Post Office. She drops some letters in the mail and makes her way back to the car, drives it north out of Curlew to the first farmstead on the left. A blue car takes her space in front of the Post Office. The fellow from the white house at 4th and Main comes out to his grey featureless vehicle and drives away to the north. Another beer truck rolls through town, I am so surprised to see it I fail to record the brand name painted on its side. The truck goes clear on through Curlew, all the way into a tomorrow somewhere else.

Rotary-Hoeing the Corn

We called it a rotary hoe: if the corn was of certain size, you could pull the machine across a field and it would tear up the soil (and hence small weeds and grasses) without damaging the crop. Rotary-hoeing set the weeds back and gave the corn some advantage.

We'd run the rotary hoe early in the season for the corn shouldn't be over three or four inches tall. We'd pull it with the Ford tractor, wheels following the empty tracks between rows of corn. A reasonably bright farm boy could handle the task; and I was a reasonably bright farm boy, I guess.

It must have been a day in late May. I must have been in fifth grade, or sixth. My father had sent me out to a far field with Ford tractor and rotary hoe. The sky had looked threatening, as it often does out there where you can see it; yet a farmer wants to waste no opportunity to cross something off his good German work list, and the cornfield did need to be worked. I was just the fellow to do it.

Occasionally stones would get caught up in the teeth of the rotary hoe and would break the stalks of corn when smashing against them, or the stone might jam a section and stop the rotary motion of that part of the hoe. A fellow had to be watchful; he had to listen. A change in sound is the quickest indication of trouble.

Each time a stone got caught in the machine, I'd stop the tractor, go back to the hoe and knock the stone loose. Each time I'd throw the stone on the flat part atop the rotary hoe: this gave the machine some weight and eventually the stones collected in this fashion would be removed and tossed onto our "rock pile" behind the machine shed.

It was a crying wind that morning, a darkening sky. I had been racing up and back in the field of corn, fence line to fence line, hoeing and collecting stones. A spit of rain, like an insult, then another spit of it. Drops of moisture stained the rocks atop the rotary hoe, giving them some speckled brilliance. You could hear the rain on the corn. I turned tail for home.

In the house, I find my father having coffee. Mom sits at the table with him. They look at me as I walk into the room.

"See," I said. "See, I do know enough to come in out of the rain."

Feeding the Cattle

When one of them stepped with full weight onto your foot, you remembered suddenly they weighed twelve hundred pounds, thirteen hundred pounds. They were Hereford beef cattle, out in the feed lot northeast of the barn, and it was feeding time. They'd seen me coming and had started lining up along the troughs we fed them in. I was slower getting out of the way than I intended to be and one of them thought to put its foot exactly where my foot was. The full weight of pain.

I slammed the steer hard with an elbow to the head; it turned to look at me blankly. What felt to me like a hard hit was nothing more than a pesky little irritation. I slammed the steer again, this time with my shoulder into its shoulder. Nothing. Talking to a steer is like talking to a rock, except rocks have some personality.

I grabbed the steer's ear and twisted hard, pushing up and away. The steer bellered and moved its head away from me; its foot followed up and away long enough for me to get my foot out from beneath it.

I climbed into the line of wooden troughs leading to the wagonload of feed. I walked between the white faces of the Herefords on one side of me, white faces on the other. The cattle pushed each other for position at the trough, and bellered. Bellering at the feed trough and long, low moans in the dark of night, that's about the extent of communication among these animals. Which is just about all you want, I suppose, for these cattle were bred for the slaughterhouse. They would be someone's steak and roast and hamburger. You wouldn't want them talking exploitation and revolution.

I made my way along the line of feed troughs between the heads of those dumb beasts and their dumb, blank eyes, towards the wagonload of feed. One bucketful, then another, and I carried the feed out to the far end of the troughs, dumped a bucket across a three-foot stretch of the trough, dumped the next one that much closer to the wagon. I repeated the task again and again and again until finally I was done with feeding the cattle.

I put the buckets back into the wagon the last time and turned to watch the cattle eat. They turned their heads sideways, stretched their necks, extended their long beef tongues to corral a share of the feed from the trough. They jostled each other for better position, like mountains pushing and shoving.

Off to the west the sun was dropping down behind the trees in the grove. Long shadows were spilled like paint. Wind, cool and soothing. The sound of chickens, the sound of a car along the gravel road in front of our place, the sound of one of my sisters calling out "Supper!"

"There has got to be more than this," I might have said to myself. I was watching the cattle feeding dumbly and I was looking at myself. Had I been bred into a life no less predetermined than the march of these steers towards the slaughterhouse, I wondered. "There has got to be more to it than feeding cattle."

"Hey!" I shouted at the evening sky, just for the hell of it, just because I could. The sound roared from deep within and exploded out of me. None of the cattle turned to look at me, not a one of them.

I went to my supper.

The Journey:

West of Curlew,
Friday, October 27, 2000, Morning

I am walking west from Curlew. I am headed down the gravel road at the north edge of the section of land I grew up on. I am walking counterclockwise today. The John Deere tractor I had earlier seen hauling dirt comes down the road towards me. I step to the side of the road. The fellow is driving right down the middle of the road like he owns it.

The tractor comes up beside me and stops. The fellow on the tractor pushes open the glass door of the cab. He speaks to me: "Are you the fellow writing his memoirs about growing up on that farm a mile south of here?" He points towards the old farmstead.

"Yeah, that's me," I say, a little surprised by his question.

"You're a Montag," he says.

"Yeah."

"I'm Hans Appel," he says. "We lived just at the southeast edge of Curlew. You remember?"

I nod. And then we're talking. Hans had moved to Curlew in 1956 and he farmed there until he "retired" a few years ago. He rents out that farm now. Since his farmhouse had been just within the corporate limits of

Curlew, he could serve as mayor for thirty-five years. He has since moved into the house he built out of town to the east, there at the edge of Vic Graff's gravel pit, where I thought our old skating pond looked like a park.

Hans and his wife had raised a fine family on the farm. None of the children are farmers, however. One has studied human genetics, one is in social work, one owns a good business in Sioux City. And so on. "I don't like to brag about my kids but they are all doing well," he says.

"Maybe my son put it best in the acknowledgements of his dissertation. He was thanking everyone who'd helped him along the way and he said 'I'd like to thank my mother and father who gave me a good work ethic.' That was the only part of the dissertation I could understand."

"Milking cows teaches you how to work," he says.

Hans seems distressed by the decay of Curlew, distressed by the disappearance of the small farms. "I bet there are a lot of farms you remember that aren't here any more," he offers.

"After Dean Backstrom died in the explosion at the house you grew up in, I said to John Spies who was in charge of that land, I said 'Do Curlew and Mallard and all of us a favor and rent that place to a young couple who wants to farm. Hell, I'll even cosign for the right fellow to help him get started.' And John said it was already in the hands of the land management company and the piece had been rented. What's more, they were going to tear all the buildings off the place. Well, I've been involved in soil conservation so I said 'Don't take out that grove of trees. At least leave the trees.' And you see the trees are still there."

"I wish the election was over," Hans says. "It scares me." His John Deere has a sticker on it supporting the Democratic candidate for governor of Iowa. "They all talk about the booming economy. It's booming for the people who've made a killing in the stock market. It's not booming for working class people. Life is still pretty hard out here on the farm and in these small towns."

"Farmers should form a union, but you know what," he says, "they're way too independent for a union to work."

"I'm semi-retired," he says. "I still have some cattle and I farm that 80 I'm hauling dirt to, to fill in some holes. I rent out the rest of my land."

"I've got a wagon that holds seventy-two bushels, it cost me $400. My tenant has two wagons that cost him $10,000 each and each of them holds 740 bushels."

"That's not a wagon," I say, "that's a truck."

"I like to say I was smuggled into the United States," Hans says. "That gets people's attention. My mother was pregnant with me and my twin brother when she immigrated. Our family has an interesting story. My mother hadn't finished school yet when my dad first came to the United States. He said he'd come get her and take her to America when she was ready and he had enough money. It was twenty years later he went back for her. He was forty years old and she was thirty-five. She waited for him."

Hans's twin brother is a retired school principal in Wisconsin, his younger brother had been a dentist in Madison, Wisconsin, and is retired too.

"And you're still farming," I say.

"Well, I've got to be doing something with myself," he says.

"Corporate farms couldn't farm the way I have," he says. He's talking and I look through the window of his cab at the sky behind him. There is a red-tailed hawk circling in my field of vision. He has been parked in the middle of the road for twenty minutes or more. To get around him, a fellow driving a tractor headed west has already had to pull partway into the ditch as he moved past.

"I put anhydrous ammonia on my fields once and I tell you what–that stuff is scary," Hans says. "I never used it again. The way I farm I don't kill the worms and the little organisms in the soil."

"I did forty acres of oats and forty acres of soybeans on my 80 this year. People say there's no money in oats. I tell you what–look at the bottom line. I don't put all those expensive fertilizers on my field and I made $200 an acre on those oats. I get the oats off in July and one of those hog operations you see around here drills hog manure into the stubble ground at no cost to me. I've got no love for those big hog operations but you can't beat them so use them to your advantage. That fertilizer costs me nothing. It'd work nicer if I had a three-year rotation on that 80."

"There by Curlew where your Uncle Larry farmed, there's nothing left at all," Hans observes. "There where you grew up, at least the grove is left to break the wind." He invites me to stop at his house for a tour of his place. He has some old things from Curlew he'll show me, and some old cars, and so on.

I tell him I'll stop tomorrow to see him.

Curlew,
Friday, October 27, 2000, Morning

Random thoughts as I walk the four miles around the section I grew up on:

Perhaps this is a story with no bad guys, this loss of all the little farms. Perhaps the end result of a hundred small decisions could not be foreseen while the decisions were being made. Perhaps the accumulation of those decisions pushed into the current emptiness.

⚘ ⚘

I remember: My mother said, "Did you tell Bryan about your dream?" I had told her that Bryan and I were spectacular heroes in my dream the night before and now I was home from a day at school.

"Did you tell Bryan about your dream?" she wanted to know.

"Mom!" I said, peeved, "I don't have to. He was *in* it."

⚘ ⚘

If they stop me and ask why do I keep walking around the section out here I'll tell them: to write down the things I remember when the land speaks to me, to write them down before they are lost forever.

⚘ ⚘

The rhythms of this farm, this land: did they help to create the poet I've become? The rise and fall of the sun, the spin of the stars in the black night, the turn of the seasons. The push and pulse of labor–making hay, shoveling corn, carrying feed to the cattle. The clatter and boom and squeal of hogs on the feed floor. All these helped to shape the poet in me, no doubt. Yet if they shaped me, why didn't they fashion poets of others around me? Why am I the only poet? How do you explain grace? Why try?

You are different and you know you are different and you know it at an early age. My cousin Robin, Larry and Pat Allen's oldest daughter, says the question is this: "Why am an ugly duck?" You don't ask yourself the question just once, she says, but over and over.

Part of the difference, Robin implies, is simply that we ask "Why?"

Why do I keep insisting on asking? The wind is the wind. It doesn't mean anything, it just blows. Does it ever wonder whence it came? I don't think so. The poet is a kind of wind rustling the grasses and corn leaves, nothing more.

⌒ ⌒

Sky the color of the tin siding of the elevator as I come into Curlew from the south. Earth the color of the wood exposed where the wind has torn the siding loose, the wood is decaying.

Palo Alto County,
Friday, October 27, 2000, Afternoon and Evening

Between Curlew and Mallard, a red-tailed hawk. Another between Mallard and West Bend. One between West Bend and Emmetsburg just before I enter Cylinder. In Cylinder I see a sign in front of a building: "This building wants to be a store." The headstone of the door says: "The Dorcas Society." Three miles from Emmetsburg along Highway 18, another red-tail.

⌒ ⌒

I am having a big piece of steak in the Dublin Restaurant at the west edge of Emmetsburg. You *know* you're in the heartland, I think to myself. I've overheard one young waitress say to another: "I told my mom I was going to run away from home and take my dad and brother with me."

Emmetsburg to Curlew,
Saturday, October 28, 2000, Morning

A wet, heavy morning. A hawk. The sky drops down and the mist shrouds a farmstead that almost disappears into greyness. Another farmstead close by shines clearly. As I approach Curlew, it is entirely lost in fog.

Cutting Pigs

"Squeal like a cut pig."

If you grew up on a farm, you might know what that sounds like. It's the sound a pig makes as the knife slices open its scrotum and a testicle is removed. It is high-pitched and intense–the kind of sound you might make if you've been so rudely treated.

When we castrated pigs, we tossed the testicles onto the bedding of the hog house floor. Another farmer might save them in a stainless steel bucket, fry them up later, make a meal of them. Connoisseurs call them Rocky Mountain Oysters. We called them pig nuts and didn't indulge. We didn't eat brain or kidneys either.

Cutting pigs wasn't a job you relished, but–growing up a farm boy in the 1950s–it was a job you had to do and you did it. At least you weren't in the house making beds and washing dishes. Cutting pigs is like branding cattle, I suppose: it's barbarous but you don't have much choice. There's no sense asking forgiveness, you just do it. Don't look for anything honorable about it, it's a job. As with a lot of things in life, it's not something you like to start, but once you're rolling it's got a compelling rhythm and you stay at it 'til the end. You don't half-shoot the dog; if you're gonna kill it, you make sure it's dead. Like playing music and making love, cutting pigs makes more sense doing it than watching it. It takes a shape of its own. Don't pretend to be horrified: we did such work so the world has pork chops and ham and bacon.

Castrated pigs gain weight more efficiently. And boar pigs that grow up to be boar hogs produce a tougher meat with a strong flavor most people find offensive. When such hogs are butchered, the meat is ground up and disguised in highly spiced meat products—bolognas and sausages. You don't get top dollar for boars when you sell them for butchering as a result of the strong flavor. In addition, in the pig world as in the rest of the universe, testosterone makes the animal more difficult to deal with. Partly it's a matter of who's in charge. Testosterone has no OFF switch. And boar pigs, like other males, have a roving eye; it takes a good fence to keep one where it belongs. So you cut the male pigs.

You want to do the job between the time the pigs are old enough to fight off infection and the time they are too big to handle. You leave each pig with two slits in its scrotum, which allow germs entrance deep into the body, so the pig has to be ready to fight infection. But if you wait too long to castrate the pigs, why then it's a wrestling match and you might learn just how much pigs like mud and you might become better acquainted with mud yourself. A pig that gets to be much more than fifty pounds is getting too big for an eleven or twelve year old farm kid to pin in place while his dad cuts it. There can be no excuses in this regard: if the pigs get too big, it's gonna take more than a farmer and his half grown sons to castrate them.

Basically, cutting pigs is a three-man job and if what you've got is a man and two boys, why the boys grow up quick. Child labor laws didn't apply to farm kids in the 1950s and if you complained you were properly labeled a crybaby. A good pair of gloves was essential to the task, and at least a long sleeved shirt, if not a denim farm coat. You walked to the hog house and entered it. You moved your shoulders up and back, up and back, to loosen up your muscles. It might have looked like you were being cocky but you were just bracing yourself for the task ahead. You stood in the smell of it then, in the dust, the manure, the blood you knew was coming. You waited for the sting of sweat in your eyes, even on a cool morning; you knew it was coming. You waited for your hair to mat up under your cap as you worked. You watched dust dance in a shaft of morning light streaming into the shed–that was the beauty of it.

The Number Two Son gets the worst job. I didn't make the rule, that's just the way it is. He has to catch a pig and hold it until the farmer is ready to cut another one. It's not fun–the pigs, remember, have been walking around in manure out in the hog lot and anything you could grab hold of would likely be slick. Number Two Son holds the pig until Number One Son is ready to flip it on its side and pin it to the floor. Sometimes the best place to get hold of the pig is by the gristle of an ear; twist and you can take the pig right down, even a big one.

Number One Son has to be steady and certain and cool. He pins the pig on its left side, putting his left elbow and forearm on the pig's neck and holding the pig's front feet bunched in his left hand. The youngster's right elbow and forearm rest on the pig just to the front of the ham. You bear down with enough force to keep the pig motionless. The right hand holds the pig's top back leg securely and helps expose the working area, the scrotum; you don't want the pig kicking or moving while the knife makes its slit. The pig's lower hind leg is left free, but if the pig is pinned properly that leg is powerless. A twelve year old farm boy aching to be a man knows he is measured by how well he keeps the pig pinned. You want the pig to fight you; it means it's strong and will survive the ordeal. But you cannot let it move. Now is the time you remember everything you learned in school about sitting still.

Handling the knife is not boy's work. It takes a father's sureness, the certainty which comes with maturity and experience. You want the cut to be quick, clean as a hot needle poked through your eyeball, dead on and accurate. This is the moment the pig screams. It is a sound different from any noise made by the other pigs snuffling about the shed waiting their turn. A distinct sound all its own. Beneath the hand of a good man with a sharp knife, the pig's testicle almost explodes out of the slit in the scrotum, the way a mouthful of food flies out of an unhappy child and halfway across the kitchen table. Another slit to the scrotum, another explosion of fluid and flesh, and you're done with one pig. You let go of it. The pig gets up and runs off. Later it will go about its business like its trauma was nothing much to worry of. It sniffs the blood in other pigs' cuts.

Depending on how many pigs you've got to castrate, you might be at the job an hour, two hours, two and a half. You might take a break, drink coffee with your father, relax the muscles in your forearms which tense up holding pigs. Because it is tough work, you don't want to spend too much of the day cutting pigs; it is tough work for the boys manhandling the pigs and for the man handling the knife.

Barn and hog shed—it was a man's world. This was the 1950s, remember, when things were separated a little differently than they are today. Men could do what they thought was men's work. And if anything was man's work, it was castrating pigs.

⌖ Cutting Pigs ⌖

As males in those days we saw ourselves as providers. We saw ourselves as tough, as in sturdy and reliable. We could do the dirty work. My dad fought Hitler. We could do what had to be done. We were not brutes, but we were not whiners either.

We didn't talk much about what we did, about what we had to do. Taciturn would be too big a word for our kind of quiet. A simple glance could speak, a nod of the head, a shrug of shoulder, a turn of the hand. These could be all the language we needed, some days. We could get kicked by a cow all the way across the barn, slam up hard against the far wall, and all we'd say was "That stung a little."

We were men–or were fast becoming men–in a world we had to wrestle a living from. We were poised between the way it used to be and the way it was gonna be, doing our best, our jaws clenched tight as the world hit us again and again.

We could do what had to be done, but we didn't want to stay at castrating pigs more than a few hours. There is only so much blood and manure you can take at any one time. Only so much scream of pigs. Only so much knowledge of pain.

Butchering Chickens

It was always the hottest day of summer, without fail, the day we butchered chickens was. It didn't have to start out hot. There could be dew on the morning grass, a faint coolness at the edge of a breeze. Yet by the time our work was finished we'd be about done in, all of us, and it would be hot, it would be very hot.

On an Iowa farm in the 1950s you pretty much expected to take care of yourself. God bless the cloth coat Republicans, eh? The only cash you might see would be the weekly egg check, that and what us kids could earn walking the neighbors' fields pulling cockleburrs, at fifty or seventy-five cents an hour. There would be the occasional $10,000 check when your father sold cattle; he held it briefly. Most of the money actually belonged to some banker and simply passed through your father's hands on its way home. When you sold hogs, much of that check paid for the protein mixed into the feed used to raise the hogs; when all was said and done, the Moorman Feed salesman saw a lot more of that money than you did. Well, you knew going into it back then that a family farm would not generate much cash, but it was the life you wanted to lead. And you did eat well, you ate very well: at least once a summer, usually more often, you butchered fryers so you could taste the best fried chicken in the world.

⪜ Butchering Chickens ⪞

The day we butchered chickens always started the night before. We'd catch the chickens in the dark and tuck them into slatted crates. This quieted the birds and allowed for efficient slaughter in the morning.

Then we'd rise early on the day set for butchering. We rose early most days, actually; sometimes—as when you are set to butcher chickens—it just seems more worthy of mention. We'd get chores done up quick and come in for breakfast. Water had to be heated in big pots on the stove in the kitchen. A lot of water, to be used later for scalding the chickens. Scalding helps to loosen the feathers, which makes plucking that much easier. Somehow amongst all those pots of water being heated, we'd manage to find breakfast.

I was only ten or eleven years old when the task of killing the chickens fell to me. The oldest child will be your natural-born killer, loaded as he is with the most the soonest in the way of responsibility; too much too early has a way of bending you. I was, at that age, too young to empathize with the plight of chickens yet old enough that it felt real good to be important. You could have asked me to do damn near anything.

My father learned to kill chickens from his father. You drive two nails an inch or so apart into the chopping block. You catch the chicken's head in front of the nails, pull its legs to stretch the neck out, then take the axe to that expanse of neck. Obviously such a method presupposes you need an axe to separate the chicken's head from its body.

My mother's method was different, learned from her mother, as I learned it from mine. It is elegant in its simplicity. You take hold of the chicken by its legs. You put the head and neck of the chicken on the ground. You put a broom stick on the chicken's neck, behind the head.

You set your right foot on the broom stick to the right side of the chicken's head and your left foot on the broom stick to the left side of the chicken's head. And then– remember you've got the chicken's legs in your hands–you pull the legs of the chicken up until its head is separated from the rest of it.

I could kill four chickens in the time it takes to tell you how to kill one.

On the farm, death is part of life. You know when they're born that they will be slaughtered–the pigs, calves, lambs. The day the chick hatches out of the egg, its days are numbered. You don't feel a need to get hardened against death, nor to shy away from it, nor to ignore it; death just *is*, another reality on a landscape of harsh realities: you look it in the eye, accept it, do what you have to do. If you have to, you knock a runt pig in the head with a hammer. If pigeon droppings have been ruining the hay stored in the barn, you climb into the haymow in the dark of night, grab the birds off their perches, and pull their heads off. There is no viciousness involved, no malice. If you want to eat, something has to die. You protect what belongs to you. If you don't think death is a central part of the deal we've made with the devil, you haven't been paying attention. And you don't want to get righteous with a farm boy or he may explain to you just how many bodies *you* are standing on.

So you have the chicken's head separated from its body. You have a choice now. You can let go of the chicken, in which case you learn the meaning of "running around like a chicken with its head cut off." Or you can hold the chicken into a bucket, which restrains the flopping around and keeps all the blood flowing to one direction. Using the bucket eliminates the dirt and debris the chicken picks up flapping wildly around the farm yard. If you let the bird run around with its head cut off, you do add a little excitement to the morning–why, a headless chicken can run from here all the way to the cornfield, damn near. There are mornings you might want to offer some lively chasing for your brothers and sisters gathered around to help with the butchering, simply so they'll settle down later on, once the real work begins.

After the chickens have stopped their flopping, the hot water for scalding them is brought out. You want the water hot. You don't want the little kids bumping up against it and getting burned. The water is poured into a five gallon bucket. You dip the chicken into it, swush the bird around. You hold onto the chicken's legs as far back as you can, to keep from getting scalded yourself. You scald ten chickens to a batch, one after another.

Possibly here is the most repugnant smell in the world, the smell of wet chicken feathers.

Ten was the number. You'd scald ten chickens, then you'd singe those ten, then take the entrails out of them. You put the whole, empty chicken into a tub of cold water and cut it up later. If you were butchering forty chickens, as was often the case, you'd do four sets of ten. If you were butchering a hundred and fifty chickens, as we did on one hot summer day, you'd have to repeat the set of ten–what– fifteen times.

Plucking a chicken reveals your own naked vulnerability: it is a thin barrier which keeps the outside out and the inside in. It becomes very obvious in the chicken's nakedness there is not much standing between the throb of life and the stillness that is death. Not for chickens, not for us.

Your worth at butchering might be measured by how well you can pluck a chicken. The bird has been scalded and is hot; if you're good, if you're really good, you can slide one hand across its body and pluck off nearly half the feathers in one fell swoop. You drop that handful into an empty feed sack where are collected, too, the chicken heads your brother has gathered up, for disposal later. Then you slide your hand across the other side of the bird, for most of the remaining feathers. This sounds easier than it is.

Brown paper bags or newspapers get balled up and put into a bushel basket or five gallon pail. A match brings the paper to flame. That flame is used to singe hairs off the naked chicken. You might think: *chicken, bird, feathers*; but chickens have their hairs too, long hairs. If you can get them, grocery bags are always better than newspapers for singeing chickens–ink from the newspaper can get onto the meat, the black flecks of burned newspaper flip so easily onto the breeze, and just maybe (a ten year old thinks) the bad news released from the newspaper into the flames could make the chicken taste bad.

Possibly here is the most repugnant smell in the world, the smell of chickens being singed.

You would singe ten chickens, then you'd open ten chickens. Cut off the feet, that's the first thing. Maybe this day the neighbor lady would be helping to butcher; she'll take home the chicken feet, cook them up for a meal. We never did that–we threw the feet away. We figured only really poor people had to eat those chicken claws; we might not have any money but we weren't that poor, ever. Cut off the feet. Cut out the craw, the sack around the neck of the chicken. Then give some attention to the chicken's plump tail. We didn't call it "the pope's nose," we were Catholic, but we knew people who did. There is an oil gland on the top side of the tail, you cut that away. When a chicken preens itself, it turns its head back and dips into that oil gland, then fluffs the oil into its feathers. The tail isn't particularly tasty to start with; removing the oil gland helps. Then you open the rear of the bird to take out the entrails.

Possibly here is the most repugnant smell in the world, the smell of warm chicken entrails.

Pulling the entrails out of the body cavity, you want to keep the liver intact, being careful not to break open the bag of gall attached to it. Gall on the liver will ruin it. The gizzard, too, gets cut out and laid aside and is cleaned later.

Now shows the advantage of the small hands of children. Tiny hands and fingers can reach way into the body cavity of the chicken and remove the lights tucked high into the bones of the back, the lungs.

If you are dressing out old hens, which you do at the end of their egg-laying career, you may find in them some whole eggs, some soft-shelled eggs, and egg yolks of various sizes. These you save–they can be used to make noodles. Take this down: the rule of thumb for noodles is two thirds of a cup of flour to one egg, no water. Add pepper and salt. Roll the mass out flat, cut into strips, drop the strips into boiling water. If you are using smaller eggs, adjust the amount of flour to the size of the egg. You've got noodles for your chicken and noodles.

Whether old hen or young fryer, the freshly-emptied bird is laid into a tub of cold water. A few, small motions and a living creature has become food for the table. There is a hose running into the tub from the nearest water faucet; a slow, steady flow from the deep well keeps the water in the tub cool throughout the day. Our fried chicken was distinctly good: at any family reunion or potluck we could taste the difference. Our single, immutable rule: get the body heat out of the chicken and get it out fast. The water in the tub was constantly refreshed, to dissipate the body heat of the first ten birds, and the next ten birds, and the next. Body heat of all those chickens. Flowing out of the tub in the water overflowing. Into the air. Heating up the hottest day of summer.

The heat of the sun, straight up. The sun directly overhead. It would be noon and time for dinner, we called it dinner then. If you were right on schedule, all the chickens had been scalded and plucked, singed and opened and set into the tubs of water waiting to be cut up.

If you were butchering one hundred fifty chickens for Doctor Walsh, to pay off a dental bill the size of Connecticut, a dental bill nine sons and daughters can ring up quickly, well, you might be behind schedule at noon. To butcher one hundred fifty chickens in a single day is a big day's work. The chickens would still have to be bagged next day, one bird to a bag—two drumsticks, two thighs, a back, both halves of the breast. If your parents should happen to go out to a dance instead of finishing up their work properly, why they might have to rise early in the morning, bleary-eyed from celebration, and they'd have to sort and bag chicken parts pretty nimbly to get one hundred fifty chickens to the dentist's office in Emmetsburg by 8:00 a.m. But that's another day's worry.

Today's worry now is a noon meal and a little piece of nap under the shade of the big cottonwoods out in the yard. We called it "the noon hour" and its duration was an hour, not a minute longer, no matter how much you want to show you can sleep all the afternoon.

The afternoon task is to get the chickens cut up. First, you inspect them for pin feathers and remove any blemishes. Then you take each bird apart. The pieces go into a fresh tub of cold water. At the end of the day, all the tubs will be moved to the basement and filled with ice water, to keep the chickens cool overnight, after which they will be bagged for freezing. But now you want to cut up the chickens. Your mother has the most experience, which shows in the scars on her index finger where she's cut herself several times while separating the drumstick from the thigh; cutting through the joint where thigh and drumstick meet, she has cut into the joint of her own finger. When she cuts herself again, she'll say that she's a slow learner.

This is how to take a chicken apart:

Pull one leg out away from the body. Cut through the crease of skin between the thigh and the body. Separate the leg and thigh from the body as a single piece, then cut through the joint between leg and thigh to separate them. Repeat this process on the other side of the bird.

Pull the wing away from the body. Cut as close to the joint of the wing at the shoulder as you can. When the wing comes off, fold it up into a neat little triangle that will stay folded upon itself. Repeat this process on the other side of the bird.

Cut through the neck as far down into the body as you can. Remove it and save for soup, or for those poor folk who say they actually like chicken necks.

Now take the breast of the chicken in one hand and the back in your other hand and bend them away from each other until you hear something snap. Cut through the back of the bird where the snap occurred; you've just removed the lower part of the back.

What remains is the breast of the chicken attached still to the ribs. Cut between the ribs and the breast along each side until the pieces separate from each other.

Flatten the breast and drive the knife through it from the back side to the front, to crack the breast bone, then split the breast lengthwise.

The ribs, you usually have to break those bones a bit so the ribs lay flat for frying.

Repeat this process forty times, or eighty, or one hundred fifty.

Usually the chickens we were cutting up back then were young and tender fryers. Sometimes in the crush of farm work, however, we let our roosters get too big before we got to butchering them. They'd weigh six or eight pounds each, which felt like twelve pounds after a day of handling them. To keep such big ol' birds from being tough to eat, we'd bake them in the oven for four hours, in pure cream. Cream was plentiful on the farm in the 1950s– we had no money, but if we wanted a quart of cream for cooking, we got it fresh from the cow, just as it was being separated from the rest of the milk. Cream keeps the chicken moist and must have in it something to tenderize the meat. We were among the farm children who said chicken cooked in cream was the best chicken ever.

By the end of a day spent butchering chickens, it would be hard not to think about eating it. Sunday dinner–crispy chicken, mashed potatoes with lumps in them just the way you like it, a smothering of gravy. You might be almost delirious in the heat of the late afternoon, thinking about Sunday dinner.

Dream time and reverie? Well, not yet. The job is not done until the chicken has been moved to the basement of the farmhouse for further cooling and safekeeping overnight. If the day has not been extremely hot, you might have been working close to the house, in which case you don't have far to carry the chicken. If it was a scorcher, you were probably set up much farther away, down near the corn crib, in the shade of the apple trees, where a breeze got funneled between the crib and the chicken house.

Now you empty water from the tubs, without spilling chicken parts onto the ground. You grab hold of a handle on this side of the tub, your brother grabs the other handle.

⮺ Butchering Chickens ⮹

You carry that wash tub of chicken to the basement. Careful down the stairs. Into the darkness of a single bulb overhead, into the only coolness of the day. Your eyes can't adjust fast enough. In the darkness, you imagine a chicken's head on the ground. You have just separated it from the chicken. You close your eyes. Still you see the beak on that head working, opening and closing, as if the chicken is calling out. A blank eye stares up at the sky. It winks at you. In spite of the day's heat, a shiver runs up your spine. You spread ice over the chicken in the tub, then fill the tub with cold, fresh water.

And your day winds down. A long day. Hot. You have evening chores to do yet, then a worry stone of moon will rise. Stars will come out. Later, in the light of a bright moon, the stars will seem to disappear, like drops of water in a hot skillet, cast iron, seasoned.

The Journey:

Curlew,
Saturday, October 28, 2000, Morning

"The Methodist Church building was hauled to Emmetsburg," Larry says. "All that's left is the bell."

It's Saturday morning. I've stopped to visit Larry and Pat Allen again. We are talking over coffee again.

"That would have been your Uncle Dale," Larry says when I tell him the fellow from West Bend told me one of the little Allen boys was quite the brawler. "Dale liked to fight. One time he knocked down five cops at a dance in Livermore. The guys he was with just hid under the table."

I tell Larry I'm going to be visiting Len and Mary Leslein later in the day. Larry says "You know your sister Kack was baby-sitting for the Lesleins and when she got home she said to your folks 'Mom, Dad, did you know Methodists don't eat bananas on Tuesdays?' 'What?' your mom said. Kack said 'I was telling Len Leslein we were Catholic and couldn't eat meat on Friday and he said he was Methodist and couldn't eat bananas on Tuesdays.' You see if Leslein remembers that."

Curlew,
Saturday, October 28, 2000, Morning

Hans Appel is not home when I stop at his house east of Curlew, so I head out to his eighty a mile west of town to see if he is there unloading dirt into the holes he was filling yesterday. He is. He is just finishing his work. So that he doesn't have to climb down out of the cab, I lift the tongue of the flat rack to the drawbar of the tractor as he backs into place. I fit the pin through the tongue, the tractor is hooked to the flat-rack, and he's ready to go.

"You go on to the house," Hans says, "I'll be along shortly."

After he arrives home, Hans shows me a 20' x 20' building that had been the first gas station in Curlew; he has moved the structure out to his place to preserve it. Attached to it are a couple of decorative beams from the old hotel in Curlew; he'd rescued them when that building was being torn down. (The decorative end of one of the beams is visible in the photograph I've seen of Miss Susie A. Easton, Curlew's Rural Route #2 carrier from 1904 to 1909.) Inside the old building Hans has the scale and an adding machine from the store in Curlew, a line shaft for running machines that had been in Lloyd Seagren's workshop, a platform scale from Critz's elevator in town, a desk and locker from the Curlew school.

Hans had owned an old Curlew fire truck but has since sold it to a fellow from New York City who'd seen it advertised in the Des Moines paper. He still has a fireman's mask and a fire extinguisher from the Curlew fire station.

Another building, another line shaft, this one from Eddie Seagren's automotive repair shop. The Phillips 66 sign on the wall had hung from a pole in front of Eddie's garage.

At the entryway to his house, Hans has set bricks into the ground to make a walkway; these came from a smokehouse that once stood behind the bank building in Curlew. Some fellow was going to haul them to the dump and Hans just couldn't stand to think they'd end up that way.

In the house he's got a silver tea set shelved in a place of honor. Hans is the only "family" his godmother has left so she gave him the four piece set that's over a hundred years old. His godmother had come from Denmark at the same time his mother did.

Also in the house there is a heavy trunk from Germany that had belonged to Harry Matthiesen when he arrived in the area before the start of the Civil War. After Hans had the trunk restored, he'd offered it back to the Matthiesen heirs but they didn't want to take it from him. "And I didn't *really* want to part with it," he says.

We both have muddy feet, so Hans and I are just looking into the house from the entryway. I see one of three beautiful doors Hans had bought at a farm auction and put into the house; the hardware for the doors came from Milwaukee where the pieces were being thrown out. Hans' wife Gwena, when she saw the door knobs, rescued them.

One great wall, facing the open space beneath the cathedral ceiling, is faced with sheeting from an old corn crib. The aged rawness of the wood is beautiful in the captured light. "My wife did the interior design," Hans says.

He says he was the first in the Curlew area to convert to electric heat back in 1969 in his old house out at the farm. Now, he believes, the electric heat in this house is at least twice as efficient as it was back then.

He bought the 80 acres the house sits on in 1970 and paid $29,000 for it. "I wouldn't take a million twenty-nine for it now," Hans says. "Money's not everything." When the house was built, a fellow with a bulldozer worked at landscaping around the gravel pit for a month.

"If I was younger," Hans says, "I'd have a wind charger. We need to be using something sustainable."

The lectern from the Church of Brethren that had stood southwest of Curlew is found in still another building. (Church of Brethren is where Hans and his wife Gwena were married.) In the same building there is a loom Hans found in a house he'd bought in Curlew; he wants to restore it and learn to weave but at the moment the loom mostly gathers dust, he says.

Hans has a lot of other antiques—vehicles and equipment not necessarily associated with Curlew but which he wishes to preserve. There's a tractor made by the Thieman Harvester Company of Albert City, Iowa, built with a Model T engine, transmission, and differential. It seems when Ford stopped making the Model T, the Theiman Brothers bought 500 leftover drive-trains and built tractors using them.

In one building Hans has a 1928 Model A rumble seat roadster, a car from the first year that Model A's were built. In another building, he's got a 1927 Model T, the last year for that model. Hans was born in 1927 and wanted a Model T from that year. "It's original cost was $525 new," Hans says. "I bought it from a minister who'd found it in Colorado and drove it all the way back to Iowa. I bought it sight unseen from the minister based on his description of it. I figured if you can't trust a Methodist preacher, who can you trust? You could drive that car all the way across the United States if you wanted to. Of course, it would take you a while."

He's got other vintage vehicles: a 1923 Model T truck with a partially wooden cab; a 1914 Model T truck restored by an old farmer who finished work on it but died before he had a chance to drive it. "We bought it at auction," Hans says.

From a more modern era, he's got a 1964 VW bug convertible with a 1200 cc engine. "If I had to part with any of my cars," Hans says, "this is the one I'd keep." He's got a 1972 VW bug with a sun roof, and a 1971 Porsche that changes to a convertible when you put the hardtop in the trunk. "The Porsche will do a hundred miles per hour in fourth gear," Hans says. "There's five gears. It rides like a lumber wagon, but it's fast."

There's the planter Hans bought in Arkansas. The fellow Hans bought it from said that when he was a kid, he and his father had hitched a mule to it and planted forty acres of cotton.

Hans is restoring a very old potato plow–"a winter project." He's building an imitation steam engine that will blow blue smoke rings, a project he'll finish up once he figures out how to transfer power from the engine to the back wheels.

Hans has an old hand-held corn planter that puts one seed in the ground at a time. An old broadcast sower you'd hang from your neck. An old sewing machine that had belonged to his mother. A pedal-powered John Deere toy tractor he rescued from the junk heap–"they sell for $1000 now." A 1926 motor to run his line shafts. A David Bradley garden tractor that had belonged to his wife's father; he has all the auxiliary equipment to go with it.

There's the big Stoughton wagon, over a hundred years old. A 1936 John Deere steel wheel tractor. A 1928 John Deere GP with a brass carburetor–"it would run more efficient with a shot of water in the carburetor. When the oil companies found out about that, they bought up the carburetor because it extended mileage and gas efficiency." There's a fanning mill and a one-ear-at-a-time corn sheller, both powered from a line shaft.

Out at the end of his driveway Hans has apple trees that are direct descendants of the original Delicious. One year the Iowa fruit and vegetable growers association took two hundred grafts from these trees and sold them at $25 apiece as a fund raiser.

Do his neighbors think he's a little peculiar, I wonder.

"Oh, yeah, they know I am," Hans says. "I was an 'organic farmer' for a few years and didn't use any chemicals at all."

Why does he keep all this old stuff he's collected? Why is he saving Curlew's history? "There's a lot of history our kids won't know unless we save it," Hans says. "That, and I just never get around to throwing anything away."

Plowing the Beans Under

"You be good kids," my mother said to us as she got into the red and white '58 Ford station wagon. We were lined up in the yard to see my parents off. They were headed to Emmetsburg, Iowa, to see *Gone with the Wind*, which had just been re-released.

"If it starts to storm," my father said, "get the big chicken house doors closed up. I don't want rain blowing in on the roosts."

"Yeah," I said.

"Thomas," my mother said, "you're responsible. Take care of your brothers and sisters." Thomas had to be responsible–he had three brothers and five sisters.

The sound of gravel crunching under the tires of the station wagon. A dust cloud like a rooster tail behind the car headed off down the gravel road. I took a quick look at the sour August sky.

Chores were done. We'd had supper and my sisters were finishing dishes. It was summer–no school, the day's work was done, we could watch a little television while my folks were gone off to the movie.

"Tom," my sister Kathy soon called. She was standing at the kitchen sink looking out the window. "Tom, the sky's getting pretty dark out there."

Indeed it was. The wind had picked up and was starting

to blow fiercely.

"Flip," I yelled for my brother, "come on. You can help me close the chicken house doors."

We weren't halfway across the yard when the storm hit. By the time we got to the chicken house we were swimming through waves of rain, great sheets of it, moving walls. The wind and the rain and the fury were blowing straight in on the chickens.

The force of the storm was holding the pair of doors open. Together the doors made a hole big enough to drive a combine through. Chicken wire in the opening kept the hens in the hen house. The rain was stinging us, stinging our eyes, the tanned skin of our faces and arms. Our clothes were soaked through. It was all Flip and I could do to pull one door away from the wall and into the wind and start to close it. It was a struggle of wills—the wind's will, two boys'.

We won the struggle.

Immediately then, on the turn of a knife's edge, we had to keep the wind from slamming the door shut. The force of the wind caught the other side of the door—we held on, held it back. The chickens were already frightened, were already piling up in the corners of the chicken house. We didn't want the door slamming to scare them further. Best we could, we eased the door closed.

The task with the second door was not any easier but now we were experienced. We knew to balance the edge of the door between wind on one side of it and wind on the other, giving us time to reposition ourselves.

Once we had both doors closed Flip and I entered the chicken house. We turned on lights. We could hear the storm raging outside; it was a freight train crashing, crashing, one boxcar onto another, crashing. Inside we started unpiling chickens from the corners of the building.

Frightened chickens pile up like that and smother each other. We worked quickly. We shooed chickens and we moved chickens and we carried chickens over to the roost. In the deepest part of each corner there were some dead birds already. We gathered up the lifeless bodies and–as we stepped back out into the storm–we flung the carcasses down along one end of the building.

Each of us tried to catch his breath in the great ocean of air and swirl and water and hail around us. We were lucky not to drown.

Hail. Now it was hailing. We ran blindly towards the house, hail stones stinging like a swarm of angry bees.

My sisters had towels for each of us. We dried our faces and hair and arms, then went upstairs to change our clothes.

The storm raged. The house shuddered. The yard light was on and we could see trees being whipped by wind. We could hear the hail stones out there, chopping.

Then as quickly as it had come, the storm was gone. Quiet. The darkness of the storm lifted and there was some band of sunset to the west. We just stepped outside, Flip and I, on our way to check on the chickens, when our Uncle Larry drove into the farmyard. He lived a mile away and he'd come over to see that we were okay. I suppose my mother had told him she and Dad would be going to the movies.

The ragged trees were dripping. The roof of the chicken house looked like it might be steaming a little–moisture on shingles that were still warm. The sky was quiet. A cat ran from some small piece of shelter towards the barn. Beef cattle started to beller. Hogs were at their feeders, lifting the covers with their snouts, letting the covers slam down, Bang, Bang, Bang, the metallic sounds echoing. The hogs did not like the storm at all. Bang, Bang, Bang all night long.

It was next morning my father went out to the fields to inspect the damage. I went with him. The leaves of the corn had been shredded and the stalks battered. The kernels were just at the "milk" stage in the ears, soft yet, the worst time for corn to be hit by hail. My father said he couldn't tell how bad the corn had been hurt but he looked grim-faced enough.

We drove a quarter mile to the west, to the hayfield. To what had been a hayfield. The outside third of the field had already been cut and baled and was just hay stubble when last we saw it. The next third of the field had been mowed and left on the ground to dry. Here, now, there was only hay stubble too. You couldn't find any of the hay that had been left to dry. It had been chopped to small pieces and had disappeared. In the innermost third of the field, where yesterday alfalfa had been standing just at the blossom stage, there was nothing. Nothing but hay stubble. We looked all the way across those forty acres and we could not tell where hay had been baled, where it had been cut to dry, where it had still been standing.

I'd seen hailstorms before.

My father had seen hailstorms.

"I've not seen anything like this," he said.

He shook his head. A moment of some dismay.

"Never," he said.

We went west on the gravel road to the far edge of our farm, then turned north. We wanted to see our soybeans yet; having examined the hayfield, we should have known it was a waste of gasoline even to bother. A forty acre field of soybeans looked as if it'd been harvested already. Only rows of raw stubble were left, evenly spaced, running straight east and west, chopped down to just above the soil, the whole field not worth a hill of beans.

"I'll be damned," my father said. "I'll be goddamned."

He turned the pickup into the bean field, left it running in the driveway there. He sat in it, his hands gripping the steering wheel, gripping and letting go.

"I'll be goddamned," he said.

He just sat there in the pickup, staring blankly at the field.

A day or so later I was on our Farmall "M" tractor pulling a three-bottom plow back and forth across the rubble of a bean crop. A crop that would never be harvested. I was numb: this is not the way a season should end. The notion of turning the beans under like this was too much for a farm boy of limited experience. Sure, we'd had hail before, but never like this. There was nothing left to the bean field, nothing that could recover the way the hay would, the way the corn might. Up the field I went, plowing, back I came. The thin strip of black dirt got wider and wider. Up and back. Soon enough the whole forty acres had been turned under.

Plowing the beans under, I put away the things of the child. Now I hurt like a man hurts.

Pretty soon it is a cold October day. My father has spent the morning out harvesting in one of his fields of corn. He comes into the house.

"Hot coffee, mama," he calls out as he enters. He means to warm up some before he goes back to work.

"I have been picking corn all morning in high gear," he says to my mother. "The wagon isn't even half full yet."

The Journey:

Curlew,
Saturday, October 28, 2000, Afternoon

When I phoned Lesleins from Larry's house, Mary answered.

"This is Tom Montag," I said. "I am the oldest of Phil Montag's kids. We lived next to you back in the 1950s and 1960s. I'd like to stop in and visit you this afternoon if that's convenient."

"What are you selling?" she wanted to know.

"I'm not selling anything. I'd just like to visit some old neighbors."

Now when I come to the door, Mary Leslein greets me warmly. "I never would have recognized you," she says. She gives me a hug.

Len turns off the sound of the Iowa-Wisconsin football game they've been watching on TV. We visit–Len, Mary, and myself. We sit in their living room. Sometimes we trip over each other with talking.

"Yeah, yeah, when was the last time we talked," Len wonders. "I think I remember your brother's funeral at Mallard. The years have a way of getting away from you."

"Still you can't sit and let the world pass you by," he adds. "You've got to get out there and see what's going past." He had turned eighty years old the past January and was intending to learn how to use a computer this coming winter.

"I remember a neighbor complaining that you start out as the young one among a bunch of old men and all of a sudden you are the old man," he says. "I was the young one once. Now all the old men are gone. I'm the old man."

"We've been fortunate, though," he adds. "We've got our health. But you never know."

Len and Mary live in Arizona the three toughest months of winter. "You know, the same thing is happening there that's happening here," he says. "The old people are dying off and we're getting to be the old ones.

"Yeah," he admits, "I remember telling your sister Kathy that Methodists couldn't eat bananas on Tuesdays. Your mom always kidded me about that."

We talk about farming.

"You know what a skid loader is?" Len asks. "It moves a lot of manure fast. I look at these young fellows with their skid loaders and I say 'I hate you guys.' I've pitched too much manure by hand not to. Things have changed."

From his farmyard, Len says, since 1953 or 1954, "I've seen sixteen sets of farm buildings taken off the land. That's sixteen farmsteads gone that I could see from my yard, standing right here. It got so I'd walk in the house for lunch and I'd say 'It's not a good day.' There went another set of buildings, up in smoke."

"If you go to the bank and you don't farm a thousand acres," he says, "they won't even talk to you. They'll say you won't make it with less. It's gotten so a fellow can't give his farm to his son because it's not enough to get him started."

"I don't know how a fellow can make it farming these days," he says. "You pay $140-$150 per acre cash rent. One fellow wanted Olsberg's place so bad he's paying $160 per acre. You pay for seed, you pay for fertilizer, you pay for diesel fuel. My renter took his combine over to West Bend for a tune-up and a few minor repairs–a few bearings and a new auger for the fines. The repair bill was $7000. He had to take his tractor in for some work–$2500."

"When a fellow started out feeding chickens for Hy-Line," Len remembers, "they gave you the chickens and they gave you the feed and you furnished the building and took care of them. Then chickens went bad and Hy-Line said you have to buy the chickens and they'd give you the feed. It was ten months later they said now you had to buy the feed too."

"Those hog barns you see everywhere," Len says, "four thousand sows under one roof. They'll have four of those buildings together. I know a fellow who drives semi all night to keep those hogs fed. Another fellow fills the feeders up during the day. Can you imagine hauling feed day and night for those hog operations, how much feed they must go through!"

"I remember your dad was quite a worker," Len says.

"I remember the fire at your farmhouse–that was 1948 and there were already a couple little ones in the house. The firemen got the fire put out but there was a lot of smoke and water damage. I still have such a clear image of your dad standing out in the yard after the fire. He stood there and I wondered: what's he going to do now?"

"We had a neighbor who built up a nice place feeding cattle," Len says. "He had feed lots and a row of those Harvestore silos. Then the bottom went out of the cattle business about the time he was ready to retire. 'What am I going to do? What am I going to do?' he worried. Well, he worried and he got cancer and he died. A young couple bought the place, it was just what they needed. The question is: what did his worrying get him?"

Curlew,
Saturday, October 28, 2000, Afternoon

"Sure, sure, I remember," says Curlew's ninety-three-year-old mayor, Russell Bohn. "Your mother worked for the elevator, up at the office. I worked out at the bin site."

How does a ninety-three-year-old man get to be mayor, even in a small town, I wonder. "I had the job wished on me," Bohn says. "I'm getting too danged old to be mayor."

Bohn moved to Curlew at age seven from Penfield, Illinois, near Danville in Champaign County. "It was a number of years ago that I saw Penfield again," Bohn recalls. "It looked then like what Curlew does now."

It was March 1, 1915; Bohn was seven years old, barely tall enough to see out the train window; the train was coming into Curlew. In Illinois the Bohn family had left warmth, sunshine, birds singing. Out the window as the train pulled into Curlew they could see snow banks clear up over your head. Bohn's mother studied the fields, the snowbanks, the bleakness: "You'll never raise corn out here," she said.

Since 1915 Bohn has lived within five miles of Curlew, most of it spent farming, raising corn. He started out farming a mile northeast of Curlew in 1934, then bought a farm four miles west and a half mile south. Sons still farm the place. Bohn retired to Curlew when he quit farming yet continued to help his sons until the past few years. "They seem to think now I'll get run over," he says. "They won't let me on a tractor anymore."

"I remember a tornado coming through Curlew," Bohn recalls. "It picked up the creamery, lifted it over a store, dumped it right onto Main Street."

Bohn remembers the celebration in Curlew when the three miles of concrete highway into Curlew got poured and Main Street was paved. There had been Woodman picnics in Curlew "a good many years" prior to that celebration as well, Bohn says. "Curlew used to be a pretty good town. It has certainly disappeared now. The stores here weren't big enough. The elevator was the same way—Ayshire bought out Curlew, West Bend bought out Ayshire, and so it keeps going."

The owner of Curlew's elevator, Dan Critz, "was wanting to get out of the business after his mother died. He got a job as a grain inspector in Dubuque and died a few years later."

"Insurance got so particular about every darn thing," Bohn recalls.

To get rid of one of the elevator's big buildings, "they dug a big hole, used a Caterpillar to knock down the building. They pushed it in the hole and covered it up."

Now all the grain from the Curlew area has to be trucked to Mallard or West Bend to be loaded onto rail cars, Bohn says.

The railroad tracks through Curlew were torn out in 1981. "The last time the train went through, everyone in town had to go down and see it pass by," he says.

"Squeek Seagren's store burnt down. The school went out. You take a school out, the community goes down."

"It's something to see kids going up and down our streets again on their bicycles," he says.

I asked Bohn about the abandoned houses in Curlew. "What they look like, they should be taken down. They should be burned," he says. "You have to wait three years for the back taxes to pile up, the matter goes to the county, then it still takes another ninety days to take action."

The house across the street is already being worked on, "to get the dimension stuff out, then they'll burn it. That house belonged to George Tressler, the first carpenter in Curlew. He built many of the other homes back then."

A fellow in Curlew is tearing down that house and others on the block to make a playground. "The only thing that will be left on that block," says Bohn, "is one house and a church. It's getting so there are not many houses left in Curlew."

Dick and Jerry Johnson had bought the two old hotels in Curlew, Bohn tells me. "They tore down one, burned the other."

Bohn had attended school two miles north of Curlew. "Lloyd Seagren moved that schoolhouse into town, behind the bank. I went to school in that building for several years, now somebody is using it as a garage."

According to Bohn, the Brechlers first farmed the place I grew up on. "There weren't buildings there yet where your house was. Then the insurance company got it, with the intention of putting a set of buildings on every eighty acres. That didn't work, they sold it, and that's when the Spies family got the farm." My parents had rented from the Spies brothers.

"Brechlers had an eight-bottom plow," Bohn remembers. "It was pulled with a big old Hart-Parr tractor. There was a platform on the plow and someone had to stay there raising and lowering each plow bottom. They plowed a straight line for a mile. Mile-long rows, that's a long way to walk picking corn by hand."

"Dean Backstrom was the last to live on the place," Bohn says of the farmstead I grew up on. Backstrom rented the farm when my parents moved to Dows.

"To settle an estate, the farm was split up among the Spies heirs," he says. "A south eighty was sold, a north eighty was sold, and the Spies family still has the rest. They custom-farm it, hiring somebody to do all the work."

"Only about one out of every eight or ten farms has anybody living on it any more," Bohn says. "Palo Alto

County's population keeps dropping. That's not good but that's the way it's going."

"More owners are leaving the trees," he says. "We shouldn't take all the trees out, this will look just like South Dakota. But they don't hesitate burning down the buildings."

Hampton,
Saturday, October 28, 2000, Suppertime

I tell my folks about my visit with their old friends, Len and Mary Leslein. My mother recalls a time that Dad was picking corn clear over on the far west forty: "I would haul it in and unload it and I had to hurry to get back out there by the time he needed another wagon. That night Leslein called Dad and asked if he could hire the fellow who'd been hauling corn that day. Leslein thought the fellow sure could hustle. 'No, you can't,' Dad told him. 'That was my wife.'"

⌒⌒

I ask about the fire at the farm house. "That would have been 1948 or 1949," Mom says. "We had you and Kack, and maybe Nancy. We just got home from attending a relative's high school graduation in Laurens. Smoke was pouring out of the bedroom. Dad grabbed the phone but it was so hot it melted onto his hand. So he got in the car and laid on the horn all the way to Curlew. The Curlew Fire Department came out and put the fire out."

"We lived in Curlew while the farm house was being repaired," my mom says. "You know where we lived?"

"Yeah," I say. "The house that stood right where Uncle Larry built his."

Curlew,
Sunday, October 29, 2000, Noon and After

I am having Sunday dinner with my Uncle Larry, Aunt Pat, my cousin Robin and her high school-age daughter Meredith. It is an Iowa dinner, a big beef roast with carrots alongside, mashed potatoes and gravy, cauliflower, salad greens, tomato wedges. There is coffee before dinner and with dinner and after dinner.

It is a grey, wet, and windy day. Rain rolls through, one great downpour after another, with spacers of gentle mist between. "Isn't this just a lovely day," says my Aunt Pat, and she means it. She likes grey, wet days. She thinks she should have been born in Seattle because Seattle's rain would suit her fine.

Another curtain of heavy rain. We talk family talk, we talk about what kind of orneriness is bred into the Allens. Larry asks if I remember the Sunday afternoon that Sunny's husband Russ went after Uncle Benny with a sand shovel. Yeah, I remember it, it is one of the essential images of my childhood. Aunt Pat remembers it too. She'd been out at a table in the yard with Benny's wife, my dad's sister Dora, while the ruckus built up and exploded. "Dora just kept talking like nothing was happening, so I just kept on like nothing was happening."

Robin remembers how much Uncle Les scared her when she was a little girl, how her cousins Dan and Roger scared her. "Uncle Les would say to his boys 'Sic em,' and Dan and Rog would be all over us."

"Uncle Les was a terror," Larry admitted, "but nobody had a kinder heart."

Robin teases her dad about his Allen traits and he notes that she hasn't escaped them. An Allen will have an opinion and doesn't care who knows about it. "Are either of your daughters stubborn?" my Aunt Pat asks me. She's got a daughter with a stubborn streak and wants to blame that on the Allens too.

We talk of cousins I haven't seen in thirty or forty years, of second cousins I've never seen. After dinner the table is cleared. Meredith has been very patient with all our talk and now she has to be heading off. She drives away in a big, old 1970s four-door sedan. "That's a good car for hitting a deer," I observe. Robin says, "In fact she hit a deer with it last month."

Larry remembers that all the kids from Curlew came out to play ball in his farmyard just south of town. His kids were halfgrown then, and the kids who came out to play ranged from the tiny and uncoordinated to the large and strong. Yet kids would walk the quarter mile to play ball on the lawn in front of Larry's house because there was one immutable rule: you hit the ball onto the road or beyond, that's an out. Sometimes a big kid, new to the game, might swagger to the plate and hit the ol' cream puff halfway to Appel's farm clear 'cross yonder. "You're out!" even the little kids could shout. The rule made it fair for the little guys and everyone played for fun. And kept coming back for more.

Robin starts to make herself a Halloween costume at the dining room table where we still sit drinking coffee. She's going to a party as the Queen of Diamonds and she's making herself a crown and cape. When she finishes and puts on her outfit, she does look like the Queen of Diamonds, having conjured the illusion out of nothing but a few scraps of fabric.

Robin says one of her sisters is going to a Halloween party as a brick. "Oh," says Pat, looking a little puzzled, "a brick?" Turns out her fella doesn't want to get all dressed up so he's going as a bricklayer. An Allen girl *would* go as the brick for her fella if he asked. Is it any wonder Robin used to have a bumper sticker on her car: BITCH. "We've got to take back those words," Robin says by way of explanation.

Leaves are coming down off the trees in clumps. Another wave of downpour pushes through Curlew. Aunt Pat is putting on *another* pot of coffee. "I hope you're not making that for me," I say. "Oh, somehow it gets used," she counters as she pours me another cup. "One for the road," she says.

Now I've spent the whole afternoon at my Uncle Larry's house, wrapped in the cocoon of family on a grey, rainy day, hour after hour, after a Sunday dinner not unlike those I remember in West Bend. Those afternoons I wondered what in the world the grownups found so interesting they could sit around a table and talk hour after hour, cup after cup of coffee. Now here I was, sitting and talking, swapping family stories and drinking coffee. A whole Sunday afternoon was gone.

Curlew,
Sunday, October 29, 2000, Afternoon

"Russell Bohn was an awfully quiet fellow," my Uncle Larry told me. "I remember waving to Russell time and again and he would keep driving his tractor and not acknowledge me. I didn't give up, though. I kept waving at him, and waving at him, and eventually he'd lift his index finger off the steering wheel to return my greeting. He's a lot more sociable now that he's moved into town."

Killing Rats

We didn't move the big wooden cattle feeder very often. It was a big bin of feed, with stations for sixteen cattle to eat at it freely. It sat in the cattle lot. Sometimes the tromp, tromp, tromp of dumb feet coming to it wore away the ground around. Sometimes the mash and mush of mud around the feeder meant we had to move it.

The feeder was built on wooden runners so we could hook a tractor to it and slide it easily. Actually moving the feeder was the humdrum part: killing the rats exposed when we moved it, that got our blood pumping.

There was no place a rat could love more than the dark space beneath the cattle feeder. Our barn cats couldn't crawl under there to kill them; a constant supply of feed was readily available: it had to be Rat Heaven.

It was Rat Heaven until we moved the feeder, then it was Rat Hell. We'd be stationed on all sides of the feeder, with baseball bats, scoop shovels, sand shovels. A good roar of engine and the tractor my father was driving would lunge forward. The cattle feeder broke loose from the ground. All the rats that had lived in the darkness beneath were exposed to full afternoon sun.

Full sun and the fury of an army of farm kids who take the theft of cattle feed by rats somewhat personally. We'd be standing at attention on all sides of the feeder as my father moved it, we'd see the rats, we'd swing into action. Wham! a steel shovel would come down on a rat. Wang! Thwud!

The first shot didn't have to be a killing shot, but should cripple the rat so it couldn't run off into tall grass and escape. Wham! Wang! Thwud!

Death squeaks sometimes. Sometimes death is silent.

Five or seven or twelve rats brought to rough justice. It was Saturday, it was a good day to be doing our dirty work. Thwud! Whump!

Soon enough my father would have the cattle feeder repositioned where he wanted it. Soon enough he came back to count our success. Five or seven or twelve rats dead. Some few may have gotten away from us. A few barn cats may have come sniffing around the business, suddenly interested.

Soon enough killing the rats was behind us. We were doing chores: in the settling light, evening stretched all the way from grove to milk house, all the way to darkness. Every time you felt something against your pant leg, you were startled and jumped. Could it be a rat crawling up your pant leg? It was known to happen. You'd close your eyes for sleep and see rats looking beady-eyed for escape.

There was always some little chance for the rats to escape, a little chance. Yet tick, tick, tick, life ground on.

Killing Pigeons

First my father moved very quietly into the haymow and blocked the opening the pigeons used to enter and exit the barn. The hole was high on the large haymow door, at the point of the roof. With the haymow full of baled hay, it was easy to reach the opening and cover it.

Then it was easy for us to reach the pigeons. My father, my Uncle Larry, and I were at the task. The pigeons perched at the top of the haymow along a metal track. On a hot summer's day, the track would carry into the cool darkness of the barn the hay tines holding a clump of bales. In the darkness of a late summer night, pigeons were perched there.

We were going to kill the pigeons efficiently, one after another, taking one off its perch on the rail and pulling its head off, then the next. As many pigeons as were using the barn for roost, that many pigeons spoiled a lot of hay with their droppings.

Some might think it more sporting to shoot at the pigeons like hunting doves. Shooting pigeons off the peak of a roof, of course, you risk putting a hole or two in the roof. Shooting pigeons, too, makes a very slow task of it: the crack of one shot scares away the others.

No. This was not going to be slow and it was not going to be sporting. The pigeons were spoiling an awful lot of hay and if we didn't do something the spoilage would continue week after week and month after month as the top layers of hay were used up, revealing clean bales. You deal with such pigeons the way you deal with rats, cold-blooded and efficient.

Our eyes adjusted to the darkness of the barn very quickly. We could easily make out forms perched on the metal track. We could see those pigeons that took flight, disturbed by our activity, and we could see where they came to roost again. To keep blood off our hands, we wore leather gloves, and we pulled the heads off those pigeons trapped in the haymow, until not a single one flew there or roosted there. Two men and an Iowa farm boy could kill a lot of pigeons in half an hour or forty-five minutes.

In the daylight next morning we collected pigeon carcasses in five gallon buckets and disposed of them. It was not so easy to dispose of the sensation one feels, the pigeon's head separating from its pigeon body. One does what he must.

Why I Don't Hunt

It was one of those rare fall days: you think you shall be fourteen years old forever, you are full of juice, you know you are immortal. I was walking the cornfield just northwest of the farmstead, walking among the broken cornstalks. I was carrying the break-action .410 shotgun I always hunted with, a gun I think had been my grandfather's, though if it was we didn't make much of the pedigree. The sky was full of blue. My feet rustled dried leaves on the rubble of harvest. I was hunting pheasants on a fine autumn day.

I suppose I hunted because I thought a farm boy was supposed to. Until that fall day I had not spent much time thinking about it. I'd shoot a squirrel for my gramma, who liked squirrel and gravy, and I'd be surprised how difficult it is to skin a squirrel. I'd shoot eight or ten cottontail rabbits in the deep snow of winter, shoot them and leave them lay, simply because there were too many and they damaged the young trees we set out. We'd visit the family of a hard-muscled tomboy I thought I was sweet on and I'd go tromping the corn fields with her brother, shotgun cradled in the crook of my arm.

And I would hunt pheasant on a fine autumn day in our own fields. It must have been Saturday. You could smell the moisture was coming out of the broken corn stalks. And your heart
STOPS.

The cock pheasant rises. The rush of it stops your heart. Stops the world. Everything so clear. The foot held in mid-step. The gun cold to the touch. The burst of bird before you. It rises in the wonderful arc that life is, the perfect part of the perfect circle. The pheasant goes up and away. The white ring of its neck is so intensely white. The red is red red. Sighting down the barrel of a shotgun, one sees everything clearly except what he feels.

The .410 was the perfect gun. If you couldn't kill it with the .410, it didn't need to die. I had friends with 16-gauge or 12-gauge shotguns, way more charge than a fellow ought to have. The .410 was enough. The pheasant was so clear. BLAMM.

The terrible moment is the instant the pheasant falls off its perfect arc. The bird crumpled and dropped out of the sky. Something was terribly incomplete. All of a sudden I recognized that something would be unfinished forever. I had broken the arc of that bird's flight. The blast of my shotgun had exploded beauty into a thousand shards. The world would not be mended. The pheasant crumpled and fell to earth.

Something in the world was incomplete and I was responsible for that.

I cleaned the pheasant. I cleaned the shotgun and set it back in its cupboard. I never again picked up a gun to kill anything.

All my life I've been waiting for that pheasant's arc of flight to be completed. All my life the bird crumples and falls to earth. What is beautiful has been broken since.

The Journey:

Rodman,
Monday, October 30, 2000, Morning

Another grey, wet morning. Dripping. Near Cylinder the red-tail hawk just north of town is where it is supposed to be. This is a good sign.

I am heading back to Rodman this morning, back the mile and a quarter to the southeast of Rodman, for another glimpse of the place my parents started out farming. It is a drab land with a languid roll to it, monochromatic in Iowa's standard fall color. The gravel road is soft with the rain we've been having; the car wants to follow the ruts instead of my steering. My parents remember a farmstead on the north side of the road—it's gone. No trace of it except in their memory.

On the south side of the road's curve, where my dad "can't imagine there's anything left," there is a newer house, a pre-fab by my guess. There is a silo that looks like it's not being used, there are steel bins, a couple big tin-sided sheds that look empty. The farm yard has plenty of grey brushy stalks of weeds. Someone lives here, but they don't keep a tidy farmstead. The land that rolls away to the south is rough, a little ragged and marshy in one place, giving way to trees in the distance, and the river. Looking south, I know what the land here looked like fifty years ago. Still, I cannot imagine the farmstead my parents started out on, the lay of the buildings, the shape of the small drab house.

A fellow in a pickup stops to investigate why I am pulled to the side of the road here.

"I'm just making notes," I say.

"Oh, I thought maybe you had car trouble. Where you from?"

"Wisconsin. When my folks started farming in 1946 they had an eighty right here."

I point my thumb off to my right.

It's pheasant-hunting season and maybe he thinks I'm intending to get a few birds where I shouldn't.

"Oh," he says, "all right." He seems reassured and drives away.

I finish my notes, then I drive away too.

West Bend,
Monday, October 30, 2000, Morning

I am having coffee again at The Villager in West Bend. The woman taking care of the coffee counter is busy with a customer in the shop. A woman in a pink sweater gets off the stool she's been sitting on at the other end of the counter; she walks the length of the counter and speaks to me. "Would you like coffee?" she asks. "I don't work here, but we take care of each other." She gets me coffee, then returns to her cup and the two women she'd been talking with. They are talking about quitting smoking, about where you can smoke and where you shouldn't. The woman in the pink sweater quit smoking a week ago.

"It wasn't hard," she says. "I made up my mind and I quit."

"There was a club meeting at Laura Montag's house," says one of the other women. "There weren't any ashtrays because she doesn't want people smoking in the house. One woman lit up anyway and she flicked her ashes on her plate and snuffed out her cigarette on it."

At some point one of the women looks down along the counter and apologizes for giving me an education in small town life.

"That's all right," I say. "I'm from a small town myself."

"Where?"

"In Wisconsin. Twenty-five miles from Fond du Lac."

"Do you know where Germania is?"

"Oh, yeah," I say, "we're about twenty-five miles from Germania."

The woman minding the store is freed up now. She comes behind the counter and gets the coffee pot. "You want some more coffee with your education?" she asks, tilting her head back towards the women talking at the other end.

Once the three women finish their coffee and leave, the woman behind the counter finds out I'm a Montag. "The woman in the pink sweater is married to a Montag," she says. "Her husband is Harold Montag."

Earlier, when I'd told the woman in the pink sweater that I'd come back to Curlew to see what was left, she'd offered that "West Bend is pretty lucky–we have so much left."

West Bend,
Monday, October 30, 2000, Morning

All the barns I've been seeing, they seem so small. Yet I don't remember ever thinking our own barn was large by comparison. If it were still standing today, I suppose I'd think it was awfully small too.

Riding the Horses

It was the end of the beginning, when I chose direct disobedience and went out to ride a horse across the late afternoon cornfield that October day. My brother Flip chose to go with me.

The light was the color of the litter of corn stalks. The air was electric with Indian summer sensation. The horses were not ours but belonged to someone in Curlew and we were boarding them: that was why we were supposed to stay off them. Yet the late afternoon sun said "Ride, ride," and we did. We didn't do it to be disobedient, we did it for the sheer wild joy of it, disobedience or not.

We let the horses run. They ran headlong down the rows of cornstalks, headed south, racing sunlight at breakneck speed. At the edge of the field we turned them and ran back north, we flew north, and the manes of the horses were caught up in the breeze that joy creates. The color of those flying manes, imagine it; imagine the color of sunlight caught in the manes, the sunlight caught in the corn stalks, the autumn smell of moisture coming out of the land, the smell of winter approaching, the smell of death settling on the land. We were racing those horses to outrun death, perhaps. For the sheer blood run of being alive.

Of course my mother had been standing in the

farmyard, in front of the house, watching our half an hour of disobedience. Flip and I did what we had to that beautiful late afternoon, that pulsing, electric day; and then my mother did what she had to. Flip and I returned to the farm yard.

"Thomas, didn't your father and I tell you not to ride those horses," my mother said. She didn't say it like it was a question.

"Yes," I said. "Yes, you did."

"And yet you went out there and rode them in direct disobedience?"

"Yes," I said. "Yes, I did."

She had the belt she used for spankings. I put my hands against the north wall of the outhouse to steady myself and took my licks. Eight, nine, ten, and she was done with me. Flip took his licks, and I stood beside him as he had stood beside me. Eight, nine, ten. I think it hurt my mother more to discipline us than it hurt us.

Yet this time was different. When she'd finished, I said what I had to: "The same kind of day, I'll do it again." My statement was not defiance, but fact. The fact is: some things you must do.

It was the last time my mother spanked me.

The Journey:

Curlew,
Monday, October 30, 2000, Morning

Once again I am walking the four miles of gravel road that encircle the farm I grew up on. As I leave Curlew, the crows in the park get very unhappy with me. They scold the way red-wing blackbirds do. Augh-augh-augh. Augh-augh-augh. The sound echoes off the tin walls of the quonset building to the left behind me. The grey sky is opening up. The sun peeks through. These crows might choke on their unhappiness; that is how crows die. I keep walking away from them, I'm heading west out of Curlew, the final lap of my home place, a kind of sadness is caught in my breath.

A quarter mile west of Curlew, a cock pheasant comes up SUDDEN out of the ditch to my left, the whrrr of its wings almost in my face. My heartbeat doubles, my breath expresses its surprise. The bird crosses in front of me and glides to the north until it disappears against the background of a grove of trees a mile distant. I am still gulping for air and the pheasant is gone.

A deer comes across the yard at Blaine Drown's farmstead, it crosses right in front of the house. It runs west in the ditch along the road for an eighth of a mile or so, then veers into a field. It's a large doe. A few moments later I hear a sound like a shotgun blast come from behind the house on the place. I do not see anyone. Another moment later, another gunshot, louder. Someone is killing something.

Broken cloud cover, broken blue sky, broken sunshine, the wind, always the wind. I'm another eighth of a mile down the road, there's another gun blast at Blaine Drown's place.

Just to the west of me, in the grove that remains where Russell Bohn's wife was born, a robin flies up and lands in a tree, its orange breast like a hunter's vest in the grey drabness. "No Trespassing" says the sign at the driveway. There is not much left to the place but trees and grass and the sound of the wind.

Maybe there are no bad guys out here where the small farms are being lost. Yet too maybe there aren't enough good guys. Someone who would have said "Yeah, I'll take a chance renting to a young couple trying to get started in farming," a farmer who would use the barn and the hog house and the chicken house on the place, a father who would dump a load of sand each summer under the cottonwoods, a place for the kids to play, a mother who would grow the sweetest strawberries in a garden's dark earth. Someone who would farm corn and beans and oats, cattle and hogs and chickens, small enough an operation that the stink wouldn't offend everybody the way those big hog operations do, sixteen thousand sows in one facility. Those operations seem to offend everybody but the shareholders looking for their few cents per share.

I'm just south of Puffy Bower's place when a pair of pheasants—cock and hen—go up, right to left, right in front of me.

A red-tail hawk hovers above our west forty. The sun flashes on the bird's breast; an invisible hand holds it aloft.

The hawk holds its place. I look away. When I look back, like my childhood, it has disappeared.

As I pass the old farmstead, what's left of it, I pee on the ground. I mark the place, this one last time I say it's mine.

Returning to Curlew for such a visit as I've made. This is a way to say good-bye to what used to be. Perhaps I am also saying good-bye to what is here now. The world has a way of changing and I do not know that I shall see this farm again.

I feel as if I have melded into this landscape, that these fields have melded into my dreams. The place creates my picture of how the world is. We understand the world by understanding where we've come from. How else to explain the longing to get back home–wherever home is–after some time away? The light we've grown accustomed to. The musky soil. A familiar wind. A pattern, our usual routine. We make our world and our world makes us. Does the container shape the water or does the water hold the container to its shape?

Night Plowing

So much of farming is not the darkness. There is the darkness of a haymow, of course, and darkness milking cows late on a winter's day. Still, much of farming is sun and green things growing.

Night plowing is a dark fall task. Late season, late day. The corn has been harvested. The stalks have been shredded, leaving a mulch on the surface of the field. The farmer's load of work does not decrease, even as the days grow shorter. Most evenings it would be my father who was plowing the darkness. There were times he'd send me out.

After school in those October days of my youth, I'd more often be found feeding cattle, watering chickens, gathering eggs. The boys' chores, they were called. Some days, though, I'd have a quick supper then dress myself warmly for night plowing. Long johns and blue jeans, a thick work shirt with a sweat shirt over it. A heavy denim work jacket, the farmer's kind, lined. A cap with ear flaps. Good gloves.

Perhaps I'd walk to the field where my father has been plowing all day, perhaps I'd drive our 1953 Ford pickup to the field's edge. "Pa," I'd say, "I can take over now." My father would climb down off the seat of the International 420. He'd walk like a man just come off a bucking horse, maybe, wide-legged and stooped. Farming is a sport for boys, for the young and resilient: grown men suffer farm labor to the deepest marrow of their bones; look at any farmer's hands. Young and full of myself, I'd climb onto the tractor. "You be in by midnight," my dad would say.

The smell of harvest. Corn stalks at the butt end of the day. You can smell the moisture of the broken stalks bleeding into the air. You know it is an Iowa farm in autumn, quite sharply and severely. The sun all day. The warmth the land has soaked up. The color of a settling landscape, the way the late light lays on it. The smell of the cornstalks bleeding. Off in the distance somewhere, the smell of leaves coming off the trees, the smell of wood smoke. Farther off, apples in a cellar.

The setting sun is a wild fire along the western horizon. All of a sudden it's the wideness of South Dakota I think I'm seeing, where the land rolls west forever, not the square and grey and certain Iowa farmland I'm familiar with. That kind of sunset—one that makes you think of eternity.

Then the moment passes. Then the sun is gone. Then you are plowing into darkness.

In the spring, in the weak spring sun, you had been in this field piling rocks onto a stone-boat to remove them from the field. You put them on the great rock pile behind the machine shed and every year the rock pile grew larger. How many more rocks are out there clawing their way to the surface, you wondered. The stones you picked up, when you touched them, they were warm with the kiss of the sun. The larger rocks you wrestled onto the stone-boat the way you'd like to get your arms around one of the girls in your class, to feel her warmth.

You had helped to plant corn in the field, dumping bags of seed into the planter, watching your father drive off leaving straight lines like claw marks where the seed has been put in the earth. You'd gathered up the empty seed sacks, put them into the pickup, later you'd burned them. You didn't plant any of the corn in the field–it was not often your father let you plant corn. A man is careful. He is judged by how straight his rows are, how straight the lines.

Sure, you had run the cultivator in summer when the corn was up. When the weeds wanted to steal moisture off the field. You'd be out there, the cultivator would be tearing weeds out of the soil or covering them up. You'd be driving those straight green lines with the shoes of the cultivator throwing dirt. You'd be watching the rows of green come rushing past rushing past rushing past. When you closed your eyes for sleep, you'd see the rows of green come rushing past. Even now you can see them.

You cultivated the field of corn and you remembered your mother had fired a hired hand who fell asleep doing the same job. He'd thought he could play all night and work all day, got home just in time for morning chores that day. Fell asleep as the tractor went down the field. He plowed across twelve rows of corn before he startled himself awake. It was an awful sight.

"You can't fire me," the hired man said to my mother.

"Yeah," said my father when he got back from town with baling twine, "yeah, she can."

You'd helped bale hay in the neighboring field, working like a man, eating at the men's table. You'd helped to plant soybeans and to cultivate them, you hauled in oats. You'd done chores, the eternal chores–the cattle, the hogs, the chickens, all the dumb beasts that depended on you.

All year the equation of success depended on you. So it seemed. So it seems as you plow on through the darkness.

It is not the darkness itself which brings the chill of

longing, of loneliness. It is what darkness does, the way it divides life into little, lighted chunks. The way night marks the end of day, so darkness separates one farmyard from another, separates the warm yellow light spilling out the window of the farmhouse from the far field where you are plowing.

Out in the field now, in such darkness, sight is not the primary sense. You feel the land more than see it. You feel the land through your hands on the steering wheel of the tractor, through the bite of the plow following behind. The smells of the world become mixed with the diesel fumes: then you can have no memory of apples. You hear the world at night, you hear it as the diesel roars, that steady heavy hum and throb, you hear it in the wind. A car out on the gravel road is merely headlights in the distance, strange orbs, not family or friend or neighbor. A bird flutters away in front of the tractor and startles your darkness. You can feel the land vibrate; the darkness becomes palpable, a taste in the mouth, fresh sheets on your bed on a hot summer's night, the world's breath, the bruise of a girl's lips pressed against yours.

The head lamps of the tractor spill a yellow glow twenty feet to the front. You become the small circle of light moving back and forth across the darkness. One might think darkness means emptiness: not always. Your senses are like the biggest men at the church picnic, wanting to stuff themselves full. Now the darkness is like water, you don't pay it notice, it is like water you are swimming through, a dark clinging liquid. The world is as large as your circle of light as you plow the darkness, and that's large enough.

The night may turn chilly but you won't notice. You are dressed warmly. Darkness is a blanket. Your chin and cheeks may grow numb in the cold air but you won't notice, not until afterwards, back at home, in bed, as you rest your head against your arm, as you drift into your lonely, lovely sleep.

What a wondrous thing is the four-bottom plow. The steel tooth of it. The plow takes a fair swath of landscape–four or five feet wide, six or eight inches deep–and turns it bottom to top. The shredded corn stalks are turned into the soil. Tender soil is turned to the surface for next year's crop. The circle of life. The turn and return.

The field is a half mile long. You plow from fence to fence. You bring the plow out of the ground at each end of the field, drive the headland to find the furrow heading back the other direction, set the plow back into the soil.

The tractor moans as the plow bites in. The tractor moans and roars. Slow, rhythmic, up the field and back, up the field and back. Though you cannot see it, the stripe of dark soil grows wider. The plow bites into the soil and the earth shudders and hums. Shudders and hums. Deep in the darkness, deep into the night.

You plow until midnight. You plow through the darkness. You cannot begin to imagine all that you are part of. The earth shudders and hums.

The Journey:

Curlew,
Monday, October 30, 2000, Afternoon

I find St. Mary's Cemetery easily enough. The only problem: in my memory, it was on the west side of the road, and the Harold Budd farm was on the east side. The world has turned itself the other way around while I've been gone. The house on Budd's place is still the big square one I remember, now the paint is badly faded and windworn. I don't know if it is still being inhabited, it looks so desolate.

I have come to the cemetery to visit my brother's grave. He was killed driving truck before he was fully twenty-one years old. The grave marker says:

> Randy P. Montag
> 1957   Son   1978
> Keep on Truckin'

There is a semi's cab and trailer etched into the stone.

Beside Randy's grave, a stone for my parents, a stone for when they will be laid to rest:

> Montag
> Philip J. 1921-.
> Oma M. 1928-.

As if I am peeking at the world through cracks in a fence, elsewhere the cemetery is full of half-memories. Some of our history is written in stone, in the gravestones here. John P. Schneiders (1945-1975) was a grade or two ahead of me at St. Mary's. Mae Schuller (1927-1998) was the mother of my classmate, Bruce Schuller.

Joe B. Wilson (1925-1973) was the father of my best friend, Bryan. Someone has suggested he'd had a heart attack when his car crossed the centerline and plowed head-on into an oncoming semi; some say it was sorrow. And then:

> Bryan Lee Wilson
> 4 Engr Bn 4
> Vietnam BSM-PH
> Aug. 29, 1947
> Nov. 3, 1968

You've known for thirty-two years your friend is dead but now you know it in the gut. Standing here looking at his gravestone, you try to catch your breath. A shadow passes, the wind fills the pine trees with emptiness, something seems to tick, tick, tick in the glow of the afternoon. I have developed a thick callus about my brother's death and so I am not as moved by seeing Randy's gravestone as by seeing Bryan's. I have not prepared myself for this intensity, I have no scar to protect me. I touch Bryan's stone; even in the full warmth of the afternoon, it is stone cold.

Stone: James Schuller (1950-1974). He was in my brother Flip's grade as I remember.

Stone: J. Norman Namer (1905-1992) and Jeannette Cone (1907-1984). I think these are the parents of my classmate Paul Namer.

Stone: Graff, Henry (Vic) 1912-. Eleanor M. 1923-1996. Vic Graff was my Little League coach. His wife has died. He is still alive, living in Emmetsburg, and he returns regularly to the piece of ground he'd farmed across the road from Hans Appel's house and the pond.

The wind has blown the clouds apart, the wind is in the pines, the wind is far off like a distant freight train. I hear the sound of truck tires on pavement a mile to the east. In all directions the farmland rolls away. It is bright here in the sun. It is dark there in shadow. There is an immense autumn checkerboard all around me. I feel the irony: I am standing in a cemetery as the world shuts down for another season.

Stone: Karen Ann Duffy (1950-1968). She was in Flip's grade.

Stone: Joseph Leuer, Jr. and Lottie Leuer, parents of Edward Leuer, who was in my grade.

Stone: Budd, Harold E. (1903-1964) and Marcella A. (1906-1981). This is the fellow who farmed right across the road. Mrs. Budd was my 4th grade teacher. She was always Mrs. Budd, I have just now learned her first name. I have always said the ending to every story is in some cemetery.

Stone: Schumacher, Eugene R. (1919-1999) and Jeanette (1925-). "Parents of Joe, Mike, Pat, Kay, and Tim." Joe was in my sister Kack's grade, I think, and the rest paired up with other of my brothers and sisters.

I go back and stand at my brother's grave. It is an incessant wind, strong and steady in the pines. Twelve feet to the south of Randy's grave, a field that had been soybeans until a few weeks ago. You wait and wait and wait and wait and wait to learn something significant or sacred at this holy moment. All that you learn has to do with wind and loneliness and the tricks that light plays with the bean stubble and the faded paint on the old square house across the road. You always wondered how Mrs.

Budd could teach at St. Mary's when her husband wasn't Catholic. In the meantime you have learned how much more forgiving God is than are the churches that act in his name. This old planet wobbles in its orbit and sometimes I suppose there is a God who steadies it. And sometimes I suppose there is not. The grass in the cemetery is a little greener than the rest of the landscape. Some day these saints will rise up. Someday my brother will start his diesel. Or not. Maybe it ends here. Maybe this is it. Maybe all there is is the Iowa wind, eternal. You want to believe there is more than a bit of warmth on polished stone, a few names and dates carved into granite, some few memories.

There is a hump of land between where I stand in St. Mary's Cemetery and our old farmstead. From where my brother is buried I cannot see where I grew up, this is fact as much as metaphor, here where my parents shall be laid to rest.

Curlew, Meditation at the Old Home Place, Monday, October 30, 2000, Afternoon

I have returned to the old farmstead and parked the car in the driveway. I want to sit here for a while and think. What is it I have been doing? What I've seen, what does it mean? I scribble and I keep scribbling.

You see mile after mile after mile of empty field, the ground worked for another season. There is a time to sow and a time to reap. A time to laugh and a time to cry. A time for the wind to blow, a time for incredible silence. A time for building up small farms, a time for tearing them down. For everything there is a season and a purpose under these shifting Iowa skies.

If you like having tomatoes and fresh broccoli in winter, perhaps you are part of the problem. Americans have decided that we'll no longer confine our diet to what is available locally. We choose not to limit our appetites. This simple decision has changed everything, or it is an emblem of the change. Any time you insist on having what you don't have, you are contributing to the problem.

The day has warmed enough that now I'm sweating as I sit here making notes.

It is plain to see that the steel bin here is rusting. You can't hear it rusting for the sound of the wind in the big pine tree, the wind in the old cottonwoods, in the grove. The sound of stiff weeds where a family had lived and grown; the weeds sway, they give and push back.

The sun keeps rising and setting. This old mudball keeps spinning and circling. The land keeps waiting for seed. Seed is our hope for eternity.

Even giving it considerable thought, I find no clear answer for the question "Why am I a poet?" A natural affliction with words? I could make dictionaries. The rhythms of the Sermon on the Mount and the first verses of John's Gospel? Only part of the answer. Perhaps I write because I read a book like *Patches* and thought someone should speak for my people and my place the way *Patches* spoke for an earlier place and time. It is only when I'm looking back that I see this as a possible explanation.

Partly it is the power of the land acting on me. The turn of the seasons shaping a farm boy who was somewhat articulate. A place and a time, pushing on me all these years. The power of specific memories. The insistent rhythms in those memories. A modest talent that comes as a gift, as grace; it cannnot be earned. The land humming in me and through me.

Some respond to the land that owns them by walking it. Some become hunters. Some stay to farm. I write poems. Many of us with the same urge, each of us manifesting it differently. The jolt of an electric juice, and we react. The poet is like the blacksmith. The poet is a kind of blacksmith, working a different kind of steel. A common urge, yes. Then the poet is not so different.

I think I write so family and neighbors shall not have lived in vain. I want to speak for them, to tell their stories, I want them to be represented in the gallery of humankind. We are not famous yet we should not be forgotten. Though I can make no good argument for why they must be remembered, I live with the conviction that it is important. There may be no satisfactory explanation. Why ask why the meadowlark sings?

⌒ ⌒

Completing my task, I can take pride in having completed it. It has been good to visit the old place. The lay of my emotions, like wind through the trees. I may leave feeling a little nostalgic perhaps, enjoying some sentiment for a glittering past that never existed. Yet certainly I walk away, too, with a true and real sadness at the loss of a true and real world.

You can never go home again because you can never again be who you were. Yet I would not be who I am if I had not walked this land, these fields, during my first fourteen years. The days that shaped me help me shape my days. I need a Darwin to chart the evolution of my successive selves—what has come forward, what has receded. What I am more of, what less. And to mark, too, the essential sacred core I carry from the farm into everything I do.

I don't want the sadness of the loss to be what is

remembered. I want to remember the joy of those years—the family, the land, the circle of life and love. Something is born and something dies: what is new grows out of the decaying mass of the old. You may water it with a few tears, but then it is time to put away sorrow, grab hold, move forward. Every year has its winter and summer, spring and fall. Every life does. Every family, every generation of families has its seasons. The alchemy of time transforms everything.

I have come back, yes, but I cannot stay. Truthfully—I don't want to stay. Only dead things lie still. Sometimes it seems like we are trudging forward so S-L-O-W-L-Y but indeed we are going forward. We have got to be making a world for our children to come back to, for their children to come searching for.

In some strange way, the farther you go the closer you get to where you were. Every day the sun comes 'round. Every life goes 'round too. You may end as you began. You may lay dying, whispering "Rosebud" or "Curlew, home." In that moment, we speak of whatever it is that owns us.

⌒ ⌒

I'll leave this place. I'll return to the big red house in Fairwater. I'll sleep and while I sleep I'll half listen to hear the wind in these cottonwoods, I'll listen for the moment the old trees crack and fall back to earth, to know what instant they no longer mark my home.

Heading Home,
Tuesday, October 31, 2000, Morning

My journey is ending. I am headed towards my Wisconsin home. I am thinking of the things I've seen and heard the past week.

Then I remember what my Uncle Larry said about

my dad's father, Henry; it seems a good emblem of the place I've come from, the time, the family:

"I learned to plow a straight headland from your grandfather," Larry had said.

"Henry would set his eyes on a spot in the distance and he wouldn't turn his head left nor right.

"He kept his eye steadied on that distant spot.

"The line of his plow, it was just as straight as could be."

Moving the Elevator

It did not seem so much like an ending as a beginning. I was halfway through my senior year of high school at Trinity Prep in Sioux City, Iowa. I was home for Christmas vacation. It was 1964.

After years of talking about it, my parents had finally bought a farm. At one point earlier, I had gone over to Dows, Iowa, to look at the place with them. I suppose it must have been during the previous Thanksgiving break. We had been driving back to Curlew, it was dark already, my father was tired. They'd been talking, my parents had, making plans, perhaps they had been arguing a fine point. There is so much to consider when you buy a farm.

My father wanted to change drivers, let my mother drive; he would rest on the way home. He had just come through a stop light in Humboldt, Iowa, at the intersection of Highway 3 and Highway 169. He pulled to the side of the road, got out of the car and walked around the back of it. My mother slid over on the bench seat into the driver's position, put the car in gear, and drove off.

"Mom!" I said. "you left Dad back there."

My mother pulled the car to the side of the road about an eighth of a mile from where my father had gotten out.

"Oh," she said. "I wasn't thinking."

"I was thinking about something else," she said to my father when he reached the car and climbed in.

"Damn right you were," my father said.

The rest of the drive home was pretty quiet. A fellow has a lot to think about when he buys a farm, and so does the fellow's wife.

People thought they were crazy, paying $425 an acre for the farmland they'd bought. No one paid that kind of money. Even God's best half section that my parents had rented for years wouldn't sell for that kind of dollar, people said. "What were you thinking," they'd ask.

My folks were dumb like a fox is dumb. In the ten or fifteen years they owned the farm, the price of farmland shot up. They sold their land for five and a half times what they'd paid for it.

Now here it was, Christmas vacation, 1964, I was home from school, my uncle and I were going to take the elevator from the old farm at Curlew to the new farm at Dows. That's a distance of sixty-some miles as the crow flies, farther than that along the backroads we would have to keep to as we pulled a forty- or fifty-foot-long elevator through one village or another, picking our way towards the new farmstead.

We had celebrated Christmas already, our last celebration at Curlew. It was a weekday between Christmas and New Year's. It was a clear day with sun and bright blue sky and fifteen degree temperatures.

A fellow puts on his long johns for a task like this–he puts on his long johns, then he puts on another pair of them. He puts on an undershirt and a shirt and a sweatshirt and a jacket and a parka. He puts on a stocking cap and pulls it down low to his eyes. He has got two pair of socks on, he's got his old shit-kickers on, he puts on a pair of rubber boots over them and buckles them all the way to the top. He pulls the hood of his big ol' parka up over his head, snugs the drawstring tight as he can make it. He puts a woolen mitten on one hand, then another. He pulls a leather mitten over each hand. The fellow is as prepared as a fellow can be. It's going to be a long day out in the cold, along the highway, you want to be warm enough to be comfortable.

The elevator, which would reach the top of a thirty-foot corn crib when in use, was cranked down so that the far end of it was only six feet off the ground. The near end of it was hitched to the back of the Ford tractor. The tractor was full of gasoline. There was more gasoline in the back of the 1953 Ford pickup.

I would lead the way on the tractor, pulling the elevator, and my uncle would follow behind in the pickup. I'd drive the tractor for twenty minutes, half an hour, then I'd stop. My uncle and I would switch places. He'd drive for twenty minutes or half an hour and we'd switch again. One of us would be out in the cold on the tractor, pulling the elevator, the other in the pickup getting warmed up.

Sixty-some miles of Iowa backroad is forever, sixty-some miles is not so far.

A quarter mile east from our farm, then a mile north. Three miles of pavement, then we crossed old Highway 17, heading east towards West Bend. We had our route mapped out pretty carefully, to avoid major highways and as many small towns as we could.

One is never so alone as he is out there in the brisk cold leading the short parade—tractor, elevator, pickup. It was crisp, it was blue sky like a winter's dream, it was yellow sun on everything, the thin layer of snow reflected back at me. The roar and rumble of the tractor. I had an intimate connection with the road, with the distance, with the going and the coming, the leaving and the staying.

There was a small spot on each cheek that burned with the bitterness of the cold, a small piece of flesh bared to the morning. My hands in the thick, wool mittens were plenty warm enough, though my fingers were feeling as if they were starting to cramp. I was gripping life's seriousness that seriously. My feet were warm. My armpits dropped a little acrid adolescent sweat even as I could see my breath. What burned was a little patch of flesh only, my cheeks; that, and perhaps an intensity in the soul where I was starting to recognize nothing would ever be the same.

How you conceive the world is not the way the world will always be.

Very soon I stopped the tractor and climbed off it. My uncle stepped out of the pickup there at the end of the elevator, an emphatic dot above an i, the sun above a silo. I saw his warm breath curl like a halo in the cold air, then the wind took the vapor away. I walked back to the pickup and my uncle climbed onto the Ford tractor, put it in gear, pulled the throttle wide open. He eased off the clutch and the elevator was moving away from me.

The pickup was surprisingly warm, though the heater was open only partway. The cab broke the wind, that's what was important, to be out of the wind. I took off my mittens and put them on the seat beside me. I pushed the hood of my parka off my head, pushed up my stocking cap. Just above the coldness of a cold cheek, a bead of sweat. Then I was rolling forward, the pickup moving at barely more than an idle. The tractor roared forward ahead of me, plowing the winter day wide open, a slash of furrow pointed off into the future, coming out of the past like time's arrow.

The old pickup didn't have a radio, yet I wasn't getting bored. There was an intensity to the task, watching the tractor ahead of me, the elevator, the pressure on the tires as the elevator moved over rough spots in the road, the bounce, bounce of the high end of it. I was the eyes of the operation, making sure the elevator was rolling smoothly, I'd pump the brakes of the pickup as a warning if a vehicle seemed to be coming up behind us too quickly.

It was my uncle's turn to drive in the cold, my turn to warm up.

My turn to reflect on the ending and the beginning. I was poised at the age one starts an independent life just as my parents were moving off the only place I had ever called home. I had been reading Thomas Wolfe, I was well aware of how hard Wolfe had found it–home, leaving home, trying to go home again. I was starting to understand that the arc of my life was going to take me out of this little universe. I would still be the first-born of my mother's womb, I would always be her first-born son, yet slowly I was pulling away, moving off, becoming an adult. Years later I would say "I'm glad to be from Iowa. Far from Iowa." I didn't mean it; it was a joke, like saying "Iowa is nice if you like pigs and corn and pigs and corn and pigs and corn, not necessarily in that order." I was helping to move the elevator from the rented farm at Curlew to the farm my parents had bought four miles north of Dows, a quarter mile west; I was rolling through a future of my own making, into another series of mysterious accidents that would find me with a good companion of a wife and two lovely daughters in a small village in central Wisconsin, another kind of home. I was spinning away from my first home, with no idea what it felt like to have a child leave home to make his own life, or her own. I was young enough I could survive my ignorance. I had been kept warm and safe in that womb of a farmstead at Curlew, and very soon I wouldn't be able to find my way back to my Iowa farm home.

Lost in the adolescent reverie, I was startled when my uncle brought the tractor and elevator to a halt in front of me. His time in the cold was up. We would change places again. We would play this little game of leapfrog all the way to the farm at Dows. My cheeks would get cold, then I'd warm up, again and again. There was no macho display of fierceness in the cold, there was no reason to play some big man when you were already doing a man's work, the job expected, everything that necessity required of you. We rolled on, heading east mostly, angling south occasionally, sometimes going out of our way to miss a tight turn or the heavy traffic of a main road. We travelled a path I have never travelled again; I could not find all those roads today if I tried. We rolled on.

My brothers and sisters would find a new life at Dows, they'd make new friends in a new school, the farmhouse on the new place would become home to them. It would never feel like home to me. I'd never spend more than vacation days there, I'd always be a visitor, even when I helped with chores, even when I worked the fields in summer, cultivating corn, baling hay.

Curlew was my home, that was behind us.

Well into the afternoon, yet soon enough to surprise me, we pulled the elevator into the yard of the farmstead at Dows. My father would greet us as if we'd done nothing more than walk across the road to the mailbox to bring back the mail.

To my dad, we'd had a job to do, and we'd done it. Yet some part of me knew there was more to it. Something had ended. Something new was begun.

Tom Montag is a middle western poet and essayist who has all along been interested in place and the literature of place. For his next project, Montag hopes to look at one town in each of the middle western states–the people, the history, the landscape–to see what it is that makes us what we are. Beyond that, he will continue working on his book about the people and places of the Fox and Wolf River basins of Wisconsin, "Middle River Tangle."

We hope you enjoyed Tom Montag's *Curlew:Home* from Midday Moon Books. For more fine literature, please subscribe to our quarterly magazine, *The Midday Moon.*

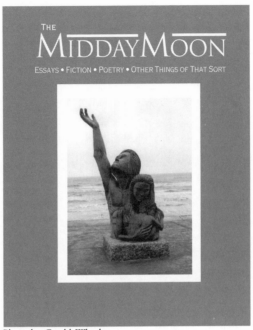

Photo by Gerald Wheeler

Name _____

Street or P.O. Box _____

City _____ State _____ Zip _____

To order the Midday Moon, please send your name, address and $16 to:

The Midday Moon
P.O. Box 368,
Waite Park, MN 56387